Clinical Self-Hypnosis

The Guilford Clinical and Experimental Hypnosis Series

Editors

MICHAEL J. DIAMOND AND HELEN M. PETTINATI

Clinical Self-Hypnosis: The Power of Words and Images
SHIRLEY SANDERS

Self-Hypnosis: The Chicago Paradigm
ERIKA FROMM AND STEPHEN KAHN

Trance on Trial
ALAN W. SCHEFLIN AND JERROLD LEE SHAPIRO

Hypnosis: A Jungian Perspective
JAMES A. HALL

Hypnosis, Will, and Memory: A Psycho-Legal History
JEAN-ROCH LAURENCE AND CAMPBELL PERRY

Hypnosis and Memory
HELEN M. PETTINATI, EDITOR

Clinical Practice of Hypnotherapy
M. ERIK WRIGHT WITH BEATRICE A. WRIGHT

Clinical Self-Hypnosis

The Power of Words and Images

SHIRLEY SANDERS, Ph.D.

THE GUILFORD PRESS
New York   London

© 1991 The Guilford Press
A Division of Guilford Publications, Inc.
72 Spring Street, New York, NY 10012

Printed in the United States of America

This book is printed on acid-free paper.

Last digit is print number: 9 8 7 6 5 4 3 2 1

Library of Congress Cataloging-in-Publication Data

Sanders, Shirley.
    Clinical self-hypnosis : the power of words and images / Shirley
Sanders.
        p.   cm. — (The Guilford clinical and experimental hypnosis
series)
    Includes bibliographical references.
    Includes index.
    ISBN 0-89862-342-1
    1. Autogenic training.   I. Title.   II. Series.
    [DNLM: 1. Hypnosis. WM 415 S215C]
RC499.A8S26   1991
616.89′162—dc20
DNLM/DLC
for Library of Congress   90-3407
                                                              CIP

I dedicate this book to my family, for making it possible:

*To my late father, Samuel Sanders, for his belief in
the power of knowledge*

*To my mother, Nellie Sanders, for her belief in
the power of imagination*

To my sister Rhoda for her belief in adventure

To my sister Evelyn for her belief in me

Preface

For many years I have been fascinated by self-hypnosis. During my early training in graduate school at the University of Kentucky, I believed that hypnosis was related somehow to mind over matter, but I did not understand this relationship. I knew that it was possible to use hypnosis to achieve certain ends, for example, to speak in public, write, teach workshops, even to complete graduate school. I learned the power of words to calm, to organize, to energize. But I had not yet learned about images. As my experience increased and my desire to understand increased also, I found little writing about the clinical use of self-hypnosis. Although a case report might include a paragraph stating that the patient had been taught self-hypnosis, not infrequently the content and wording of the self-hypnosis instruction was lacking.

Because I believe that the match between therapeutic words and images and patient experience is critical, I have brought together from my personal experience, from my patients' experience, and from the work of other hypnotherapists a description of how patients are taught self-hypnosis. I attempt to show what words, formulas, and images are used to verify and capture a bit of an experience of the power within— the power of the individual to transform meanings via words and images. Because the area is so new to research, many conclusions have not yet been published widely but are my own. However, I have attempted to relate the material to the collective thinking when possible.

The major thrust of this book is to show the quality of the self-hypnotic experience as well as at what specific goals the self-hypnosis experience aims. The power of words and images is a reflection of the patient's power within to think, self-direct, and change. The power stems from the meanings generated by the person, not by the words in themselves. In addition, the power reflected in words and images opens new possibilities of experience that can only be demonstrated by looking at individual examples, for the experience is unique for each individual. Individuality may be masked by general group analysis. The contradiction between the science and the practice, the tough-minded and the tender-hearted, continues.

The time is ripe to present an initial organization of clinical material on self-hypnosis that will clarify the early roots of self-hypnosis in man's basic struggle against nature, going back in time as far as the written word. In this book, the scientific roots of hypnosis and self-hypnosis are traced in an effort to clarify yesteryear's bequest with current experience. Our ancestors have left practical wisdom that provides the underlying structure for psychotherapy. The history of folk medicine and ancient medicine has consistently shown man's concern with control of life by combining charms, spells, incantations, and words to stave off the effects of the unknown and the unexpected. This historical review is meant only to reveal the methods our ancestors used and is not meant to endorse the philosophy that they believed. The red thread that we will follow is the thread of the word as symbol, representation, wish, and suggestion that something be changed: sickness to health, weakness to strength, confusion to understanding, mediocrity to creativity. The power of the word and the image is the power generated by the patient to transform meanings and experiences via words and images.

In addition, the moment is ripe to relish the variety of techniques, theories, and approaches to self-hypnosis and present them in summary form for all to see. Not everyone teaches self-hypnosis in exactly the same way, nor would we want them to. The unique creativity generated in self-hypnosis is stimulating. Yet it is possible to glean some general principles that apply to all.

I realize that in order to capture the unique transformations, a limit may have to be placed on scientific documentation. The major aim, however, is to present a compendium of ways to use self-hypnosis, a state-of-the-art presentation. Because serious research and theoretical conceptualization are only just coming to the fore, the research and theory presented are not meant to answer all questions but merely to present some of the questions that are currently being asked. In addition, the clinical use of self-hypnosis is more advanced than the scientific explanations, which are only just beginning. It is exciting to be on the cutting edge of this new frontier.

Because of space limitations, this book does not cover the full range of heterohypnosis research and theory but rather focuses on the practice of self-hypnosis and research related to that practice.

WHO SHOULD READ THIS BOOK

This book is directed at the mental health professional interested in clinical problems who wants to use self-hypnosis in his or her practice. Although it contains basic information for the beginning hypnotherapist, the material spans a number of levels to include the advanced hypnotherapist as well.

This book permits comparisons between different orientations of self-hypnosis and provides examples of the types of problems that can be addressed by self-hypnosis. Each orientation is presented objectively, without criticism or evaluation. Consequently, I hope that clinicians, researchers, and students will be able to delineate more clearly the way they talk about, study, or use clinical self-hypnosis.

STRUCTURE OF THIS BOOK

This book consists of four sections. Part I presents a clinical introduction and historical antecedents of self-hypnosis. Part II discusses theories of heterohypnosis and relevant research in self-hypnosis. Part III consists of practical applications of self-hypnosis by clinical orientation as well as by disorder. Each application is described, and a clinical example is presented. Implications are discussed. Self-hypnosis in the personal life of the clinician—a view toward self-relaxation, creativity, and self-understanding—is included. Part IV summarizes and discusses conclusions and implications for the future.

There is a need to describe the broad array of theories and techniques used in clinical practice. This book is a first attempt to organize this vast multiplicity.

Since self-hypnosis can only be known by experiencing it, I leave you to explore your inner world by reading, attending, and experiencing.

Acknowledgments. I sincerely thank my colleagues for the support and feedback they have so generously given me during the development of this volume: Billie Strauss, Mitzie Eisen, Erika Fromm, Michael Diamond, Mary Clarke, and my sister, Evelyn Sanders Shimoni, who was always available. Also, I am indebted to Sharon Panulla, Rowena Howell, Sarah Kennedy, and all other staff members at Guilford Press for their help and support.

Contents

PART I. INTRODUCTION

Chapter 1. Clinical Self-Hypnosis in Practice 3

Chapter 2. Historical Precursors to Self-Hypnosis 16

Chapter 3. Psychological and Sociocultural Roots 39
of Self-Hypnosis

PART II. THEORY AND RESEARCH

Chapter 4. Theories of Hypnosis, Self-Hypnosis, 59
and Psychotherapy

Chapter 5. Research in Self-Hypnosis 84

PART III. DIAGNOSIS, INTAKE, AND APPLICATIONS

Chapter 6. Evaluation 107

Chapter 7. A Multiplicity of Applications: 125
A Uniqueness of Response

Chapter 8. Pain Management 142

Chapter 9. Psychophysiological Disorders   157

Chapter 10. Children, Psychotherapy, and Hypnosis: 177
            A Therapeutic Triad

Chapter 11. Self-Hypnosis for the Professional   191

PART IV. SUMMARY

Chapter 12. Conclusions and Directions   209

Appendix   215

References   219

Index   238

PART I

Introduction

CHAPTER 1

Clinical Self-Hypnosis in Practice

The body says what words cannot.
—Martha Graham

The idea that people can experience self-induced hypnosis has been described in many healing contexts and in many different cultures, but scientific recognition and experimental demonstration of self-hypnosis is only now becoming a serious focus of attention. In the clinical literature, clinical self-hypnosis has often been described as similar to, if not identical with, heterohypnosis, leaving the reader to assume that self-hypnosis needs little explanation. Nonetheless, the ways are so numerous that self-hypnosis is used clinically that the novice hypno-therapist may well become confused and overwhelmed by the extant diversity.

As a starting place, this book attempts to clarify the confusion and the diversity through an initial organization of the goals, uses, and. techniques that have been reported by clinical hypnotherapists using self-hypnosis as part of a treatment approach. Little definitive research evidence is yet available to bring order into this complicated arena. Although controlled studies of variable interaction are just beginning in self-hypnosis and heterohypnosis. I am unaware of any such studies in the area of clinical self-hypnosis. Nonetheless, many hypnothera-pists teach their patients creative approaches to self-hypnosis in the clinical situation in a diversity of ways. To help this new field develop, it is necessary to sort through the multiplicity of ways that self-hypnosis is taught and to sample the multiple ways of using self-hypnosis in the clinical situation.

This chapter provides a description of clinical self-hypnosis, as well as highlights areas for using self-hypnosis within a psychotherapy framework. Although some areas are not covered in this volume, specific areas are sampled to demonstrate the diverse ways in which many hypnotherapists may use self-hypnosis. The interaction between psychotherapy and self-hypnosis is yet largely an unexplored arena, and the two sources of input may at times seem paradoxical. The ways that these powerful influences interact with patient variables and other contextual variables are yet to be revealed in the literature.

Because of the diversity in approaches, techniques, and rationales, there is no one approach that can be considered to provide the best methodology to implement self-hypnosis training (Crasilneck & Hall, 1985; Kroger, 1977; Erickson, 1980a). The therapist, the context, the patient, dimensions of self-hypnosis, and the problem itself all interact, contributing to the patient's truly unique response to self-hypnosis.

CLINICAL SELF-HYPNOSIS

A first step in organizing clinical self-hypnosis is to define it and differentiate it from self-hypnosis, which is a superordinate concept. Clinical self-hypnosis is but one aspect of self-hypnosis, and it has its own aims and goals. In my view, clinical self-hypnosis is an adjunct to a major treatment approach, be it individual hypnotherapy, individual psychotherapy, group therapy, or family therapy. The therapist teaches the patient self-hypnosis as a way (1) to participate actively (in a motivated and purposeful way) in the treatment process and (2) to reinforce self-mastery. The patient is given the opportunity to participate actively because the therapist, by providing a safe environment and support, facilitates psychological health by suggesting helpful words and images to which the patient ascribes meaning. In addition, the therapist remains available to the patient if questions arise. Clinical self-hypnosis is part of an overall treatment program rather than a simple self-help technique.

Much confusion surrounds the terms of self-hypnosis and auto-hypnosis. Some theorists identify all hypnosis as self-hypnosis (Spiegel & Spiegel, 1978; Erickson, 1948; Cheek & LeCron, 1968). Others view self-hypnosis as a self-directed state (Romen, 1981). Still others consider self-hypnosis to be a self-initiated state (Fromm et al., 1981; Brown & Fromm, 1986). Often the term self-hypnosis is used interchangeably with autohypnosis (Kroger, 1977). This practice leads to mounting confusion. On the other hand, some view autohypnosis as a reflexive, biological state (Ludwig, 1983; Gardner & Olness, 1981). Because of this confusion, I present autohypnosis and self-hypnosis as the same experience in contrast to a more reflexive biological state, although I realize that not everyone will agree with this formulation.

I believe that a reflexive, automatic reaction to threatening situations is quite common in life. The trance, seemingly triggered by a threatening or extraordinarily demanding situation, enables us[1] to carry out quite complex behaviors. The ability to enter an automatic trance is neither taught nor self-directed; rather, it appears to be instinctual or survival-directed (Ludwig, 1985). I propose a new name for this instinctual or survival-directed trance, "archetypal"[2] self-hypnosis, which appears to serve as a model or template for other trance states that are taught, induced, or triggered by drugs. The term archetypal has been chosen precisely because it refers to an instinctual template or first form for adaptive behavior. Those automatic trance states that occur in a pathological situation, such as those seen in posttraumatic stress syndrome and multiple personality, are also derived from the archetypal self-hypnosis but are not used adaptively. Although these states initially developed to protect the individual from trauma and extreme stress, like other survival techniques that have been overused they no longer serve an adaptive function and become part of the pathological system itself. These states then need to be modified by treatment (Bliss, 1983; Frankel, 1976; Spiegel, 1986a).

While clinical self-hypnosis and self-hypnosis share many important characteristics, as discussed in Chapter 4, they differ in important contextual ways. These contextual differences are sufficient to define each separately. Self-hypnosis, in contrast to clinical self-hypnosis, is a self-directed, self-induced state (Fromm et al., 1981). In this state, the person is both the subject and the operator, paradoxically self-inducing a trance. The early reports of self-magnetized individuals reflected this self-induced experience. More will be said of self-magnetism in Chapter 2. Albert Moll, an early psychologist who integrated self-hypnosis into the general subject matter of psychology, distinguished between self-hypnosis, which is self-induced, and autohypnosis, which is triggered not by another person but by something else outside the subject (Moll, 1891/1925). This topic will also be covered in Chapter 2.

It is my view that self-hypnosis is possible because of the archetype of autohypnosis that serves as a model for alteration of conscious-

---

[1]Us here refers to patients and other therapists who have experienced or described this phenomena.

[2]In the Jungian sense of archetype: a first form or template.

ness. Although the functions and the experiences of self-hypnosis and archetypal self-hypnosis are different, both are trance states or altered states of consciousness. In Chapter 5, I review some relevant research about self-hypnosis as an altered state of consciousness.

Clinical self-hypnosis, on the other hand, refers to a self-hypnotic state that is first taught to the patient by the therapist and is monitored by the therapist, who reviews the words and images (with their con-comitant meanings) that the patient has used in home practice. The home practice is self-induced and self-directed by the patient according to guidelines discussed in the session. These guidelines or rules of procedure may be directive or nondirective, authoritarian or permissive, structured or nonstructured, depending on the theory and orientation of treatment. In order for self-hypnosis to be relevant to psychotherapy and to the research situation, some input must be given to the patient (subject) in order to assess its impact on the patient's (subject's) response. Patients enter therapy with a variety of cognitive styles. Some patients, such as very anxious or panicked individuals, have difficulty focusing their attention, whereas others, such as obsessive–compulsive individuals, have difficulty expanding their attention. For this reason, I believe that any theory of clinical self-hypnosis must take into account a continuum of ego functions that can be affected by self-hypnosis.

Thus, in clinical self-hypnosis, the patient may learn to use self-hypnosis effortlessly, either in an expanded or a more restrictive manner, depending on the patient's needs. In addition, some patients have a greater tolerance for unconscious input, whereas others are unable to cope with such input. The importance of gauging or titrating the amount of unconscious input must be emphasized, and reasonable limits must be set to prevent overwhelming or retraumatizing the patient. The therapist's monitoring of home practice through the medium of verbal report, written or spoken, is critical until the patient becomes more receptive to input from the unconscious. Chapter 4 discusses these distinctions in more detail.

The term self-hypnosis "practice" is used to indicate that the patient initiates self-hypnosis away from the therapist. Practice refers to a mode of proceeding to enter self-hypnosis. It does not connote willful, deliberate behavior in the sense of forcing oneself to do something. Rather, practice provides the opportunity for the patient to enter self-hypnosis, consequenttly affecting various ego functions such as ego receptivity, attention flow, primary process thought, deautomatization, and fantasy (Fromm, 1981). According to McConkey and Sheehan, the notion of subjects being requested to *try* (i.e., to make an effort) to experience suggested events effortlessly is a paradox that can be seen across the range of traditional hypnotic suggestions (McConkey & Sheehan, 1982). The request may seem to present a double bind (Haley, 1967), or it may refer to motivated or purposeful behavior in the sense that a response, even an effortless hypnotic response, is motivated, purposeful, intentional behavior. Because it has the malleability to be affected by motivation or purposefulness, clinical self-hypnosis can be taught as a useful reinforcement of hypnotherapy.

Areas of Use for Self-Hypnosis

The general areas in which self-hypnosis can be used are varied. Particularly in clinical self-hypnosis, defined goals are important criteria of success in hypnotherapy. These goals are not necessarily aspects of self-hypnosis, but rather, they are goals defined by the patient and therapist together and ones that can be realized through the use of self-hypnosis by the patient. Whether these goals are in some way related to self-hypnosis can only be answered in the laboratory. Chapter 5 reviews the current basic research in self-hypnosis.

Among the areas where self-hypnosis has proven effective are the following:

1. *Skills development.* Practice of self-hypnosis has been found effective to increase readiness and dexterity in the execution of physical activities such as sports and dance, artistic activities such as musical performance and art creations, or intellectual activities such as studying for and taking tests.

2. *Skills improvement.* Refining skills and enhancing performance through self-hypnosis practice has been found effective.

3. *Relaxation.* Self-hypnosis facilitates the reduction of tension and enhances comfort and relaxation. It is a self-regulatory method that leads to relaxation as demonstrated in the clinical situation.

4. *Goal achievement.* The use of self-hypnosis will facilitate reaching the goal set by the patient. Possible goals are limited only by one's imagination.

5. *Attention focusing.* Those persons who have short attention spans can learn to increase the duration of attending via self-hypnosis. This use of focused attention may be less optimal than in heterohypnosis, but nonetheless, the patient can learn to increase significantly the span of attention with practice.

6. *Creativity.* Self-hypnosis appears to increase the creative productivity of those who use it.

7. *Sports.* Because of its skill-enhancing properties and concentration focusing, self-hypnosis facilitates sports performance.

8. *Public speaking.* Self-hypnosis is useful to prepare speakers to present in public.

9. *Test-taking.* By enhancing concentration skills, promoting the development of good study habits, enhancing retrieval skills, and reducing anxiety, self-hypnosis serves as an excellent tool for students. They tend to prepare more adequately and to perform more skillfully after self-hypnosis training.

10. *Social anxiety.* Anxiety in social situations can be reduced via the practice of self-hypnosis, combining desensitization, problem-solving, and imagery rehearsal techniques to reduce anxiety. Self-hypnosis facilitates anxiety reduction.

11. *Phobias.* Specific phobias such as fear of flying can be reduced with self-hypnosis in combination with relaxation techniques and anxiety reduction techniques.

12. *Transcendence and self-growth.* This nondirected state for self-exploration and mind-expanding experience heightens ego receptivity to unconscious experience and expansion of experience as major goals. By transcendence, I mean going beyond blocks to new solutions. I do not believe a person can transcend his or her physical limitations; however, I do believe people can transcend blocks and tap their inner resources more deeply. Transcendence and self-growth require an expansion of awareness, a blending of primary process unconscious imagery with consciousness (secondary process thinking).

Although there may be other ways of conceptualizing the underlying processes, clinically, these activities share a common core that includes tension, anxiety, and diffuse attention. This core of discomfort interferes with concentration and performance. Self-hypnosis, because of its effect on mind and body, can reduce tension and anxiety, and affect one's focus of attention. The resultant relaxation and altered attention, on a continuum from diffuse to focused, stem from self-hypnosis practice regardless of the skill to which it is being applied (creativity, art, sports, public speaking, or taking tests). Learning self-hypnosis is one way to cultivate those behaviors or ingredients that can maximize one's skill performance. According to Fromm et al. (1981), the use of hypnosis and self-hypnosis affects a number of continua within the ego. In her view, certain of these continua correspond to ego structures coordinated by the integrative functions of the ego. She identifies ego receptivity–ego activity (an openness to unconscious input and an active orientation of the ego); unfocused, free-flowing attention (without censorship and order)–concentrative attention (focused and narrow, but deep); primary process (primitive, instinctual, and unconscious thinking)–secondary process (ego directed and elaborated); deautomatization–automatization (voluntary behavior vs. involuntary); and fantasy–reality orientation (reverie, daydreams, fantasies vs. specific reality thinking). Transcendence and growth are enhanced by the effects of self-hypnosis along this continuum (Fromm et al., 1981). Additionally, clinical self-hypnosis can be used in many cases of frank psychopathology. This area is discussed in "Applications."

Goals

For some patients, specific goals can be achieved more easily if they are clearly labeled or if appropriate expectations are set. For example, if you wish to fly without fear, you need to present that experience as a possibility in your imagination. Positive suggestions set up a positive, self-fulfilling prophecy. Negative suggestions, on the other hand, trigger a negative self-fulfilling prophecy, frequently leading to failure. For other patients, opening a window to the unconscious and allowing thoughts, images, sensations, and perceptions to occur effortlessly will lead to insight and understanding. The importance of evaluation in clarifying what approach is taken depends in part on the interaction of complicated variables such as patient variables like personality and problem, as well as contextual and therapist variables such as orientation and theory of self-hypnosis.

In hypnosis and self-hypnosis, the subject or patient learns to be less aware or critical of his or her behavior in order to explore more fully the total experience. The patient will, in heterohypnosis and in waking therapy sessions, generate imagery that is relevant and helpful as well as imagery that may lead to feeling overwhelmed. In order to maximize success, the therapist may suggest or fine-tune patient images that are most helpful by reinforcing them via posthypnotic suggestions. Thus, the patient may be asked to experience those images related to specific goals, such as:

- to release tension
- to gain insight
- to find a new solution
- to restructure an idea
- to heighten positive feelings
- to reduce negative feelings
- to enhance a sense of self-control
- to develop healthy habits
- to transform a sensation from unpleasant to pleasant
- to remove a symptom
- to substitute a less disabling symptom for a more disabling one

Of course this list is not exhaustive. The goals will be dependent on the nature of the patient's problem and the resources available.

Phenomena

The general phenomena of self-hypnosis are similar to those of hetero-hypnosis. According to the Chicago group (Fromm et al., 1981), both heterohypnosis and self-hypnosis are altered states of consciousness reflecting a reduction of reality (lowering of the generalized reality orientation, as described by Shor, 1959) and an increase in absorption to inner experience (Tellegen & Atkinson, 1974). These phenomena, according to Fromm, are structural variables in self-hypnosis as well as in heterohypnosis.

More specifically, in self-hypnosis, the individual experiences a greater quantity of imagery than in heterohypnosis or normal states of consciousness. Free-floating associations are often experienced as free-floating images. This primary process thought is characteristic of self-hypnosis. The imagery reflects content that is important in decipher-ing the patient's dynamics. Psychotherapists have long valued imagery as a powerful clinical tool. Carl Jung, for example, realized the value of imagery in the exploration of early childhood memories. Jung described the psyche as consisting essentially of images. He describes these "as a series of images and not an accidental joining or sequence. Rather, the images form a structure that is full of meaning and pur-pose. It is a picturing of vital activities. And just as the material of the body that is ready for life has a need for the psyche in order to be capable of life, so the psyche presupposes the living body in order that its images may live" (Jung, 1958, pp. 325–326). He believed that imagery serves two important functions in psychotherapy. First, imagery is a means of perceiving mind–body unity, and, second, imagery is symbolic of meaningful memories and feelings that are repressed or dissociated.

In clinical self-hypnosis with patients, as compared to hetero-hypnosis, consciousness is altered, as is concentration. It may be ex-panded or constricted, depending on the requirements of the situation. As we will see with normal subjects, attention in self-hypnosis appears more expanded (Fromm et al., 1981). In addition, time distortion experiences are common. Time may be experienced as expanded, even cosmic, or reduced to a microscopic experience in both situa-tions. Generally, more time disorientation appears in self-hypnosis than in heterohypnosis (Johnson, 1979). Affects may be heightened or diminished. This aspect of hypnosis and self-hypnosis renders it as particularly helpful in the therapeutic process. Affects may be heightened, for example, in abreaction to obtain release; or they may be diminished, for example, in cognitive control strategies used to gain control. According to Fromm et al. (1981), this phenomenon reflects the vacillation between ego receptivity and ego activity. Self-hypnosis then may help in titrating the affects, that is reducing them or facilitating them when necessary. Brown (1985) and Gruber (1983) describe hypnotic techniques useful in stabilizing affects.

Self-perception of the body also appears changed (Schneck, 1966). Sensations of heaviness, lightness, warmth, and coolness occur. Perceived changes in size, in connections between body parts, and changes in tension and/or relaxation are selectively described by patients during self-hypnosis. This effect is in part a reflection of the decrease in the generalized reality orientation as well as the physiological effects of relaxation that may occur in self-hypnosis.

Self-perception of voluntary control also appear changed. The patient may experience a sense of involuntary or automatic behavior. Feelings of floating, spinning, and "things are happening" may be experienced. Some patients become quite anxious during these experiences and may not be able to tolerate them. Others find these experiences exciting. Still others can contain them. Not every patient describes all of these experiences. Since the perception of one's self in self-hypnosis is subjective, there may be experiences that are unique or more individualized.

HYPNOTIC IMAGERY IN THE CLINICAL SITUATION

Although there are a multiplicity of ways that patients will experience imagery, the following examples are taken from a variety of patients in my practice. These examples do not imply that these imagery experiences are the only ones possible or that they are in some way better than others. They simply provide specific examples taken from patients in self-hypnosis using spontaneous imagery.

An undergraduate student with test anxiety experienced blankness when taking a test. Whenever a test was scheduled, she became so anxious that she could not prepare for the exam. In self-hypnosis, she spontaneously imaged herself studying in a garden surrounded by many colorful flowers. At home she practiced self-hypnosis studying in a garden and found that she was able to concentrate on her books and notes. At her next exam, Susie brought a colorful flower with her. She passed the exam with flying colors. In this example, spontaneous hypnotic imagery generated powerful meanings through colorful flower imaging. The flower she took to the exam was partly a transitional symbol, that is, it reinforced a comfortable, safe self-experience (Winnicott, 1953). In this example, spontaneous hypnotic imagery reflected powerful meanings through colorful flower imagery.

Thus, we see that the patient may self-administer specific suggestions in which there is an illusion of enablement, as for example, "because I have practiced relaxation, I find myself drifting, drifting off to sleep." Indirect suggestions depend on conditional contingencies according to Erickson (1980a). They do not depend on an act of will.

A second patient, Joe, had difficulty sleeping. He would fall asleep for 1 or 2 hours, but would awaken and would generally browbeat himself for being awake. He then learned to enter self-hypnosis when awaking from sleep. He self-suggested relaxation. First, he would take three long slow deep breaths and relax every muscle, followed by the self-suggestion, "because I have practiced relaxation, I find myself drifting off to sleep." He was able to do just that. He learned that going to sleep was dependent on the conditional contingency of relaxation. His physiological and psychological response to self-hypnotic suggestion enabled him to sleep normally and naturally.

Guided imagery used as positive suggestion for success, then, can be useful when used in covert practice of new success-oriented behaviors. It can strengthen conscious and unconscious ego defenses by reinforcing and validating competence.

Another patient, Mrs. J., was thinking of going to work after 20 years of being a wife and mother to three children. She was quite anxious about interviewing for a job, although she believed that once she started working, she would do fine. Quite simply, she felt no one would take her seriously at an interview. She was able to imagine herself going to an interview in which she described as well as experienced herself in the following way: "I experience myself becoming more confident, more able to express my feelings at an interview, at work, or wherever I am." She did indeed get a job after her first interview. Thus, the free-floating imagery that can be tapped in self-hypnosis can be useful to glean insight and emotional understanding as it opens a window to the unconscious: that is, the patient becomes more ego-receptive as attention expands.

Still another patient, Dot, a middle-aged school teacher was bingeing late into the night. She felt out of control of her eating and feared gaining weight. Her bingeing was related to some unconscious motives that required uncovering. In hypnosis and in self-hypnosis, Dot began to look at the images that came to mind. She found that the images were related to sensual feelings that she usually denied or repressed. Bringing these feelings to the light of consciousness enabled her later to seek out a meaningful relationship with a man.

One patient, Jack, found himself to be very stressed-out at work. He forgot things, experienced high levels of tension and anxiety, and was on the brink of panic. He began to practice formal relaxation exercises, much like those described by Jacobson (1929). Each day he practiced, alternating tightening the muscles and loosening the muscles, starting from the feet, the legs, the body, the arms, even the muscles of the head and face. Over a period of months, he mastered the tension and was able to improve his work situation. Thus, this patient practiced progressive relaxation as part of every day life. Such daily practice can minimize the build-up of tension and fatigue.

A patient may also spontaneously facilitate memory experiences or hypermnesia. "I am going back in memory to that time when I was 10 years old in school, and I was frightened." The benefits of hypermnesia include abreaction and freeing up of vital energy. Thus, many faces of imagery spontaneously emerge in clinical self-hypnosis.

SELF-HYPNOSIS AND AFFECT

In self-hypnosis, affects are more easily accessed, much like opening a window to the unconscious. Nonetheless, an optimal level of affect is necessary in both hypnotherapy and psychotherapy in order to help the patient to work through problems. Without the combined power of intellect and affect, change may be jeopardized. Excessively high levels lead to feelings of being overwhelmed. Too little affect may lead to flat intellectualization. The optimal level of affect is that which integrates.

For example, Jane was fearful that she would not be able to write her doctoral dissertation. In hypnosis, we could discuss the fears and examine her motives for finishing or not finishing. We could look at symbolic meanings represented by the doctoral dissertation. It represented growing up, taking responsibility, putting her thoughts on the table to be judged. And we would go beyond the here and now by looking at the future through her imagination: What would it be like when she had finished her dissertation. The emotions connected with completion of the dissertation involved a combination of pure joy and intense fear. We clarified how her ambivalent feelings, attitudes, habits, and expectations prevented her from working effectively and now we could also tap an entirely different set of feelings, attitudes, habits, and expectations that would permit her to bring both her competence and her motivation together, a self-integration that ultimately permitted her to complete her work.

In this case, a new balance between thought and action replaced the precarious destructive dissociation or separation of thought and action. Of course, self-hypnosis also can be experienced in a more automatic, unfocused, and free-floating manner leading to expanded awareness. As we will see, there are a variety of approaches and techniques, and in clinical self-hypnosis one may combine a number of these approaches.

The multiplicity of ways that self-hypnosis can be used in psychotherapy is staggering. Indeed, self-hypnosis appears deceptively simple, as reflected by the previous examples. Change occurs at several levels within the individual: It occurs at the level of self-perception, affect, and cognition. It occurs at the level of self-esteem. And it occurs at the behavioral level as well. When these transformations occur in a synthesized manner, they comprise powerful change.

The technique of self-hypnosis itself can be taught in a striking variety of ways. Self-hypnosis is a tool that is not self-evident. It can vary according to the psychotherapy theory used; it can vary according to the hypnosis theory used; it can vary according to the specific patient and his or her ability to use self-hypnosis. And it can vary according to the style of the therapist. Fromm and Kahn believe that the interaction within the patient between structural variables such as absorption and content variables such as imagery leads to a variety of unique responses (Fromm & Kahn, 1990d).

The connecting theme of this book is to highlight the transformation of meaning and experience perceived by the patient and contained in his or her words and images. The possibilities are manifold. At the same time, this book attempts to clarify a variety of ways for the hypnotherapist to use self-hypnosis in the clinical situation, ways to explain it, and ways to teach it. For this reason, the focus is placed on the bridge between heterohypnosis and self-hypnosis, those suggestions, verbalizations, and instructions that are given to the patient to help him or her to enter self-hypnosis, that is, to create a therapeutic set. The patient's experience is subjective. Current research is sorting out the relevant variables and their complicated interactions, and with time the clarifications and understanding will come. The nature of self-hypnosis and its rich phenomenology can be explored elsewhere (Fromm & Kahn, 1990a). I have included chapters on the history of self-hypnosis, as well as ones exploring the theories of hypnosis and self-hypnosis (which are just beginning to be articulated). In addition, relevant research is cited. The inclusion of these areas is important to maintain a realistic and scientific perspective through which clinical issues can be addressed. We begin by looking at the developmental history of self-hypnosis to understand more fully its intricacy. As the controlled study of self-hypnosis is just beginning, with evolution over time, the place of meanings held by words and images may itself change. Only time will tell.

CHAPTER 2

Historical Precursors to Self-Hypnosis

The history of self-hypnosis has been indisputably neglected. By and large, self-induced trances before experiments in animal magnetism were associated with magic, witchcraft, and alchemy. What is overlooked in this historical sequence is the fact that the occult experience was the predecessor to the scientific one. These experiences were attempts by man to control his world. Spontaneous trances frequently accompanied man's attempt to gain control of his world, and these attempts have been reported for at least as long as the written word. Because the study of science was so primitive, essentially man sought answers from supernatural sources, the prevailing belief at the time to explain causality, since man had not yet discovered his own ability to cause change. In an effort to gain perspective, I review those early beliefs and practices that appear to be the early precursors of self-hypnosis. Because self-hypnosis was not to be conceptualized for many centuries, the self-induced trance, as associated with healing and change, was not recognized as a natural phenomena in its own right but was viewed as an epiphenomenon of hypnosis.

The history of self-hypnosis has included eras in which the following thematic perspectives have predominated:

1. *Spiritual perspectives* include the power of words, rituals, meditation, and sleep cures.
2. *Religious perspectives* include prayer, posturing, and biblical quotations.

3. *Prescientific perspectives* include observations of mind–body correlation, changes in belief toward humanism, recognition of man's inner life.
4. *Scientific perspectives* include animal magnetism and self-magnetism.
5. *Medical perspectives* include the contributions from Liebault through Freud.
6. *Psychological perspectives* include Coué and autosuggestion, positive autogenic training, tape-assisted self-hypnosis, written instructions.
7. *Sociocultural perspectives* focus on style, directive and nondirective paradigms, dynamic paradigms, and social expectation.

SPIRITUAL PERSPECTIVES

The one thing in the world, of value, is the active soul
—Emerson, *The American Scholar*

The spiritual perspective on healing was the earliest form of therapy in that explanations were intimately concerned with meaning and life. The history of folk medicine and ancient medicine has consistently shown man's concern with controlling life and seeking guidance for the future. Because man did not know what to do, he turned to external guidance and external control by combining words, actions, and objects to stave off negative effects of the unknown and the unexpected such as illness. The appearance of illness was attributed to forces outside the control of man. Yet the power of words in the healing process has been demonstrated universally, in the Hindu Sanskrit, Egyptian hieroglyphic, the Babylonian cuneiform writings, and other early writings.

In order to understand fully current mythology about hypnosis and self-hypnosis, we need to look back to these magical rituals. Current interest today demonstrates a specific movement back to early myths in an effort to understand man's cosmology. Professor Joseph Campbell devoted his life to this task. He wrote extensively of the myth that he conceived to be the foundation of life: the spontaneous shift of ideas from sentiments to consciousness (Campbell, 1976). Increasingly, the importance of myth in the development of life and culture is revealed (Hamilton, 1940). The importance of myth in the development of hypnosis and self-hypnosis needs to be revealed.

In the primitive times of human history, magic occupied the domain of phenomenology that has now been succeeded by science

(Ghalioungui, 1973). It represented an attempt to explain and to control life (Jaynes, 1976). Judging the ancient past by modern standards is akin to judging Viking longships by the Queen Elizabeth II. The Viking barks were efficient and effective for their time, but we would not want to sail the ocean in them today. Judging the past by the present leads to myths, opinions, and denial of these roots. In this book, the scientific roots of self-hypnosis are traced in an effort to clarify yesteryear's legacy and practical wisdom with current experience.

Confronted with the paradox of life, man has traditionally sought answers. Jaynes (1976) postulates that primitive man held dialogues with himself in order to find his answers for meaning, health, and life—dialogues between the right and left brain. Later, as consciousness expanded, the conversations within were transformed to prayer with an external diety. Hinduism presents a religion in which each person participates in God. The belief is that a part of the deity exists in each individual, and therefore, each person is in part divine (Bloomfield, 1964). Thus, profound religious and existential communications were experienced within the individual. Healing practices were generally carried out by the educated priests and medicine men, since illness was attributed to malevolent acts of evil spirits (Muthu, 1930). The priest relied on "his own religious feelings" (Ghalioungui, 1973, p. 42), and the practice of healing was restricted to those who possessed a higher, deeper knowledge of the secret nature of things. Appeals to the gods were made orally or in writing (Jaynes, 1976). By the powerful words and images designed to coerce and control "deities" that contributed to the illness, the words of power healed.

The apparent marriage between magic and religion was one of convenience in that both dealt with occult, superhuman forces of nature in an effort to control these for the benefit of man (Ghalioungui, 1973). However, a hierarchy of power existed, with the learned priests having the greatest authority and the magician having less, much like the distinction between the professional and the lay person today.

Words and Actions

The role of words has held a primary place throughout the history of man. For this reason, I briefly describe the role of words within various contexts such as actions, sacrifice, rituals, the use of the mantra, meditation, music, and charms. Therapy was based on rituals or words and actions of worship (prayer), sacrifice (abstinence and action), and purification (cleansing) (Ghalioungui, 1973; Jaynes, 1976; Campbell, 1976). Specific rituals included incantation, prayer, and sacrifice. The verbal prayers, bolstered by actions of sacrifice and purification, generated powerful expectations. The setting, the rituals themselves, and the words heightened the expectations and motivation of the patient, and consequently, they affected the outcome.

Incantations consisted of "words of power" (Jaynes, 1976). The words had power because they enabled change in the life of the individual; that is, they propitiated the gods, and they ousted the demons, the then-believed cause for illness. Within the Egyptian culture, the extant belief was that the words were a great mystery and should not be revealed to the general populace lest they be misused. Perhaps this secrecy was the shamanic way of limiting the practice of healing and was deemed necessary because so many people lacked understanding. Nonetheless, the secrecy intensified the power of the words and the priesthood.

In ancient India, the priest could appeal to the gods orally or in writing, since his education permitted him this flexibility. The treatment provided by the priest was highly verbal and ritualistic, consisting of words in the form of incantation and prayer and activities consisting of sacrifice set forth in the learned writings. In a real sense, the approach to healing was holistic. That is, therapy addressed itself both to mind and to body (Ghalioungui, 1973). Prayers, hymns, sacred dances, and medicines in the form of herbs were combined to enlist godly help and to expel evil demons. Words became powerful weapons to foil the demons, thus restoring well-being. Whereas early man believed that help was external, his words and his rituals in the healing situation may be construed as constituting a self-hypnotic approach.

Sacrifice

Sacrifice was an action designed initially to charm the gods and to gain their favor. Later, it was viewed as a way of participating in the spiritual experience (Ghalioungui, 1973). For example, a burnt offering is reduced to smoke and ashes. This transformation of a material substance into an ethereal quality demonstrates that change is omnipresent. As the ritual transforms matter into spirit, the word transforms fear into hope. According to Jung (1958), "the priest and the congregation, in their service, move along a progressive continuum[1] from purification, consecration, exaltation, and spiritualization" (p. 160). Transformation in this sense is a demonstration of God's power. In modern science, self-transformation may be attributed to one's personal power to change.

[1]This continuum reveals a transformation.

Rituals

In addition to words, rituals were an important part of healing practices. Early rituals included washing, anointing, and perfuming. The use of water in healing and hypnosis through the years, for example, suggests a pathway from ancient practices to more scientific times (Edmonston, 1986). Rituals or activities were believed necessary for change to occur.

Words, however, have continued to dominate healing because language accompanies and shapes action; meaning attaches to behavior. The nature of language and its relationship to the body are complementary. Body and mind interact. Language is a trigger for brain activity within the individual, and language can be a response to brain activity; for example, a word or idea can trigger a variety of responses such as movement, thought, feeling, or self-control. In ancient times, these responses were believed to come from the gods. In his role as intermediary between the gods and the patient, the priest would invoke: "Tis thou who canst grant me the means of saving all" (Ghalioungui, 1973). The response to this invocation was given in sleep in the form of a dream. Because dreams were regarded as divine, coming from the gods, efforts were made to increase dream activity and to enhance the clarity of the vision. During body sleep, the opportunity for communication between the gods and the soul was considered maximized because it was believed that the soul was awake. First, the priest chanted, and the patient repeated the chant. The patient then retired to the shrine of the god whose inspiration was desired and slept in the portico of the temple (Ghalioungui, 1973). The patient had achieved a state of readiness and had only to wait for something to happen, that is, to have a dream. This expectancy reflects the power (defined by the patient) of images. The dream sometimes contained the diagnosis, but also, frequently, it contained the cure. Dreams, as we understand them today, contain day residues, unconscious meanings and conflicts, and unfinished business. Dreams can hold the resolution of that conflict and thus present an image of the cure.

The Mantra

Another way of using words of power was the chanting of a mantra (Bloomfield, 1964). A mantra is a spoken charm or hymn addressed to the gods. Mantras were used for many purposes. Specific mantras and charms existed for prayer, for hope, for protection, for harmony, for avoidance of discord, and for success. The repetition of the mantra was intended to charm the gods to help and to entreat the evil spirits to leave. Some mantras sound like hypnotic inductions. According to Edmonston, the Charm of Assignation most closely approximates an induction procedure (Edmonston, 1986).

> The mother shall sleep, the father shall sleep, the dog shall sleep, the lord of the house shall sleep . . . O sleep, put thou to sleep all people with the magic that induces sleep. . . . (Bloomfield, 1964, pp. 105-106)

Thus, words were important tools to negotiate with the outside powers controlling life and to obtain guidance from these powers, the gods. Man was not yet self-reflective, so he was unable to use words to direct himself. Today, our scientific body of knowledge includes the use of words to direct oneself through self-suggestion.

Meditation

Meditation consisted of clearing and purifying the mind, focusing attention away from the world, and turning the attention inward (Ghalioungui, 1973). Meditation, although undirected, leads to a profound alteration of consciousness and a variety of changes in physiological as well as mental functioning. These changes may be even more profound than those found in hypnosis, which is more focused and directed by hypnotic suggestion.[2] According to Shapiro, meditation is ineffable, beyond words, whereas he does not believe that hypnosis and self-hypnosis have this quality (Shapiro, 1984).

In meditation, suggestions are given as hymns, instructions, and verbal incantations before the actual practice of meditation, which is experienced by the individual alone (Bloomfield, 1964). The early roots of self-hypnosis can be recognized in meditation practices. Although the court is undecided, proponents can be found who claim hypnosis and meditation are alike (Benson, 1975) and others who claim they are decidedly different (Shapiro, 1982). Finally, in meditation, the contents of thought are unimportant; the major focus is on the meditation experience itself (personal experience).[3] Early meditation expe-

---

[2]The power of words in primitive times had to do with the ability to enlist the aid of outside forces.

[3]When I visited India in 1986, I learned how to practice transcendental meditation (TM). I found that there are many steps in refining meditation, requiring considerable practice—20 minutes every morning and 20 minutes every evening. My subjective experience of TM in comparison with my personal practice of self-hypnosis is that TM happens or unfolds, whereas self-hypnosis is actively directed. In those instances when I permitted self-hypnosis to be less directed, the experience of trance became more like that of meditation.

rience provided an opportunity to communicate with the gods, that is, mindfulness or selflessness; however, in hypnosis and self-hypnosis, the contents of thought—its very meanings (e.g., images, dreams, affects, reveries) are important. Research today continues to seek physiological distinctions between the states of meditation and self-hypnosis (Davidson & Goleman, 1977; Brown, 1977; Fromm, 1977; Van Nuys, 1973; Walrath & Hamilton, 1975). Because no clear-cut differences have been found to date, most theorists today believe the difference lies in the subjective experience itself.

Music, Dance, and Rhythm

Music, dance, and rhythm provided other means for man to communicate with the gods. In ancient China, as early as the 18th century B.C., music, dance, and rhythm were used to enable individuals to commune with the dead in an "ecstatic" state. The later Mesmeric crises resembled these ecstatic states.

Scholem (1941), Denny (1904), Stoll (1904), and Bowers and Glasner (1958) describe the early use of posture and verbal repetition by the Chinese people. As Bowers and Glasner (1958) describe, "she sits down on a low chair and bends forward so that her head rests on her knees. Then in a deep measured voice, she repeats three times an exorcism, whereupon a certain change appears to come over her" (Bowers & Glasner, 1958, pp. 54–55). Posture and repetition are important also in meditation and other altered states of consciousness, for example, attainment of religious ecstasy.

During the fifth century B.C., sleep temples where people came for a 9-day incubation or sleep treatment were very popular in Egypt, Greece, and Rome (Ghalioungui, 1973). During the treatment, the goddess Isis would reveal herself to the sufferer and offer diagnosis and treatment. The Greeks, in contrast, would dream of Aesculapius, the god of medicine, who would cure the individual or give treatment instructions (Bullfinch, 1979). Aesculapius could communicate at two levels with his patients: at the somatic level of the symptom and at the spiritual level. His spiritual communication, that is his treatment by words, identifies him as the father of rapport (Ghalioungui, 1973; Bernheim, 1980). In these sleep temples, involuntary cures were attained when the patient achieved a state of readiness or receptiveness through what now might be construed as autosuggestion. The setting, the instructions, and the "treatment" itself prepared the patient to expect a dream that was understood to be a direct communication with the gods. Moll describes autosuggestion as self-triggered by the doors of perception (Moll, 1891/1925). What the patient heard, saw, felt, and experienced were all via sensory pathways. The patient understood that the gods would communicate with him through a dream. Are these preparations not the very triggers of autohypnosis?

We may conclude, therefore, that the ingredients of incubation or sleep treatment were an association of spoken word, amulet, and trance (Bernheim, 1891/1980). An altered state of consciousness combined with words of power appear to be commanding demand characteristics as described by Orne (1965).

Charms

As part of the treatment, charms (objects believed to possess some occult or supernatural power) such as an amulet were used to reinforce the words of power. These objects were believed to exert an irresistible power to please, attract, fascinate, or influence (Deleuze, 1825/1982). The charm was combined with words to fascinate the gods as a treatment intervention. Sometimes water was used to "magnetize" the charm, which enabled the patient to treat him- or herself with the "magnetized" charm or amulet (Deleuze, 1825/1982). This reference to self-treatment by the patient via a transitional object is an important link to clinical self-hypnosis. The transitional objects used today include biofeedback, scripts, and tapes.

Nonetheless, hypnosis and self-hypnosis today continue to rely heavily on the power of words to affect the self. We have seen the early recognition of the power of words in the earliest scriptures: words incite, motivate, and soothe. Of course, they can also be destructive. Words can lead to hope and motivation or to fear and despair. Words become tied to symbols and take on the powerful meaning of those symbols. Words then impact: They can energize, inspire, or torment. Words of power can lead to a self-fulfilling prophecy.

Although they were not identified as such in earlier civilizations, demand characteristics existed in such situations. The preparations given to patients heightened their expectations that something would happen. When they were ready, something indeed did occur, such as a dream or an image, leading to revelation, that is, a bringing to light of that which had been hidden (Easton, 1989). The proceedings, as described, resemble autohypnosis, a state in which an external event triggers a subjective experience. The descriptions gleaned from early history imply the operation of demand characteristics: the situation, the expectations, the states of readiness, dreams and unconscious revelations, and, most importantly, the power of words to induce change.

RELIGIOUS PERSPECTIVES

A religious perspective on healing is reflected in the Bible and religious teachings. According to Wolff (1951), several of God's activities were hypnotic. God was the necessary and sufficient cause for healing and health. Thus, when illness struck, prayer, ritual, and sacrifice are sought.

In the ancient Celtic nations of Britain and Germany and in parts of Gaul, the Druid priests used a combination of music, rhythm, and dance to influence the gods. Healing candidates were trained in purging, cleansing, dancing, and the medicinal preparation and use of drugs. The powerful use of words attributed to the Druids included a belief in their ability to kill a person with rhymes and rhythms (McCullock, 1911, p. 326). Although contemporary scholars disclaim this belief as unfounded, such beliefs at one time generated strong demand characteristics.

In our time, rhythmic aspects of induction are viewed as musical. Rhymes are important in communication because of the musical rhythm associated with the words. Rhythm provides a bridge to the familiar and the known. In primitive times, such as the time of the Druids, melody itself expressed an idea. In acts of healing, that idea was related to cleansing, purifying, and the transformation from illness to becoming well. In modern times, music and rhythm have been found to affect mood and energy level; for example, soft, quiet rhythms induce relaxation.

Writings from the Old Testament contain several references to hypnotic-sounding behaviors (Glasner, 1951). The Bible refers to Adam's sleep or *tardemah*: "And the Lord God caused a deep sleep to fall upon Adam" (Genesis 1:3). In the Book of Isaiah (55:11) it is written: "So shall my word be that that goeth forth out of mouth. It shall not return unto me void, but it shall accomplish that which I please. . . ." Another biblical passage describes the "holding of the eyes." This notion of the power of the eye in inducing trance is widespread. The early precursors to the power of the eye can be found in Genesis (44:21), "to set the eyes" on anyone is to view him or her with favor. In Matthew (20:15), the "evil eye" figuratively speaks of the envious or covetous (cf. Deut. 15:9). In Hebrews (4:12), the following indicates the power of God's Word: "For the Word of God is quick, and powerful, and sharper than any two-edged sword." God's Word was imbued with His Power— "The Word once spoken runs an independent course and it possesses an intrinsic force—a creative principle" (Genesis 1:3). In Jewish mysticism, rabbinical scholars such as Abraham Ben Eliazer have recommended what appears to be a practical self-hypnotic technique: "Concentrate on the great name of God; to imagine its radiant letters between their eyes and to fix all their attention on it" (Scholem, 1941, p. 143). Such practical maxims have become part of Jewish oral law.

The New Testament also has citations emphasizing the power of words to affect us, although the connection had yet to be made that man could give personal meaning to words. Words were considered powerful because their meanings came from God; for example take the passage "In the beginning was the Word and the Word was with God and the Word was God" (John 1:1). What greater power can exist than the Word of God? Saint Paul described himself in a state of trance in which his mind and body were separated while praying in the temple at Jerusalem (Acts 22:17). In fact, the word trance comes from the Greek word *Ekstasis*, which denotes the state of one who is "out of himself." Such were the trances of Peter and Paul (see Acts 10:11, 11:5, 22:17). The trance or ecstasy was an absorbed state of mind preparing for the reception of a vision (see also Cor. 12:1–4).

Hebrew poetry focuses on man's relation to God. In the Hebrew scriptures there are three distinct kinds of poetry dealing with this relationship: the dramatic Book of Job, the lyrical Book of Psalms, and the didactic Book of Ecclesiastes. This poetry is quite distinct from that found in western nations because it has neither metre nor rhyme, but rather consists in the mutual correspondence of sentences or clauses, called parallelism or thought-rhyme. While hypnotic suggestions can be made with rhyme, the type of parallelism found in Hebrew poetry, where the same idea is repeated with the same words (see Ps. 93:2) or with different words (see Ps. 22), is more conducive. The idea may be expressed in a positive form in one clause, a negative in another (see Ps. 40:15), and/or may be repeated in the same verse at intervals. The use of repetition is common in giving hypnotic suggestions as is that of gradation, where the thought of one verse is resumed in another (Easton, 1989).

Even today, the perception of mind being separated from body is a frequently described experience in hypnosis, meditation, and self-hypnosis. A patient may describe the experience of observing his/her body below while floating near the ceiling. Another patient may learn in self-hypnosis to separate or dissociate a body part such as an arm that is painful from his/her mental experience.

The power of words in religion provides a channel for man to gain control of his life and understanding from God. The Word expresses God's power to act. Words are used in prayer to thank God, to ask for God's help, or to seek quiet acceptance. Words of prayer renew hope and courage. They offer a model of behavior to be imitated. They are powerful indeed.

Formal prayer moved the patient one step closer to the possibility of self-hypnosis. Because of it the patient could appeal directly to God on his or her own behalf. The dialogue itself could be direct. Yet any change was attributed to the will of God and not to the will of the patient.

PRESCIENTIFIC PERSPECTIVES

As dependence on external forces decreased, prescientific explanations for causality emerged to account for healing therapy. History reveals the increasing awareness of the mind's influence on the body. Early descriptions of such mind–body interaction have been found in writings dating back 3,000 years. For example, the fakirs in India induced trance states by themselves. In such a self-induced state they appeared to feel no pain and to engage in seemingly unbelievable physical feats.

The dawning understanding that thoughts can affect illness and health underlies the discovery that man can reason and arrive at conclusions. The notion that the mind can function somehow independently of experience has led to a new humanistic concept of man's place in the world and to a belief in the powers of the mind. The following are some examples of this new recognition grounded in self-awareness and in the growing realization that the mind could somehow affect the body.

Mind–Body Interaction

The Greeks provide us with a variety of allusions to the mind–body connection. For example, Hippocrates noted that "when the eyes are closed, there are times when the soul can discern diseases in the body." The Greeks believed that the operation of the soul was revealed from the "light" or understanding obtained in dreams.

Examples of this phenomenon abound in classical Greek mythology. For example, Chiron, the centaur and Prince of Thessaly, had fascinated his student Aesculapius for the purpose of discovering a remedy to cure the foot of Hercules. In this myth, the state of fascination, a precursor to hypnosis, generated enlightenment or knowledge.[4] Another myth described Epimenides, in a cave who fell asleep and

[4]Fascination refered to the healer's ability to influence the patient.

remained a long while in that state. When he awoke, everything had changed. The explanation for this experience was that he had dismissed his soul from his body and had recalled it at his own pleasure. The myth highlights the self-induced separation of soul (mind) from body. Plotinus, the Neoplatonic philosopher, described the familiar presence of feelings without conscious reference. He believed that unconscious inferences spring from perceptual experience.

Early philosophy was patterned after Plato and Aristotle (Vlastos, 1971). Plato maintained a radical dualism between ideas, or ideal forms, and material things. His teachings split spirit and rationality, essence and imperfect material reality, body and mind. Aristotle, on the other hand, unified form and matter with the principle of inseparability. His unification of form and essence, body and mind, lays the basic foundation for the possibility of self-directed hypnosis as a real and meaningful concept. In addition, Aristotle introduced the concepts of potentiality and actuality, allowing for change and transformation to occur.

Roman Emperor Marcus Aurelius in his "Meditations" declared: "Our life is what our thoughts make it" (Aurelius, 1945, p. 33). St. Augustine deduced the presence of the unconscious in his description of the great power of man. St. Thomas Aquinas discussed processes in the soul of which man is unaware. Dante, with a different perspective still, described the potentiality of the unconscious, referring to the fact that shameful memories are often forgotten.

Shakespeare's works show great awareness of unconscious experiences and nonvoluntary behaviors (McHovic, 1981). For example, in *Macbeth* Lady Macbeth is observed "with her eyes open but . . . their sense shut" by the doctor of physic and a waiting gentlewoman; Lady Macbeth speaks and rubs her hands together as though she were washing them, oblivious to what is taking place around her (*Macbeth*, Act 5, Scene I, beginning Line 29). In *King Lear* the description of Lear's temporary madness thematically mirrors his inability to see actuality when he was sane (Act 4, Scene 6, beginning Line 153). And in *The Tempest* Sebastian, brother to the King of Naples, describes Antonio as if . . ." in a strange repose, to be asleep with eyes wide open, standing, speaking, moving and yet so fast asleep . . ." (*The Tempest*, Act 2, Scene 1, beginning Line 215). These examples reflect the presence of unconscious experiences that could be a consequence of a self-induced trance.

The Abbé De Faria noted subjects who went into trances upon crossing his threshold even before he could perform an induction (Bramwell, 1956). Thus, the foundation was developed over many centuries for a dynamic interaction of mind and body that implies the existence of experience beyond consciousness. This pathway simultaneously contributed to the possibility of a psychodynamic theory of the unconscious but also to the possibility of a dynamic, interactive use of self-hypnosis: A mind divided into conscious and unconscious components makes directed self-hypnosis meaningful.

Beginning of Self-Direction

During the Renaissance, Western man began to exhibit dissatisfaction with a passive orientation to the world. Renaissance man rebelled against the limitations imposed by the learned priests and the secrecy of the intellectual sphere. At the same time, man affirmed the power of his reason to determine, express, and achieve the good. This era enabled man to become aware of capacities, strengths, and powers to direct his own life. As self-direction became more explicit, belief in religion weakened. A figure–ground reversal was occurring; a transformation in which power for change could come from within the individual.

The church and religious healers, to gain the confidence of sick and ailing people, focused on the power of the imagination to cure. Words were again used to transform. Musuae (1562), as quoted by Bernheim (1891/1980, p. 8), described an "infallible method for successfully concluding a pregnant woman's labor," consisting of reciting some pages from the Songs of David. This quote appears to be the first reference to childbirth aided by words. In it, words were transformed into healing tools.

Between the 15th and 17th centuries, the focus on rationality and personal power conflicted with the belief in demonic possession. Many people were accused of being possessed by spirits, demons, and evil forces. On the other hand, Paracelsus, in the 16th century, believed that everything in the world derived from divinity but that maintenance of worldly things came from the stars. He hypothesized that these two influences endowed man with a double magnetism, generating an effective secretion in animated things. His thinking led to the eventual theory of animal magnetism and to the origin of magnetic medicine (Ellenberger, 1970). According to Edmonston, Paracelsus anticipated Freud as well since he described the compelling force of imagination (Edmonston, 1986).

Magnetic cures were described by Van Helmont, a priest, who attempted to prove their validity (Ellenberger, 1970). At this time, interest in alchemy swelled precisely because it symbolized transformation from a lesser good to a greater good. Just as baser metals could be transformed into gold, so man could be transformed from a lower level of development and achievement into a higher one, by way of magnetism. In 1774, Jean-Joseph Gassner, a priest very interested in exorcism, instructed a patient on what she could do to heal herself (Ellenberger, 1970). This instruction in self-healing appears to be the first explicit reference to the individual's power to help himself.

The Enlightenment, in which primacy of the role of reason was championed, arrived in Europe around 1775. Ignorance, superstition, and tradition suddenly were no longer tolerated. An antireligious trend was apparent. It was at this time that the German philosopher Kant wrote of the power of the mind to be master of one's morbid feelings through simple delusion: "the leaving behind by man of his self-caused minority. Minority is the impossibility of using one's own reason without the guidance of another . . . have the courage to make use of your own reason" (Kant, 1781). In effect, training of the will and controlling the emotion were given precedence as capacities under cerebral control.

Until Kant (1781), all experience and reality were presumed to reside outside the person. The mind was believed to be only a blank screen that reflected perceptions. Immanuel Kant brought about a radical change in philosophy: He switched the focus away from the concept of mind as *tabula rasa* to a new perspective and thereby opened a new way of looking at the world.

In the *Critique of Pure Reason* (Kant, 1781), Kant proposed that knowledge existed separate from sensory experience. In fact, he believed that the mind, rather than being a blank tablet, is equipped with its own pure concepts. In fact, the mind organized the flux of sensory impressions in substances, qualities, and quantities by means of these concepts. Rather than the mind being a receiver, it was conceptualized as active—active in interpreting the world. Kant theorized that the categories of the mind organize the sensory flux, giving meaning and relationship prior to direct experience. This new turn in philosophy leads to a shift away from the external world of nature independent of man's interpretation to the active inner world of interpretation and powers of the mind as the essential key to what we experience and what we know. Since it is only possible to use self-hypnosis in a deliberate way, rather than as a reflex, if the mind can function independently from the external world and can engage in activity and self-experience, we are greatly indebted to Kantian philosophy. Thus, by the latter part of the 18th century, the foundation for the experience of a self-directed hypnosis had been laid.

SCIENTIFIC PERSPECTIVES

As more systematic explanations emerged, healing and therapy were also systematized. The history of hypnosis is replete with potentials related to the eventual development of self-hypnosis. Animal magnetism and what I term self-magnetism[5] were noted at parallel times. For this reason I now review this development.

Animal Magnetism

Anton Mesmer, a 18th-century Viennese physician who believed in the influence of the planets on the human body, plagiarized a then-existing theory for his dissertation (Pattie, 1967). Initially, Mesmer used magnetic steel plates in his "treatment" of disease. He taught that a fluid, when universally diffused, influenced the earth, planets, and all animated bodies. He called this fluid "animal magnetism." The visible state induced by the fluid he called mesmeric sleep. Mesmer began with external magnets and then moved from the external magnets to the therapist's inner ability to influence magnetic fluid through his or her own movements. These movements were known as the mesmeric pass. Mesmer attributed the locus of power to the magnetist himself. He had transformed power from supernatural forces to the power of the therapist.

Mesmer also used the baquet, a round oak tub that permitted treatment in groups. Magnetic cords were used to mediate magnetism externally to the patient. This group technique anticipated self-hypnosis in that the patient was able to experience magnetism in the group situation, even if the magnetist did not touch him or her directly. A self-initiated crisis was not recognized by Mesmer; rather, he believed that a crisis was caused by his own very strong powers to affect others.

The genius of Mesmer was to apply the theory of animal magnetism to illness by demonstrating scientific principles that were accepted at that time. He reduced illness and cure to one basic underlying principle: Illness was an imbalance of the universal fluid, and cure was a correct distribution of the fluid. Having "scientific" guidelines enabled Mesmer to approach illness in a pseudorational manner, with a set of procedures and goals (Tinterow, 1970).

The Marquis de Puysegur (1751–1825) was a French aristocrat who described artificial somnambulism. He observed and reported a

---

[5]Self-magnetism was an observation that some people who had repeatedly been magnetized could throw themselves into a magnetic state at will.

calm, sleeplike state during mesmerism. He noticed that when mes-
merized his subjects were both awake and asleep. Thus, he was the
first mesmerist to demonstrate the coexistence of internal and external
sets of ideas and attitudes in a single individual within the somnambulistic state (Deleuze, 1825/1982). Puysegur, too, believed that the
effective ingredient in mesmerism was the will of the magnetizer (de
Puysegur, 1837).

The Abbé de Faria, a 19th-century Portuguese priest, described
artificial somnambulism or lucid sleep (Ellenberger, 1970; Tinterow,
1970). de Faria equated natural sleep and lucid sleep. He selected good
subjects on the basis of sleep ability. This recognition of differential
sleep abilities presages the notion of hypnotic susceptibility and individual differences. Clearly, he screened his patients for hypnotic susceptibility.

On record, de Faria was the first magnetizer to report that the
power to enter the hypnotic state lies within the subject (Tinterow,
1970). This observation became crucial for the future development of
self-hypnosis. In addition, de Faria recognized that his own demeanor
vis-à-vis the patient respected the patient's power. For example, his
induction was frequently one word, "dormez" or sleep, permitting the
patient to bring about this result. Finally, de Faria was the first person
to say that subjects could undergo surgery without pain when in a
somnambulistic state. Indeed, de Faria's reciprocal approach to the
patient anticipates the theory of suggestion and the naturalistic pacing
and leading used by the Ericksonians today.

Deleuze, a respected 19th-century French naturalist, also advocated animal magnetism. According to Pattie (1967), Deleuze reported
that hypermnesia was a characteristic of trance. He also reported that
in waking and trance states the somnambulist seemed like two different persons. Thus, he had superceded de Faria in anticipating the
notion of multiple ego states.

Because he was well respected, Deleuze was able to bring magnetism back to respectability[6] by advocating privacy, comfort, and
avoidance of interruptions. He fostered self-collectedness. Patients
reported a perception of warmth, heaviness, and suffocation (Deleuze, 1825/1982). This notion of fostering self-collectedness appears
to be a move toward self-hypnosis.

Shortly thereafter, Dr. Elliotson reported a sleeping patient who,
in the sleep state, predicted that she would come to her senses on a
specific date. This suggestion predates Erickson's use of date-naming

[6]Deleuze defended magnetism after it had been thrown into disrepute by the Paris
Commission.

by the patient for cure. In addition, Elliotson used paradoxical techniques with patients. For example, he simultaneously told a patient not to eat, and in the same breath advised her to eat (Bernheim, 1891/1980).

At about the same time, James Braid demonstrated subjective and suggestive elements of magnetism in 1846 (cf. Tinterow, 1970). Independently, he rediscovered the subjective origin of hypnosis. He observed both his own student hypnotizing himself and a girl hypnotizing herself by looking at her wall. Braid concluded that patients can throw themselves into nervous sleep. In addition, Braid believed that the brain can receive, without conscious awareness, external impressions and act on these impressions, again without awareness (Bernheim, 1891/1980). Brain was himself fascinated by the phenomenon of self-hypnosis and engaged in his own personal explorations of self-hypnosis.

Thus, although the phenomenon of self-hypnosis was not understood by the 19th century, it was observed. Most theorists believed that the ability to enter a magnetic or hypnotic state by oneself resulted from repetition of entering hypnosis. After a number of repetitions, the person could then throw him- or herself into a mesmeric or hypnotic state. I have labeled this phenomenon, which was considered more an epiphenomenon than a phenomenon in its own right, self-magnetism.

Self-Magnetism

Durant also observed that certain people could induce their own magnetic states without a magnetist. Observing gypsies, he found: "Each one within themselves [sic] is both magnetizer and the magnetized, without any fluid whatever emanating from a second person" (Durant, 1837/1982, p. 17). He believed that the process of self-magnetizing was a simple act, and he was able to induce his own magnetic state.

Whereas self-magnetism was often looked upon with suspicion, the use of an amulet for a few minutes to magnetize the patient was considered acceptable for definite treatment purposes as prescribed by the doctor (Deleuze, 1825/1982). Deleuze and others believed that too many repetitions of magnetism would weaken the will.

Animal magnetism was a popular theory at one time. The observations of the state appeared to validate it. Patients *did* respond to the "magnetic" treatments, even if only because of their imaginations. Animal magnetism, then, seems to be the first systematic use of the imagination to help patients with illness (Tinterow, 1970). The reports of self-magnetization anticipate the phenomenon of self-hypnosis just around the turn of the 19th to the 20th century.

By the end of the 19th century, Albert Moll, a psychologist, had placed hypnosis within the proper subject matter of psychology. He recognized the operation of individual differences as well: "The hypnotic process is a continuum, one which includes the waking state" (Moll, 1891/1925). He wrote five editions of a text on hypnosis that is still remarkably modern. Moll recognized that some people can generate a self-initiated hypnotic state: "There are cases in which the idea of the appearance of an affect is not aroused by a second person, but is generated by the subject himself" (Moll, 1925, p. 58). Like his predecessors, Moll believed that an act of will can allow the idea of hypnosis to become so powerful that hypnosis is induced (Moll, 1891/1925, p. 28). A second route to self-hypnosis is through repetition. When a subject is frequently hypnotized by another person, he or she can enter autohypnosis.

Moll differentiated self-suggestion from autosuggestion, which is generated by an external cause interacting with the subject himself, such as a blow or a threat. Autosuggestion appears to be an automatic response that serves as a protective mechanism, leading to indirect suggestion (Moll, 1891/1925).

Autosuggestions, according to Moll, are made in different ways, the various paths of perception. Each of the organs of sense is a door of entrance for suggestion. Moll believed, however, that the most common pathway for suggestion was speech and the performance of a movement accompanying that speech. Thus, Moll was attuned to the power of words. In training subjects for hypnosis, Moll believed that both individuality and habit play a major part and that repetition and practice are necessary. His description presages modern behavioral and cognitive strategies.

As early as the mid-17th century in England, Friends or Quakers, who lived in accordance with the "Inward Light," believed that they were able to commune directly with God by turning their attention inward. They emphasized a direct relationship between the believer and God, and did not seek the services of an intermediary clergyman. The Quakers believed that the opening of the "Inward Light" would help reduce the suffering of the ill and needy. In America, the Quaker settlements fostered quietism, which stressed trust in the "Inward Light" and demanded little external activity beyond the powerful silence of the meeting. In Europe, the 19th-Century German Mesmerists emerged incorporating both Franz Anton's belief in animal mag-

netism and spiritualistic notions into their religious beliefs. Simultaneously, the New England spiritualists Andrew Jackson Davis, Phineas
Quimby, and Mary Baker Eddy were known for their work in the
spiritualistic movement that combined religious beliefs with the applied health movement. The period of transition from mesmerism to
spiritualism can be recognized as a time that the lay person or non-
professional used techniques similar to those used by the mesmerists,
while attributing the results to the will of God. Stage hypnosis also
became popular during the end of the 19th century.

MEDICAL PERSPECTIVES

A medical perspective on healing was organized around the practice
of medicine. The medical period of self-hypnosis began with Braid in
1843, when he personally used self-hypnosis. Shortly thereafter, Liebault claimed that anyone could teach himself to influence his own
body by concentrating attention on a simple thought, as reported
below. This perspective focuses on techniques that the patient could
use to influence his body: concentration, a desire to get well, and the
power of words to cure.

Continuing this professional use of words in the service of treatment, James Braid (1795–1860), a Manchester doctor, renamed magnetism by coining the term "neurohypnotism." He carried out experiments, including self-hypnotic experiments in which he personally
used self-hypnosis. He demonstrated that (1) when hypnotized, subjects did what they were told to do; (2) when brought out of hypnosis,
subjects forgot what had happened. He believed that forgetting indicated a dual state of mind, implying the existence of an inner world of
being. This inner world he felt to be important for the development of
self-hypnosis. In addition, his positive use of suggestion anticipated the
Nancy school (Bramwell, 1956).

Influenced by Braid around 1850, a well-to-do country doctor
named Ambroise Auguste Liebeault used verbal suggestions with his
patients. He explained to them that he neither exercised nor possessed
mysterious powers. He put to rest the then major myth about hypnosis.
He offered more scientific explanations and presented curative or
positive suggestions. Like Braid, he believed that the phenomenon of
hypnosis was purely subjective. In addition, he believed that anyone
could teach him- or herself to influence his or her own body by
concentrating attention on a simple thought and the desire to get well
(Ellenberger, 1970). This positive emphasis on suggestion presages
Coué and his use of positive suggestion.

Charcot's Medical Model

Jean-Martin Charcot (1825-1893), a world-renowned neurologist in France who established the Paris school, believed mistakenly that hypnosis was pathological and was a characteristic residing in the patient. He attempted to explain hypnosis according to specific phenomenon: lethargy, catalepsy, and somnambulism. Charcot attempted to explain the underlying cause of these stages of hypnosis as being physiological (Charcot, 1977). His explanations were not substantiated. Nonetheless, he gave the phenomenon of hypnosis credibility. He influenced many physicians, among them Sigmund Freud. He did not add to the fund of knowledge about self-hypnosis, although his recognition that the hypnotic state was attributable to the patient was correct, because his recognition was clouded by the misunderstanding that hypnosis was an indication of pathology.

The Subconscious

A student of neurology at Salpetrière, Pierre Janet (1859-1947), a brilliant French therapist, became interested in the phenomenon of hypnosis, and only now is being rediscovered for his many gifts to psychotherapy. In his work with patients, he discovered the operation of subconscious fixed ideas (Janet, 1920). To him we owe the term subconscious. In addition, he identified intermediate levels of subconscious ideas that might become fixed through association or substitution. Such association or substitution led to a narrowing of the field of consciousness or dissociation. Finally, Janet stressed the role of rapport in therapy in which the patient exhibits a permanent state of suggestibility toward one person only (Ellenberger, 1970). Janet theorized that hysteria is the result of a congenital weakness of the mind. In this view, he followed Charcot's medical model. Nonetheless, Janet developed a comprehensive theory of hysteria, hypothesizing that hysterical symptoms resulted from the presence of subconscious automatic fixed ideas that were dissociated and affected the patient, even though out of the patient's conscious awareness. Hypnosis in Janet's view permits the identification and reintegration of these dissociated ideas.

Hypnosis and suggestion were separated in Janet's thinking. That is, suggestion could occur without hypnosis, and hypnosis could occur without suggestion. Janet's legacy to self-hypnosis is the recognition of dissociation and automatic fixed ideas. In addition, his analysis of the conduct of man (Ellenberger, 1970), that is, the separation of bodily conduct and speech, is a critical observation relevant to the concept of the mind–body relationship, so essential in understanding and treating psychosomatic problems.

In therapy, Janet believed in the healing qualities of sleep. Thus, he taught patients the best way of preparing for sleep. He prescribed a number of spaced pauses during the day to foster suggestion independently from sleep. During these brief time-out interludes, the patient practiced suggestion. Janet required practice in fine-tuning and mastering the technique.

Janet's descriptions of subconscious ideas, dissociation, and the narrowing of the field of consciousness all hold relevance for self-hypnosis. He methods presage modern behavioral and cognitive techniques.

Suggestion

Professor Bernheim, a convert of Liebault, presented the notion of suggestion. "If the mind accepts an idea as true and the idea is reasonable, it tends to actualize itself" (Bernheim, 1891/1980, p. 33). Thus, in Bernheim's eyes, hypnosis is treatment by suggestion. Suggestion is an action by which an idea is introduced to the brain and accepted. Bernheim pointed out the value of repetition: Any suggestion must be accepted by the self to be successful. He believed that "experience teaches that the simplest and best method for impressing the subject is by words" (Bernheim, 1891/1980, p. 63).

Auto-Hypnosis

Josef Breuer (1842–1925), an internist, recognized spontaneous autohypnotic states in hysteria. In his famous treatment of Anna O (Breuer & Freud, 1893/1957), he described the manner in which two states of consciousness exist side by side. He explained that those behaviors that occur during autohypnotic states are frequently forgotten; that is, the patient is amnesic regarding what happened. Because of the unavailability of these memories to consciousness, the hysterical symptom remains restricted to the autohypnotic state. In addition, because the spontaneous autohypnotic state tends to recur, the symptom is strengthened by the repetition. Repetition has been advocated by the early clinicians in strengthening the symptomatic behaviors as well as newly learned behaviors. Autohypnosis as a way of providing curative suggestions by repetition paved the way for the possibility of understanding habitual reveries. It also permitted understanding of behaviors that appeared quite paradoxical, for example, automatic behaviors, resistance to new learning, and multiple personality.

Breuer was responsible for the "talking cure" leading to abreaction of feelings. His description of Anna O's treatment is a classic picture of a spontaneous altered state of consciousness (Breuer & Freud, 1893/1957). The talking cure, in the hypnoid state, revealed crucial forgotten material. The patient remembered both what had happened and the feelings that had accompanied the event. In this manner, he speculated that a patient could remember what happened and express those feelings that had been split off from conscious awareness. The symptom then disappeared. The talking cure became very popular, and Sigmund Freud continued to collaborate with Breuer.

From Hypnoid Hysteria to Defense Neurosis

Sigmund Freud (1856–1939) was a neurologist who soon became interested in the treatment of hysteria. He learned the practice of hypnosis from Charcot at Salpetrière and later collaborated with Breuer in treating hypnoid hysteria with the abreactive method. In 1887, Freud used hypnosis in a conventional way to facilitate suggestion (Tinterow, 1970; Ellenberger, 1970). Initially, he supported the idea of autohypnosis. In fact, he wrote a paper describing the phenomenon. However, he found that not all patients could be hypnotized. In addition, he came to believe that his hypnotized patients fabricated fantasy material would forget it when the trance was terminated. He further felt that hypnosis distorted the therapeutic relationship. Therefore he abandoned hypnosis in 1892 in favor of his new analytic method of free association. He explained that autohypnotic behavior was superfluous and misleading. Rather, he substituted the defense neuroses for hypnoid hysteria (Freud, 1962). In the same vein, he deemphasized the role of dissociation. Instead, he gave particular emphasis to repression. Freud was uncomfortable with hypnosis for several reasons. He was dissatisfied because he could not hypnotize every patient, and because those who were hypnotized frequently did not enter a deep state (Kline, 1958). He found the transference reaction to be so strong as to lead to acting-out behavior by the patient. Finally, Freud found that many patients developed new symptoms after the abreaction. Thus, he came to believe that autohypnotic behavior was superfluous and misleading, bringing about the temporary demise of autohypnosis (Kline, 1958, 1967, 1972).

Nonetheless, Freud's method of psychoanalysis presents some interesting similarities to the hypnotic situation. The patient is relaxed in a supine position on the couch with eyes closed. The patient is instructed to free associate, that is, to say whatever comes to mind without censorship. This situation is similar to self-stimulating situations that trigger spontaneous self-hypnosis. The act of focusing on one's inner world leads to a fading of external realities into the background, much like the process described by Shor of the fading of the generalized reality orientation (GRO) in hypnosis (Shor, 1959).

In addition, the patient, reclining on the couch, experiences a partially stimulus-deprived state, having only the ceiling to look at. Situations of stimulus deprivation can trigger a spontaneous hypnotic state.

One might wonder how psychoanalysis would have unfolded had Freud not abandoned hypnoid hypnosis. The theory might have been even more comprehensive in that it would include a variety of unconscious structures, rather than a unitary unconscious that contains paradox and confusion (Bliss, 1986; Kline, 1958; Ellenberger, 1970).

Shor, in Freud's defense, appreciated Freud's abandonment of hypnosis as a therapeutic method because hypnosis at that time was "too unwieldy, artifact-laden and encrusted with transference and countertransference problems" (Shor, 1979a, p. 32).

CONCLUSION

This chapter has discussed the history of self-hypnosis by reviewing aspects of the history of heterohypnosis and healing. Self-hypnosis or self-magnetism was viewed with interest as a pathological aspect of magnetism. Only as man was able to exalt the mind and reason could self-hypnosis be viewed as a phenomenon in its own right.

My view of clinical self-hypnosis as an adjunct to psychotherapy and as a means for individuals to transform themselves from within through the power of the mind, by altering pain perception, reducing anxiety, and modifying maladaptive behaviors rather than relying on either supernatural or mediating healers, is part of the currently accepted philosophy of science. It should be noted, however, that while self-hypnosis does affect normal habit modification, selected behavioral symptoms, and possibly immune enhancement, it doesn't have much power over illnesses caused by microorganisms or chemical/genetic abnormalities. Nonetheless, future scientific developments may reveal other ways to construe both these phenomena and self-hypnosis itself as the philosophy of science evolves.

In the next chapter we look at psychological–sociocultural influences on the conceptualization of self-hypnosis as a clinical tool.

CHAPTER 3

Psychological and Sociocultural Roots of Self-Hypnosis

Man is a social animal.
—Seneca

This chapter surveys the history of self-hypnosis from the turn of the century to modern times. The journey moves from past to present, from the mind's ability to be affected by others to self-directed change in more permissive and indirect ways of using self-hypnosis. Theories during the 20th-century focus on the power of the interpersonal impact itself as hypnotic processes were viewed as more psychological and interactional. Hypnotic theory combined with linguistics and philosophy led to a social interaction theory between the subject and the therapist. The social interaction itself became the focal point. Since autohypnosis and self-hypnosis were considered variations of heterohypnosis, little concern was given to account for the intrapersonal interaction occurring within the personality, that is, the interaction among conscious directive self, responsive self, and observing self, an intrapersonal interaction. Rather, self-hypnosis was viewed as a variant of heterohypnosis.

As we have seen, the clinical study of self-suggestion for therapeutic purposes began in the mid-19th century. The presentations were primarily those of self-observation. As early as the time of Ambroise

Liebault, the belief existed that anyone could teach him- or herself to influence his or her own body by concentrating attention on a single thought and a desire to get well (Ellenberger, 1970). Liebault himself focused on the expectation of the power of the patient's mind to affect the body. The therapist suggested in a quite directive manner what to do.

This theme was more finely developed by Mannasseit in 1876, who asked his patients to focus attention, and thereby expectation, on a single part of the body in order to cause different effects. He believed that the deliberate narrowing of attention to a specific site led to physical change (Ellenberger, 1970). In this instance, direct suggestion from the therapist led to focusing attention and to maintaining the expectation that both physical and affective changes would occur. Shortly after, Botkin (1876) reported using self-suggestion in surgery to cure himself of fatigue and leg pains. He found that specific relief occurred in response to his own self-suggestion. Botkin had discovered the power of self-talk (Ellenberger, 1970).

Charles Baudouin from the Nancy school, which focused on the importance of suggestion, discussed the concept of suggestion and self-suggestion with his patients (Baudouin, 1922). He taught them self-monitoring by requiring them to keep a personal journal. He appears to be the first therapist to require such self-observation.

However, it was Vogt in 1893 who noted the great practical value of autohypnosis and recommended it for preventive purposes (Ellenberger, 1970). He believed that people could use autohypnosis in order to prevent illness, pain, and other problems. Prevention became an important use of autohypnosis. It is interesting how the value of autohypnosis increases as the times demand a "natural way of preventing and ameliorating problems and disease anticipates the "wellness programs" that abound today.

The first hypnotherapist to identify mentally healthy individuals as the best subjects for hypnosis and self-hypnosis was Bramwell. He explained that healthy persons were better able to control voluntarily their focus of attention (Bramwell, 1903/1956). Bramwell described self-suggestion as a conscious act that directs the mind to regulate itself. Such self-regulation leads to a readiness for specific action. Bramwell appears to be addressing the interface between mind and body, attention and performance, language and action. During his preliminary explanations to the patient, Bramwell expressed his belief that the patient hypnotized him- or herself. Bramwell then provided therapeutic suggestions such as that "he should sleep well, both free from headache and depression" (Bramwell, 1956, p. 75). According to Bramwell, the central object in all therapy by suggestion ought to be the development of the patient's control of his or her own organism (p. 179). Bramwell appears to be a leader in fostering self-control, much like the early fostering of self-collectedness described by Deleuze. While patients are in hypnosis, they are told that they can relax themselves without the need of someone talking to them, and can give themselves suggestions.

Hilger used self-hypnosis to treat insomnia. He taught his patients: "It is quite sufficient to breathe in a quiet rhythm, and to repeat to one's self by syllable, 'I may now rest, I do not need to work now,' and then to say, 'I do not need to make any plans now,' then say, 'I may now sleep. I am sleepy, I will now sleep, I sleep now.'" (Hilger, 1912, p. 60). This direct approach focused on a specific goal: sleep. We see the influence of rhythm, repetition, and sleep associations. The predictable rhythm leads to the expectation of sleep.

In 1925, a French apothecary, Emil Coué, interested in the work of Bernheim and Liebault, taught the public how to use self-suggestion formulas. Generally, he employed strong personal conviction and positive thinking in a repetitive manner to teach people how to give themselves suggestions. Because he worked with large groups of people, he seemed to function more as a teacher than as a therapist who would limit the size of the group for more individual monitoring. His method was deceptively simple. He asked his patients to murmer every night when comfortably settled in bed and on the point of dropping off to sleep, in a low but clear voice, this little formula: "Every day in every way, I am getting better and better." The patient was advised to recite the phrase like a litany 20 times or more a day. (Coué, 1922, p. 26). His emphasis on positive suggestion was influenced by the Nancy school. He believed that it is impossible to think of two things at the same time, following a reciprocal inhibition model. Coué explained "every thought that completely fills our mind becomes true for us and has a tendency to transform itself into action" (1922, p. 38). He believed, as did Liebault before him, that the power to change lies in the subject. Building on the suggestive hypotheses of the Nancy school, he believed direct self-suggestion was powerful. Being very sensitive to the power of the unconscious, Coué believed that the patient possessed the power to access the unconscious. Because this access was more available when one was near sleep, Coué taught his listeners to use self-suggestion on awakening and falling asleep.

Believing in the necessity of practice, Coué instructed others to practice and to modify the technique to meet their needs. Coué contended that the "force of the imagination is in direct ratio to the square of the will" (Coué, 1922). He, as did many others at that time, believed that the will was the identified force in carrying out self-suggestion.

Coué's method is particularly important in the history of self-hypnosis, since he generalized the use of suggestion to cover the specific activity of directly giving suggestions to oneself. One may argue that conscious self-suggestion may not be self-hypnosis. Coué, however, believed that conscious self-suggestion could access the unconscious and lead to action, for instance, a carrying out of the self-suggestion. In this sense of opening a window to the unconscious, self-suggestion appears to fit in with the notion of an altered state of consciousness.

Self-hypnosis was employed by Stanislavsky in an expanded way to train actors, for example, in their craft. Specifically, he heightened emotions during the acting experience by focusing on a specific affect, like anger: The actor felt angry and experienced himself as an angry person.

Stanislavsky expanded the base of hypnosis in using self-hypnotic exercises to improve a skill, albeit an acting skill. Specifically, self-hypnosis improved acting performance by heightening emotions. Actors rehearsing an affect such as anger would become angry until that anger was omnipresent. Such an alteration of affect leading to an alteration of one's total awareness appears to concur with the notion of an individual becoming so absorbed in a role that the person has entered a state of self-hypnosis.

CLINICAL PROGRAMS

A program of progressive muscle relaxation was developed by a psychologist, Edmund Jacobson (1929). This program focused on the mutuality of muscle tone and emotional reaction, an example of the mind–body interaction. He trained the patient to concentrate and to observe a specific sensation. Training was carried out two to three times per week, supervised by the therapist. The patient also had to practice at home for varying lengths of time, for example, 3 minutes at a time once or twice a day for 1 year. His prevailing practice model was that of discrete, spaced trials. Whereas Jacobson did not identify his program of progressive relaxation with self-hypnosis, Edmonston (1986) reported a long history of the relationship between relaxation and hypnosis. Both relaxation and hypnosis in his view have been historically equated in many theories, observations, and measurements of hypnotic susceptibility (Edmonston, 1981). In addition, the method of progressive relaxation seems particularly relevant to the history of self-hypnosis because it provides a home practice component away from the therapist. The patient used the program at home, alone, before returning for more training with the therapist.

THREE METHODS OF SELF-HYPNOSIS

Three methods of autohypnosis were developed by Salter (1951). The first was autohypnosis by posthypnotic suggestion. Simply, he told the hypnotized patient that posthypnotic suggestion makes it possible for him or her to do hypnosis by him- or herself. He assured the patient that he or she would have no trouble awakening. In hypnosis, he administered a simple posthypnotic signal that the patient could use to recreate the trance at a later time.

A second method Salter used was to provide the patient with a script, that is, general written instructions. The patient was then asked to memorize the instructions. Salter assured the patient that these instructions were not to be used to hypnotize anyone else. The patient repeated the memorized passages to him- or herself either aloud or subvocally: "I feel very comfortable. My arms are so relaxed and heavy. I feel so very comfortable and relaxed. My whole body feels comfortable and relaxed. I just want to sleep."

The third method of self-hypnosis was an early attempt to turn control over to the patient:

Now I am fast asleep, in the deepest possible hypnotic sleep; I am in a deep sleep, as deep as the deepest hypnotic sleep I have ever been in. I have complete auto-hypnotic control of myself. I can give myself auto-hypnotic suggestions and awaken whenever I wish. I can talk to the person who gave me these autohypnotic instructions. Yet I will still remain fast asleep. I will follow such instructions as he gives me, yet I shall still have autohypnotic control. (Salter, 1951, p. 429)

The instructions Salter then gave included posthypnotic suggestions, memorization of self-hypnosis scripts, and fractional self-hypnosis.

No review of the literature would be complete without a discussion of Lewis Wolberg, who taught his patients self-hypnosis by written transcript. In effect he taught, step-by-step, the self-induction of hypnosis. He included tests of hypnotic depth such as arm catalepsy, among others, as well as challenges such as "finding it impossible to open your eyes." Wolberg wrote a two-volume book, *Medical Hypnosis*, that has been an important textbook on medical hypnosis since 1948 (Wolberg, 1948).

MODERN PERIOD

The role enactment theory of Sarbin (1950) ushered in the modern period. In this view, the subject takes on the role of the hypnotized person within the limits imposed by his or her expectations, skills, self-conceptions, and by the demands of the situation. The therapist, part of the social interaction, takes on the role of the hypnotist. In this view, hypnosis is hypothesized to be a specialized kind of social situation. This theory is mentioned here because of the relevance of viewing hypnosis as a social situation, in which, for example, persons outside the patient influence the patient's response. Rather than viewing the therapist as the cause of change, an interaction between therapist and patient contributes to change.

Meanwhile in the hypnosis laboratory, Weitzenhoffer (1957) presented a series of exercises performed alone by the trainee for 1 hour a day. The exercises included *the pendulum, the falling test of self-suggestion*, and *eye catalepsy*, among others. As the trainee progressed in using self-hypnosis, the practice was increased to 2 hours per day. Weitzenhoffer placed control and responsibility in the subject. That is, the subject could accept or reject suggestions from the therapist. The subject practiced heterohypnosis techniques of autohypnosis; that is, the subject directed him- or herself in thought. Weitzenhoffer's approach included one long practice session per day, an approach consistent with psychoanalytic practice and with meditation.

For the reader's information, the chevreal pendulum, the falling test of self-suggestion, and eye catalepsy are described below as modified for self-hypnosis.

The chevreal pendulum presents the subject with a small bob hanging on a thread. He or she is told to hold the pendulum that is formed over a ruler and to look fixedly at the bob. He or she will soon notice the bob starting to swing along the ruler, even while remaining passive and refraining from making any deliberate movements. The experimenter demonstrates how it starts swinging and then gives it to the subject, who provides his or her own instructions based on the experimenter's.

The falling test of self-suggestion is actually the postural sway test of suggestibility, modified for use in self-hypnosis. The subject stands still, relaxed with his eyes closed, and self-suggestions are given that he or she is either falling forward or backward. Scoring is based on the amount of sway obtained during a given period of time. The more sway experienced, the more suggestible is the subject.

Eye catalepsy susceptibility is modified for self-hypnosis. The subject closes his or her eyes. The self-suggestion is then given that he or she will not be able to open them. His or her difficulty in doing this when self-challenged is used as a basis for scoring susceptibility (cf. Weitzenhoffer, 1957, pp. 11–12).

One innovator in 20th-century hypnosis was Milton Erickson, who outlined his rationale for a new concept of trance as a period of creative reorganization (Erickson, 1980a, p. 38). According to Erickson,

> the induction and maintenance of a trance provides a special psychological state in which the patient can reassociate and reorganize his inner psychological complexities and utilize his own capacities in a manner in accord with his own experiential life. Therapy results from an inner synthesis of the patient's behavior achieved by the patient himself. The cure develops from the patient's experience of reassociation and reorganization of his own experiential life that eventuates in a cure, and not simply the development of responsive behavior. (Erickson & Rossi, 1983)

In addition, the Ericksonian approach is flexible. According to Beahrs (1982), Erickson's approach begins with (1) starting where the patient is, (2) gaining gradual control over the behavior, and (3) demonstrating that change is possible. Suggestions themselves can be open-ended; one such as "you can just be aware of how you react" will elicit response tendencies. Thus, an open-ended suggestion increases the likelihood that the individual will respond in a way that is characteristic of him or her.

In the Ericksonian approach, self-hypnosis goals include (1) becoming one's own therapist, (2) developing confidence in the ability to gain control, and (3) receiving reinforcement of the therapist's suggestion (Erickson, 1980a, 1980b).

Erickson (1980b) fostered trust of one's unconscious: "If you go into an auto-hypnotic trance you must trust your own unconscious to pick the right things for you to do" (p. 61). In his view, hypnosis provides an important learning experience:

> Each person learns in his own way. You went into the trance in rapport with yourselves. In auto-hypnosis you can go into the trance in rapport only with yourself. Your first orientation should be to your situation: that you want to go into the trance; that you do not handicap yourself in any way; that you can rely upon your unconscious mind to answer the doorbell or the telephone. You can meet any contingency. (Erickson, 1980, pp. 61–63)

Milton Erickson was a genius in permitting the patient to use his or her own self-hypnosis in his or her own way.

AUTOGENIC TRAINING

Autogenic training as formulated by Schultz and Luthe (1959) involves seven well-defined standard exercises. The standard exercises are (1) heaviness, (2) warmth, (3) cardiac regulation. (4) respiration, (5) abdominal warmth, (6) cooling of the forehead, (7) termination of the exercises. Termination of the exercises involves a rigid, step-by-step sequence, flexing arms, breathing deeply, and opening eyes. Each exercise is mastered before one continues onto the next. Practice may be extended 1 hour or more. General self-instructions include: my arms and legs are heavy; I am at peace now; my solar plexus is warm. Instructions are provided for each exercise. Mastery of the basic exercises takes about 2 to 3 months. Advanced meditative exercises included experiencing selected feeling states and obtaining answers from the unconscious (Schultz & Luthe, 1959). Autogenic training fulfills the definition of self-hypnosis as understood today in the sense that it leads to an alteration of consciousness, absorption, and heightened sense of imagery.

THE 1960s ONWARD

In 1961, Erickson, Hershman, and Sector wrote a book based on their workshops on hypnosis. They taught self-hypnosis by means of posthypnotic suggestions. The self-hypnosis instructions are part of the heterohypnotic induction. For this contextual reason, I illustrate the entire verbalization in context:

> In a self-induced state, allow the unconscious to rule. Remove the conscious element . . . Our subconscious is always aware that there are many unfulfilled ideas or tasks. Some may be initiated or partially completed. Each person must accomplish auto-hypnosis in his own way. Should your desire arise in you and you find yourself awake . . . you may repeat the same relaxing procedure, the same technique and repeat it less and less frequently as you learn to remain asleep the entire night. (Erickson, Hershman, & Sector, 1981, pp. 194–203)

Seymour Hershman (1981) gives his version of the verbalization to teach a patient self-hypnosis:

> The technique that I am about to teach you is very easily accomplished . . . Take two minutes or less several times a day . . . Seat yourself in a chair during these periods . . . Pick out a spot similar to the spot you selected here. Stare at it and recollect the feelings and sensations that you experienced here . . . You will begin to feel the same sensations of relaxation . . . Remind yourself of several things. First that you have the ability to relax . . . You can use this type of

relaxation under any periods of stress or anxiety. Remind yourself that you have the ability to produce anesthesia. (Erickson, Hershman, & Sector, 1981, p. 197)

CUING FOR SELF-HYPNOSIS

William Kroger describes autohypnosis as a specific technique taught by the physician. Autohypnosis depends on the nature and type of posthypnotic suggestions given to the self (Kroger, 1977). Kroger believes that a well-conditioned patient can hypnotize him- or herself by a prearranged cue that acts as a stimulus for the conditioned response, autohypnosis. In that state, receptivity to ideas and capacity to examine these ideas for their inherent values is increased. Kroger believes that suggestions given to oneself are more meaningful than suggestions given by the therapist. This hypothesis has not yet been tested.

Kroger recommends practice to foster the learning of self-hypnosis. He recommends six sessions of 2 to 10 minutes throughout the day as of more practical value than lengthier ones. Kroger prescribes ending each session with the subject stating that he or she will enter autohypnosis more readily with each practice session, that he or she will follow all the autosuggestions to the best of his or her ability, and that he or she will terminate each session by suggesting that he or she will feel relaxed, motivated, and confident: "To achieve the best results you must carefully consider what you wish to accomplish. Through self-exploration you can establish reasonable goals for improvement" (Kroger, 1977, p. 87). Thus, Kroger consolidated the learning of self-hypnosis through the use of posthypnotic suggestion reinforced by home practice.

MASTERY

Herbert Spiegel and David Spiegel use self-hypnosis with patients to teach self-control and to help them gain mastery over their experience. One consequence of this mastery is to curtail dependency on the therapist. The Spiegels believe that the ability to enter self-hypnosis lies with the patient. After heterohypnosis (using the eye roll technique), the patient is assigned self-hypnosis exercises during the session with the posthypnotic suggestion that the patient may hypnotize him- or herself to reinforce a particular behavior or strategy. Patients are not encouraged to return for repeated sessions of formally induced hypnosis. Rather, the patient is instructed to practice hypnotizing him- or herself. Practice is assigned for 1 or 2 hours during the first week.

Initially, privacy is necessary so that the patient can practice the eye roll and arm levitation. After the first few weeks, the patient can modify the induction in two ways: (1) by closing eyes first before rolling up eyes, and (2) by letting the arm touch the forehead. These modifications enable the patient to practice self-hypnosis at home or at work, even with other people around. Practicing for 1 to 2 hours enables the patient to create a private signal system between the patient's mind and the hypnotic suggestions (Spiegel & Spiegel, 1978).

Harold Crasilneck routinely teaches self-hypnosis after the patient has experienced heterohypnosis several times (Crasilneck & Hall, 1985). Self-hypnosis instructions initially are given while the patient is in hypnosis induced by the therapist. As instructions are given, the patient is instructed to think them through as the therapist says them out loud. Later the patient repeats the words of the induction in the presence of the therapist. Sentences are phrased as if the patient him- or herself were saying them (Crasilneck & Hall, 1985).

Erik Wright uses self-hypnosis to help the patient experience a sense of self-control, to deepen trance, and to provide home practice. He asks the patient if he or she would enjoy learning more about the process of autohypnosis. Communication with the unconscious is established by ideomotor finger signaling:

> In a moment or two, I shall take your right hand and place it on your left shoulder. That is what you will do when you want to continue with auto-hypnosis. It will be a signal to the inner part of your mind to quickly review all your previous experiences with going into trance in a very short time . . . when you have reached the level of relaxation . . . your right hand will slide from your left shoulder and come to rest on your lap. This will be your signal to yourself to maintain this restful state of quiet, comfortable peacefulness for the length of time you have set for yourself for restoring your sense of well-being and energy . . . you can prevent escalation of tension as well as [sic] experience self-renewal. (Wright, 1989, p. 55)

Erick Wright's focus on self-control shows connections to Deleuze and to Bramwell. The use of a kinesthetic cue, "the right hand will rest on your lap," is one interesting way for the patient to maintain self-hypnosis.

Garver (1984) reports that when patients have learned self-hypnosis, they can and usually do use the same cue given to them when entering the hypnotic state. Garver proposes eight steps or techniques that he believes reduce the conscious critical screening and enhance the success of even the most average hypnotic subject. The therapist first guides the patient through the eight steps and then the patient is asked to perform the procedure alone.

He proposes that the patient (1) plan the suggestion first and keep it positive. The preprepared suggestion is heightened with visual imagery. Garver advocates that the patient imagine him- or herself in a particular situation, responding to that situation in exactly the manner that he or she wishes, feeling good. (2) Employ the entry cue, that is, use the cue learned in heterohypnosis. (3) Employ neutral imagery. A neutral experience such as time out is different from suggestion. (4) Move to suggestive imagery and mentally shift gears by placing oneself in a suggestive imagery environment, seeing oneself responding exactly as one would want to in that place. (5) Return to neutral imagery or time out. (6) Reorient. (7) Use posthypnotic suggestion for posttrance feeling. (8) Employ the exit cue.

BINDING SELF-HYPNOSIS TO HETEROINDUCTION

Fred Frankel provides directions to the patient while the patient is still in heterohypnosis. Pointing out whatever the patient accomplished with heterohypnotic induction, Frankel suggests that he or she is capable of accomplishing similar effects alone, by simply going through in practice sessions at home the steps carried out in the session. Frankel then repeats a description of these steps, whatever they might be, and ends by offering a description of how the patient can end the trance with a backward count of 3 to 1 and open his or her eyes. The patient is then invited to end the trance that Frankel has induced. In this manner, Frankel binds the self-hypnosis firmly to his induction. This training is achieved usually in the first trance experience (Frankel, 1976, pp. 103-110).

APPRECIATION OF INDIVIDUALITY

Erika Fromm has no written descriptions of verbalization to teach her patients self-hypnosis. Rather, her approach is an ideographic one— she tailors the instruction to fit the needs of the patient. Generally, she induces heterohypnosis first and then tells the patient that he or she now should wake up, then put him- or herself into a self-hypnotic state, going through the same kinds of experiences that he or she has exerienced with her—if these experiences were effective—but that the patient could also find his or her own ways, if that is preferred (Fromm, 1985, pp. 209-222).

David Soskis also teaches the patient self-hypnosis through heterohypnosis. He posits three necessary conditions for positive response to
self-hypnosis: active concentration, a willingness to respond, and an
absence of interference. Additionally, he points out that there is a
playful or fun element in self-hypnosis that leads to a very pleasurable
experience. Both patient and therapist enjoy the playfulness of successful self-hypnosis (Soskis, 1986).

MULTIPLE INFLUENCES

In any hypnotic situation, a variety of extra-experimental influences
exist that are unique to hypnosis (Orne, 1959; Rosenhahn, 1969). They
derive from many sources. In the clinical situation, these influences are
even more complicated. They consist of: (1) the attitudes and expectancies of both the therapist and the patient; (2) the nature of situational cues such as implicit and explicit cues, direct and indirect
suggestion; (3) the nature of the subject's talents and psychological
make-up; and (4) the biases of the therapist, including both theory of
hypnosis and theory of psychotherapy. In addition, according to
Fromm and Kahn (1990d), interactions between important content
variables (imagery), structural variables (absorption, fading of the
generalized reality orientation, and focus of attention), and personality
factors all contribute in unique ways to an individual's experience of
self-hypnosis. Although clinical research on self-hypnosis has not yet
looked closely at these interactions, the following ones need to be
included.

Attitudes and Expectancies

The attitudes and expectancies of both the therapist and the patient
significantly interact and influence the response. During hypnosis,
many cues are implicit or indirect. Milton Erickson and his followers
capitalize on implicit cues or indirect hypnotic techniques. Indirect
cues provide an illusion of choice whereby the patient can choose, for
example, which chair to sit in, but implicitly there is no choice about
sitting. This intervention, at least on the surface, appears permissive. In
self-hypnosis, practice instructions too may be given in a direct
manner as in autogenic training or in an indirect manner: "just allow
your unconscious to decide." The patient in self-hypnosis will undergo
quite different experiences in relation to direct imagery practice. Perhaps this assignment will generate more reality imagery or a more
narrow focus of attention, whereas a more indirect assignment may

lead to a broadening of attention. This hypothesis is yet to be tested. At the present state-of-the-art, little is known about these specific aspects of clinical self-hypnosis.

An even less direct approach presents suggestions embedded in ordinary conversation. Erickson hypothesized that the unconscious responds to embedded suggestions without conscious awareness (Erickson, 1966). In addition, indirect suggestions may be given where the patient has to make a choice as another route to the goal. The combined suggestions are powerful indeed.

Explicit cues are direct and spelled out. Traditional hypnosis tends to provide literal phrasing, direct suggestion, and clear instructions as a way of providing a direct structured approach to hypnosis. This stance tends to be authoritarian.

Subjectively, some theorists favor indirect suggestion over direct suggestion. It has not definitively been demonstrated that one type of suggestion is superior to another. Also, care in controlling factors such as length of time to give suggestion, latency of response time, and number of different suggestions embedded in conversation versus clarity of direct suggestions need to be studied. Another factor that needs clarification is attention span. Does the patient become satiated with one type of suggestion when it is used exclusively? I wonder if the novelty of changing types of suggestion enhances the hypnotic trance and receptivity. This aspect can be studied in the laboratory. In a similar vein, in self-hypnosis practice does a patient change from direct to indirect spontaneously and thus move from a more narrow focus of attention to a broader one? Fromm and Kahn (1990a) have found evidence for this type of shift. Lynn, Neufeld, and Matyi (1987), on the other hand, have not found any evidence that one type of suggestion is better than another.

T. X. Barber addresses the issue of attitudes, expectations, and motivations by describing hypnosis in cognitive terms such as thinking along with the hypnotist. He believes that attitudes, expectations, and motivations are the essence of hypnotic behavior and questions the validity of the term hypnosis. (Barber, 1969, 1979; Barber, Spanos, & Chaves, 1974). Brown and Fromm (1986) describe this notion of thinking along with the hypnotist as self-hypnotic behavior.

Personal Properties of the Subject

The patient brings idiosyncratic properties to the hypnotherapy. The neurolinguistic programming theory capitalizes on this aspect (Bandler & Grinder, 1975). Diagnosing whether the person is most suited for visual input, auditory input, or kinesthetic input provides important parameters. Does the patient require abstract metaphor, a feeling experience, or a visual image? Fine-tuning the communication to a patient's maximal level of acceptance or ego receptivity furthers the teaching of hypnosis and self-hypnosis. The therapist may better teach self-hypnosis to the patient with such information.

The patient's talents and psychological make-up are important contributing factors. The question of personality characteristics needs further clarification. Erika Fromm and the Chicago school are currently involved in studying this aspect as it relates to self-hypnosis (Fromm et al., 1981).

Bias

Simple bias of the therapist will affect the hypnotherapy. The overall orientation of the therapist will bias the treatment situation along the lines of that therapist's orientation. We look at this aspect of hypnotherapy in Chapter 4. The nature of situational cues such as implicit and explicit suggestions, the nature of the subject's talents and psychological make-up, and the biases of the therapist are all significant factors affecting treatment outcome. They significantly interact with the patient's response to self-hypnosis, that is, with trance depth, absorption, conscious and unconscious choices, in ways and degrees that have yet to be found.

HOW TO TEACH SELF-HYPNOSIS

The literature reveals that there is great diversity in the manner that self-hypnosis is taught to the patient. It is not possible to describe all the possible ways; the following examples reflect just a small variety.

The first induction is generally a heteroinduction, administered by the therapist. By providing a structured teaching environment, the therapist maximizes learning of the altered state. The therapist provides a comfortable hypnotic environment (Sacerdote, 1981).

The interaction between therapist and patient enables the hypnotic environment to develop with input from both. This interaction may be permissive, non-directive, and aimed at more open ego-receptivity to the unconscious, or it may be structured, directive, and aimed at ego-receptivity to strengthening ego functioning and self-control. The therapist suggests that the patient can access this same environment on his or her own. This suggestion is actually a posthypnotic suggestion (Bramwell, 1903, 1956; Edelstein, 1981; Clarke & Jackson, 1983).

Individual therapists will draw on their own styles, which may include some of the following suggestions. The therapist may intersperse associations that self-hypnosis practice will lead to the successful ego-syntonic goal that was agreed upon. For example, a tense patient learns to associate self-hypnosis practice with feeling more in control of his or her body, such as "relaxing if you want to relax." Further posthynotic suggestions may be given to bind home practice with heterohypnotic experience: "When you want to relax, need to relax, you can relax by sitting quietly. Take several long, slow deep breaths and enter a comfortable state of self-hypnosis that is just as relaxed and comfortable as this state of comfort and relaxation." Further, specific conditional suggestions may be given: "If you want to relax, then you can relax by taking a deep breath, picturing the beach" (Erickson & Rossi, 1980a). The action naturally follows on the heels of taking a deep breath. Specific problem-solving suggestions may be given as well: "And if you find yourself tensing up, what else can you do?" (Sanders, 1976). Finally, reinforcing and motivating suggestions may be given: "It becomes easier and easier to relax and to feel comfortable."

Self-hypnosis may be anchored by practice: "With practice, the art of relaxing becomes easier, more automatic, a habit, so that soon you may not even have to think about it." Or, it may respond to an imagery and analogy suggestion: "Just as you can picture the beach and how comfortable and relaxed you are at the beach, in the same way you can experience yourself at the beach and feel the comfort and relaxation again now." Age regression suggestions may also elicit a response: "Perhaps you can remember a time when you were little and you had a secret place—a place that was yours, where you felt really comfortable. It may be your very own room, a special chair, the woods, a tree house. Just allow yourself to go back in time to that secret place."

Amnesia, too, may be invoked: "Now that you are becoming so comfortable, so relaxed, you think more positively of the many ways that you can relax and succeed actively at relaxing, forgetting those things that are not relevant to relaxation, as if those things did not even exist. What is more relevant and important right now is the knowledge of your personal power to access and to maintain when you want, the pleasant action of active relaxation."

These additional techniques may also be employed. (1) The open-ended suggestion: "Just allow yourself to become aware of whatever images, feelings, or sensations float effortlessly into awareness." (2) The scheduling suggestion: "I wonder when you will choose to relax in an active manner, will it be in the morning, at noon, in the late afternoon, or at bedtime (Erickson & Rossi, 1980). Often useful is (3) the time distortion suggestion: "I wonder how long you will choose to relax in an active manner: 1 minute, 5 minutes, 10 minutes? When it's pleasant, the time passes so quickly. Where there is little time, much can be accomplished in just a few brief moments" (Erickson & Rossi, 1980).

Finally, when the patient is ready to leave the hypnotic state, dehypnotizing may be employed: "Now just enjoy the wonder of recognition of your accomplishment, knowing that you can do this for yourself when you want, where you want, how you want. Now just count back from 5 to 1, and at your own rate of speed, open your eyes to the here and now."

Some patients have experienced self-hypnosis from reading, watching someone else, or self-discovery and can enter their own hypnotic state. In my practice, I have asked this type of patient to enter self-hypnosis on his or her own and let me know when he or she is there. Then I ask for permission to participate in the patient's experience.

SUMMARY

What is evident in the modern history of self-hypnosis is that man is a social animal. We learn language, meanings, and realities through the interactions we have with others. Even altered states of consciousness may be learned through interaction with others. The hypnotherapist as other validates the patient's experience. Clinical self-hypnosis as a therapeutic tool is both similar to and different in primary ways from the self-exploration in which the curious individual may become engaged. The person seeking help perceives that he or she is unable to explore on his or her own in a positive way that would be helpful. He or she seeks help in order to receive structure, guidance, and/or feedback. Although eventual self-exploration may be an integral part of future therapeutic goals, the therapist needs to monitor, to provide feedback, and to validate what is happening in the therapy in order to insure that the patient is able to cope, to integrate, and to grow. Hypnotherapy requires the benign guidance of the therapist as described by Eisen and Fromm (1983).

As we see from the research of the Chicago group (Fromm et al., 1981), subjects went through an adaptation to the experience of self-hypnosis. Presumably those who could not adapt dropped out of the study. The subjects who continued throughout the study entered trance more quickly, more easily, and at times more deeply than their initial attempts.

We know from meditation studies (Shapiro, 1982; Carrington, 1977) that some subjects in meditation develop high levels of anxiety because of the time spent alone in meditation. If some patients are unable to adapt to the experience, then research must address what characteristics may be indicative of positive adaptation and what characteristics may be counterindicative.

In the clinical situation, I believe that the therapist must titrate self-hypnosis at levels the patient can tolerate and move to ever-increasing goals. In this way the patient will not feel isolated, overwhelmed, or hopeless. Rather the self-hypnosis experiences can lead to a storehouse of increasing self-esteem. It is important to note that I use the term "practice" metaphorically. It represents effortless self-hypnosis experience rather than willful, deliberate behavior.

We have come a long way from animal magnetism, a phenomenon attributed to the power the magnetist had over the subject. Early suspicions appeared that the magnetic process really stemmed from the subject. Then, early observations of gypsies throwing themselves into a "magnetic state" triggered the curiosity of Braid, Durant, and Moll. Now we believe that the subject holds the power to enter self-hypnosis and to use that altered state to his or her own advantage. Unfortunately, without direction, the use of self-hypnosis as a therapeutic tool may interefere with mastery if the patient is not yet ready for such communication with the unconscious. Thus, a slowly increasing exposure to unconscious content must be monitored by the therapist. The requirements that self-hypnosis first be initiated by the therapist but self-directed by the patient, and monitored by the therapist during the session are consistent with a total treatment approach. When the patient is ready, that is, when he or she is able to tolerate and cope with unconscious content, then he or she may begin to initiate self-hypnosis.

At the current state of knowledge, we have many questions but, unfortunately, too few answers. Thus, the diversity must be explored and eventually be subject to hypothesis testing. Nonetheless, it is apparent that there are a variety of ways to work clinically with self-hypnosis. The therapist's treatment philosophy may at times be in seeming paradox to the phenomenon of self-hypnosis, that is, the patient is asked to try, to practice, to allow him- or herself to enter hypnosis. This paradox between effortless experiencing and "intentional" responding runs throughout the range of hypnotic responsiveness. Psychotherapy involves some direction and monitoring, whereas self-hypnosis reflects effortless and diffuse attention. We now look at theories of hypnosis and self-hypnosis to see how these aspects may be integrated.

PART II

Theory and Research

CHAPTER 4

Theories of Hypnosis, Self-Hypnosis, and Psychotherapy

> Nothing is permanent but change.
> —Heraclitus

Description and theory of hypnosis, like the remarkable faculty of the chameleon for changing its color, also are remarkable for their propensity to be explained in a diversity of ways. Each specific theory underlying the therapist's practice today influences a patient's response. Expectations, goals, rationales, and self-observations all will affect the patient's response. According to Orne, "the effects of the 'role-play artifact' on the manifestations of hypnosis [seen clinically] demonstrate that phenomenon of hypnosis may result from the subject's preconceptions of what hypnosis is, implicit cues by the hypnotist as to what he or she thinks it should be, and the particular techniques of trance induction" (Orne, 1959/1965, p. 91). In my view, treatment too sets up expectancies and implicit as well as explicit cues. Changing any aspect of expectation, goal, rationale, and self-observation will cause interaction with other relevant variables, both specific and nonspecific, contributing to treatment outcome in some complex manner. For this reason, the current popular theories of heterohypnosis[1] are reviewed as a means to clarify

---

[1]Brief descriptions of heterohypnosis theories are included because hypnotherapists using self-hypnosis endorse a specific heterohypnotic theory. Theories of self-hypnosis are just beginning to emerge, but more work needs to be done.

the demands inherent in the treatment situation. Theory is reflected in the manner in which self-hypnosis is taught by the therapist. It is a contextual variable.

Because self-hypnosis is in its infancy and little research is available as yet to generate a conclusive theory of self-hypnosis in the clinical situation, this chapter focuses on theories of heterohypnosis and self-hypnosis. Although no conclusive theory exists about how self-hypnosis facilitates psychotherapy and most professionals do follow a specific hypnosis theory, there remain a diversity of such approaches. Nevertheless, few studies have been done clarifying the complex interactions between psychotherapy and hypnotic facilitation. Mott (1982) considers hypnosis to be a facilitator of a specific form of therapy such as dynamically oriented psychotherapy or behavior therapy. He recommends the importance of clarifying just how hypnosis interacts with the basic approaches to psychotherapy. Jean Holroyd suggests several ways that clinical hypnosis seems to facilitate psychotherapy. Attention changes and changes in imagery, dissociation, and accessing the unconscious are just a sampling of phenomena that seem enhanced in some way by hypnosis (Holroyd, 1987). In addition, clinicians hold to a specific theory of psychotherapy as discussed in Holroyd's article (Sanders, 1987). Kumar and Pekala found that both state and trait factors interact, contributing to the resulting hypnotic experience (Kumar & Pekala, 1987). No such study has yet been completed in clinical self-hypnosis. Finally, Erika Fromm's pioneering work in self-hypnosis theory is discussed (Fromm, 1975a; Fromm et al., 1981).

This chapter describes the most popular theories of heterohypnosis and summarizes them by describing the implications generated by each theory for psychotherapy or hypnotherapy. Nonetheless, I make a distinction between a theory of hypnosis and a theory of psychotherapy that also interacts potently with the unique ways that clinical self-hypnosis will be used and experienced by the patient. The theory of psychotherapy is referred to as orientation to psychotherapy.

THEORIES OF HETEROHYPNOSIS

State Theory

A state theory of hypnosis implies that the hypnotized person is in a state discontinuous from his or her usual state of awareness. This theory presupposes that the hypnotized subject can transcend usual behavior and experience. That is, the subject can experience unusual phenomena such as anesthesia, hypnotic hallucinations, and changed somatic behavior. The following presents an example of a state theory.

According to Orne, the principal features of the hypnotic state are seen as changes in the subjective experience of the subject. These changes are characterized by (1) discontinuity from normal waking experience, (2) a compulsion to follow the cues given by the hypnotist, (3) a potentiality for experiencing as subjectively real distortions of perception, memory, or feeling based on suggestions by the hypnotist rather than on objective reality, and (4) the ability to tolerate logical inconsistencies that would be disturbing to the individual in the waking state (Orne, 1959/1965, p. 121). Orne believes that the distinguishing characteristics can be found in the subjective experience of the subject.

Neodissociation Theory

The neodissociation theory as conceptualized by Hilgard (Hilgard, 1977) focuses on degrees of dissociation. He describes multiple cognitive control structures that operate simultaneously and of which we may not be aware. The executive ego is the central control structure that plans and organizes. Simultaneously, cognitive control structures have some autonomy with their own inputs and outputs. In hypnosis, the relationship between multiple cognitive control systems is altered. In self-hypnosis, there is a split between executive functions that observe and simultaneous hypnotized functions that become active. Within hypnosis, the executive monitoring functions have been limited until their full capacities are reactivated by terminating hypnosis. The neodissociation theory proposes degrees of dissociative experience. State changes occur only when dissociations become sufficiently widespread (Hilgard, 1979a, p. 69).

Trait Theory

A trait theory of hypnosis signifies that hypnotizability is a personality trait that can be measured reliably from one time to another (Hilgard, 1965). In addition, a trait theory presupposes the notion of individual differences on a reliable continuum of hypnotic talent in which individuals differ. These individual differences may vary in degree of hypnotizability, from low hypnotizability to high hypnotizability. Low-hypnotizable patients are considered poor hypnotherapy candidates. By selecting high-hypnotizable patients, the treatment effects are maximized.

Neurophysiological Theory

A neurophysiological theory of hypnosis embraces the notion that hypnosis is associated with physical changes in the cerebral cortex and the central nervous system. Pavlov's theory of partial cortical inhibition is the most well-known (Pavlov, 1941). Of course, as Weitzenhoffer points out (Weitzenhoffer, 1957), the close relationship between mental and neurophysiological events dictates an overlap between this view and other views. According to Das (1965), inhibition is a protective mechanism necessary for the survival of the organism. Because of selective inhibition of certain parts of the cortex, hypersuggestibility is possible: "a concentrated excitation of a definite stimulation, sensation or its trace . . . ." (Pavlov, 1941, pp. 108–109).

Another form of conditioning is verbal conditioning or ideomotor conditioning whereby the word becomes a stimulus setting up a conditioned reflex of a physiological nature. Hull, for example, hypothesized that suggestions were habit phenomena (Hull, 1933). According to Hull,

> a continous stimulation by words associated with a particular act will bring about the act, whether these words are those of the subject himself or of some other person. The most critical evidence indicating the reality of ideomotor action is that when a subject merely observes an action, he tends automatically to execute it. (Hull, 1933, p. 393)

According to the present hypothesis,

> the physical substance of an idea is a symbolic or pure-stimulus act. The proprioceptive stimuli arising from such acts, usually spoken words, are assumed when combined in certain patterns to have acquired during the previous history of the subject, through the process of association or conditioning, the capacity to evoke the reactions of which they are the names. (p. 393)

Thus, physiological conditioning binds words to responses. Words are empowered to generate reactions.

Psychoanalytic Theory

Gill and Brenman (1959) describe hypnosis as being "a regression in the service of the ego." A hypnotic induction leads to such a regression.

According to the authors: "The hypnotic state is an induced psychological regression, insuring in the setting of a particular regressed relationship between two people, in a relatively stable state which includes subsystem of the ego with various degrees of the ego apparatus" (p. 23). By limiting sensory–motor experience and amplifying transference, the regression is facilitated.

Ferenczi (1956) describes hypnosis as follows: "The capacity to be hypnotized and influenced by suggestion depends on the possibility of transference taking place, or more openly expressed . . . the transference . . . like every 'object love' has its deepest roots in the repressed parental complexes" (p. 177).

Thus, regression and transference are posited by the psychoanalytic theory.

Thinking along with the Therapist

Another way of conceptualizing what happens in hypnosis involves what T. X. Barber (1979) describes as thinking along with the hypnotist, a nonstate theory. Rather than talk about trance, the therapist focuses on outward behavior. Barber views the subject's positive attitudes, motivation, and expectancies toward the test situation as evidence of the subject's ability to think with and to imagine vividly those things that are suggested by the hypnotist. Methodically, he reviews the vast array of hypnotic literature with his view as the organizing glue, and with little ado, he concludes that the notion of a hypnotic state will inevitably become a historical curiosity. This alternative view of hypnosis as a nonstate is hotly debated.

Roletaking

More recently, Sarbin and Slagel elaborated on the view of hypnosis as social role enactment. They speculated that physiological response is associated with the degree or intensity of organismic involvement, that is, acting out the role of the hypnotic subject. According to Sarbin, the role of the hypnotized person is defined within limits imposed by expectations, skills, self-concept, and demands of the situation. One may enact this role to the fullest of one's physiological and psychological capacities or merely enact it on a superficial level. This theory according to Sarbin is a naturalistic one, stemming from the available knowledge of psychology and physiology within a social context (Sarbin & Slagel, 1979).

THEORIES OF SELF-HYPNOSIS

All Hypnosis Is Self-Hypnosis

Clinically, many hypnotherapists subscribe to this belief that all hypnosis is self-hypnosis (Erickson, 1948; Kroger, 1977; Spiegel & Spiegel, 1978). Erickson believed that self-hypnosis and heterohypnosis demonstrated basic phenomena. He identified them as the same process; that is, all hypnosis is self-hypnosis. Erickson and his followers fostered unconscious learning in an unstructured experiential situation. As a result of experiencing sensory–motor, perceptual, and cognitive changes (hypnotic phenomena), the patient has all the learning experiences necessary to create the sensory–motor, perceptual, and cognitive changes on his or her own. Erickson maintains that it is unnecessary to know how this learning takes place. The important ingredient is that the patient's unconscious knows more and can teach the subject more than he or she realizes.

The philosophy that all hypnosis is self-hypnosis may be reassuring to the patient in a clinical situation. Such a belief may strengthen the autonomy of the patient and enhance his or her coping skills. By definition, the patient controls the trance state. On the other hand, some patients may be threatened by so much autonomy and may feel a keen separation from the therapist.

Thus, from a research perspective, all hypnosis is not self-hypnosis. From a clinical perspective, the patient may be reassured or become anxious if he or she believes that all hypnosis is self-hypnosis. In my practice, my patients have favored the notion that all hypnosis is self-hypnosis. Of course, the matter is open to empirical study. Weitzenhoffer (1989), for example, believes that all hypnosis is a variant of heterohypnosis and that self-hypnosis is a pseudohypnosis because it is limited.

Altered State of Consciousness

Recently, however, based on the descriptive, quasiphenomenological methodology suggested by Shor (1979b), the belief that all hypnosis is self-hypnosis was significantly challenged by the seminal work of Erika Fromm and the Chicago group (Fromm, 1975b; Fromm & Shor, 1979; Fromm et al., 1981). In this fundamental work, comparing self-hypnosis with heterohypnosis, the authors found that both heterohypnosis and self-hypnosis were characterized by absorption (Hilgard, 1975; Tellegen & Atkinson, 1974) as well as the fading of the general reality orientation (Shor, 1959, 1962a; Shor & Orne, 1965). The self-hypnotic subject experiences absorption in his or her own inner experiences, and while in the self-hypnotic state, he or she subjectively experiences the fading of the general reality orientation. These phenomena characterize altered states of consciousness in general. The facts illustrate that self-hypnosis is an altered state of consciousness. However, as we shall see, both hypnosis and self-hypnosis do have some phenomenal differentiating characteristics. According to Fromm and Kahn (1990a), expansive, free-floating attention and ego receptivity to stimuli coming from within are state-specific for self-hypnosis, whereas concentrative attention and receptivity to stimuli coming from a single outside source are state-specific to heterohypnosis. Also characteristic for self-hypnosis is imagery, rich, sequenced, and/or segmented, in greater quantities and more personally meaningful than in heterohypnosis (Fromm et al., 1981).

Self-Hypnosis as a Self-Directed State

Fromm et al. (1981) described several definitions of self-hypnosis. Self-hypnosis may be viewed as a self-directed state. She reasoned that in a liberally defined self-hypnosis experiment the hypnotist may provide suggestions. This situation may be entitled experimenter-initiated suggestion. The subject responds to those suggestions in his or her own self-directed manner, that is, in terms of communications that the subject produces during trance in response to E-defined suggestions. I believe, at least initially with many patients but not all, that in the clinical situation self-hypnosis follows more appropriately a self-directed model rather than a self-initiated model. With this definition, comparisons with heterohypnosis are more straightforward. When tasks are not predefined, it is difficult if not impossible to make comparisons or to assess the effectiveness of self-hypnotic intervention. Nonetheless, with E-defined suggestions, the range of possible response is more limited. In the clinical situation, the therapy is directed at helping the person to solve a problem or reach a goal. The range of possible responses must at the same time be broad enough to allow for individual variation, but it also must be directed enough to lead to a healthy solution. Thus, the range of responses possible must in some way be a compromise between no limits on self-hypnotic behavior and no alternative response styles.

Self-Hypnosis as a Self-Initiated State

In a self-initiated self-hypnosis situation, the subject creates his or her own suggestions for induction and/or trance, thereby enacting self-initiated suggestions. According to Johnson (1981), this definition would require a spontaneous self-hypnosis format. This model is fitting for self-growth, creativity, and research. The focus is on human hypnotic potentialities rather than on normative experience or measurement of specific change or transformation. In treatment, however, progress must be measured. Behavior change or self-growth must be monitored. Without some defined criteria, such evaluation becomes impossible. In addition, some patients may be able to self-initiate trance, but frequently they are fearful of their unconscious and need to develop the trust and ego strength that will make self-initiation possible. Of course, for some individuals, the outcome of treatment may enable them to engage in self-hypnosis as a self-initiated state. For others, this goal may not be possible.

Laboratory-Defined Hypnosis

Subjects learn about hypnosis once they are in the laboratory. They receive information during the preinduction interview, the standardized trance experiences, and frequently during training sessions. These experiences lead to a set for experiencing self-hypnosis. The advantages of this set include a standardization of experiences recognizable to the investigators. According to Fromm, the main disadvantage pertains to the definition of self-hypnosis. The trance experience so defined is no longer in a strict sense self-hypnosis (Fromm et al., 1981). The wording and practices of standardized hypnotic susceptibility scales are accepted as defining laboratory hypnosis. Johnson (1981) believes that this compromise is necessary in the laboratory to insure comparisons between subjects and between studies. Without some standardization, comparisons are not possible.

Hypnotist-Absent Self-Hypnosis

Fromm points out that the importance of the hypnotist's presence during self-hypnosis depends on how self-hypnosis is defined. In hypnotist-absent hypnosis, no hypnotist is present. In the strictest sense, self-hypnosis does not require the presence of the hypnotist. The subject can initiate self-hypnosis alone. In the clinical situation, the patient generally needs to learn how to initiate self-hypnosis, although some patients enter a spontaneous but undirected and unintended trance. In the clinical situation, these spontaneous trances may be resistances (Bliss, 1983, 1986; Miller, 1984). Others may reflect adaptation (Balsam, Dempster, & Brooks, 1984), or even reflect both aspects of resistance and facilitation (Shengold, 1978). Home practice of self-hypnosis is one example of hypnotist-absent self-hypnosis. It is initiated by the patient.

Hypnotist-Present Self-Hypnosis

In hypnotist-present self-hypnosis, the hypnotist may be present. However, he or she may remain silent. The hypnotherapist may speak without giving specific suggestions, or he or she may give suggestions in a modified or reduced form (Fromm et al., 1981).

I believe that the hypnotist-present self-hypnosis model is compatible with those situations in which the therapist teaches the patient self-hypnosis and with those situations in which self-hypnosis practice is monitored. So too, the complex interaction of multiple variables colors the patient's response to self-hypnosis; that is, depending on the patient, the nature of the problem, and inherent personality factors such as ego strength, any of these models may apply in an appropriate clinical situation. Initially, clinical self-hypnosis may require more interaction between therapist and patient during sessions (hypnotist-present) and patient-directed response during home practice, which is hypnotist-absent. Both situations are important. As therapy progresses and the patient becomes more able to cope actively with anxiety and become more receptive to input from the unconscious, then less interaction between therapist and patient becomes necessary.

Clinical Self-Hypnosis

Clinical self-hypnosis, in my view, refers to a self-hypnotic state that is first taught to the patient by the therapist and is monitored by the therapist by reviewing words and images and their meanings that occur spontaneously both during the session and away from the therapist. The patient's spontaneous experiences are shared with the therapist during the therapy hour. This sharing may be in the form of journal entries, associations, or discussion. The monitoring of these experiences is an essential part of psychotherapy.

EXISTENTIAL-PHENOMENOLOGICAL THEORY

Observing how the patient uses self-hypnosis and the ways that self-hypnosis affects him or her is critical to hypnotherapeutic intervention. I believe it is possible to study clinical self-hypnosis through an existential–phenomenological framework such as described by theorists such as Rollo May (1958, pp. 3–35), Kierkegard (1954), and Heidegger (1962). Such a framework would emphasize the subject's confrontation with his or her self-hypnotic experience. Using a technique of deep self-reflection and putting aside the influence of the everyday world, the demand characteristics, the subject is free to review his or her personal and unique experience. The self-hypnotic state can be revealed in the reflections of the subject about the sense of automatized behavioral reactions, the sense of quiet and aloneness, and the sense of meaningful peak experiences.

To study self-hypnosis phenomenologically, one needs to bracket the usual concerns about whether or not self-hypnosis is a state. It requires a focus on the here and now, unfolding by way of a pure description. The phenomenological method maximizes understanding of the inner world of another individual. The focus of attention is on the phenomena themselves, without recourse to standardized measurements (Merleau-Ponty, 1963). He objects to analyzing parts of consciousness and holds that the organism as a whole is the phenomenon to be studied. Consciousness can only be known as it is both experienced and as it experiences. Perception, imagination, judgment, and feeling are all acts of consciousness that are directed at something intended. I believe a more orthodox approach to phenomenology of some of the more subjective aspects of self-hypnosis experience would complement Shor's quasiphenomenological approach and would enable the researcher to uncover additional ties between self-hypnosis and the alteration of consciousness. Such a view would permit a rich study of symbols containing both apparent and hidden meanings. In addition, such study would permit the understanding of the relationship between subject and experience. These pure descriptions could be used in a convergent manner along with more traditional observations. Fromm's method of combining clinical phenomenological methods with rating scales and questionnaires is a powerful way to study self-hypnotic phenomena. It is a very stimulating compromise based on Shor's quasiphenomenological approach. It does highlight the human experience of the subject.

IMPLICATIONS FOR THERAPY

To some degree each of these theories holds relevance for both the patient and the therapist. Although these theories of hypnosis all highlight a specific outcome of the hypnotic phenomenon, they also share some similarities. However, the difference is based on emphasis. The theory of state differences sets up expectations that the patient will experience a change in state and in awareness. Thus, a hypnotic induction can be a therapeutic tool in itself. The hypnotic induction leads to a state of awareness that is "different" from the patient's usual state of awareness. For example, rather then perceiving things in terms of anxiety, fear, or helplessness, the patient may experience relaxation, comfort, and quiet competence. The emphasis is placed on the notion of a change in perceived state of awareness.

Within the neodissociation theory is an assumption that new learning can occur within the hypnotic state because the usual barriers to new learning may not be available in hypnosis. In addition, concealed or covert experiences may be retrieved using the hidden-observer paradigm. Cautions are indicated, since the hidden-observer paradigm is subject to demand characteristics.

The possibility of state-dependent learning is maximized by this theory. Of course, when the hypnosis is terminated, the paradox exists that the new learning may no longer be available. According to Hilgard, "the essence of hypnotherapy is to integrate the dissociated aspects of consciousness and, in some instances, to manipulate dissociations for the benefit of the person . . ." (Hilgard, 1975, p. 78). I believe that the therapeutic task is integration and reorganization.

The trait theory emphasizes the notion of individual differences and degrees of hypnotic talent from low hypnotic susceptibility to high hypnotic susceptibility. In addition, the trait theory presupposes that hypnotic talent will correlate with other personality characteristics such as fantasy, thinking in images, and absorption in inner experience. The emphasis is placed on hypnotic talent as a personality characteristic (Hilgard, 1965). Persons who are low in susceptibility may not be viewed as good hypnotherapy candidates. Thus, it may be possible to select good hypnotic subjects who may respond to treatment, but it may be possible also to deny a very motivated patient but one who has low susceptibility to hypnosis.

The non-state theory emphasizes observable behaviors in the form of attitudes, motivations, and expectancies. The therapist assumes that these behaviors reflect the ability of the patient to think with the therapist and to imagine vividly those things suggested by the therapist. Change will be reflected in terms of changes observed in attitudes, from negative to positive, changes in motivations, and changes in expectancies, the letting go of extraneous thoughts. These changes are observed directly and are not associated with an overall change in state.

According to T. X. Barber, conceptions of normal human abilities or potentialities will be broader as subjects are viewed not in a trance but awake and normal (Barber, 1975). However, Barber really does not address the issue of hypnotherapy.

The implications of a physiological theory are that the therapist and patient both expect changes to occur on a physiological level. Given the close relationship hypothesized between mind and body during hypnosis, the patient anticipates that psychological experience will lead to physical changes. The therapist will maximize this relationship by suggesting specific physical changes, such as central nervous system changes, cellular changes, and changes in respiration, heart rate, temperature, and so on. The goals also will focus on such change.

In the role-taking theory, the social interaction between the therapist and patient is emphasized. The therapist, in his or her role as hypnotist, and the patient in his or her role as hypnotized patient, work toward changing expectations, skills, and self-conceptions the patient holds regarding him- or herself. By working to change the role from patient to person, the therapist highlights the importance of enacting this role to the fullest of one's physiological and psychological capacities. In their review, Sarbin and Slagel (1979) concluded that observed alterations in physiological processes were not specific to the hypnotic trance. However, they did conclude that symbolic processes produce changes in biological processes (pp. 299–300). They postulate that the concept of organismic involvement in role enactment can be monitored by appropriate psychophysiological and physiological techniques. The task is not transcendental, but rather it is a specialized kind of role situation.

Viewing hypnosis as a verbal conditioning situation permits hypnotherapy to follow a covert conditioning model such as that of Cautela (1967). In this view, covert rehearsal follows the principles of conditioning.

The psychoanalytic theory of hypnosis provides an opportunity for the therapy to facilitate access to primary process thinking. In addition, it allows for changes in the organization of thought processes in hypnosis. According to Gruenewald, Fromm, and Oberlander (1979), the effects of increased accessibility and degree of primary process expression appear to be functions of each individual's structural and dynamic characteristics and level of psychological adjustment. Of course, situational and interpersonal variables are important. It is their view that adaptive regression can take place in hypnosis, but this regression is not equated with entering hypnosis per se (Gruenewald, Fromm, & Oberlander, 1979, pp. 633–634). It also appears those patients who are not well integrated, hypnosis might lead them into areas they are not prepared for.

CLINICAL ORIENTATIONS TO SELF-HYPNOSIS

Because clinical self-hypnosis is part of an overall psychotherapy treatment plan, even self-hypnosis is taught within a specific psychotherapy orientation. The psychotherapy theory and rationale the therapist presents to the patient will reinforce behaviors conforming to that psychotherapy theory and rationale. Thus, a behavioral orientation will generate behaviors and understandings unique to that orientation, such as contingencies, reinforcements, and trials. A psychoanalytic approach will spawn free associations, dreams, and transference. Just as the therapist's theory underlying hypnosis and self-hypnosis is an important aspect of demand characteristics, so is the therapist's orientation to therapy in general a powerful influence on treatment outcome. Because of space limitations, it is not possible to review every possible creative orientation to psychotherapy. Rather, we will review hypnotherapist orientation to psychotherapy, including eclectic, psychoanalytic, behavioral, physiological, and humanistic orientations that appear frequently in the literature.

ECLECTIC ORIENTATION

Eclectic hypnotherapy draws from a wide variety of theories. In effect, it combines behavioral, psychoanalytically oriented, physiological, and naturalistic techniques where appropriate. These therapists tend creatively to combine techniques that work with specific patients. Generally, eclecticism is an empirical approach where the patient's response dictates the technique. Such therapists are flexible and relate rationale and theory to the patient's problem and response (Abroms, 1969).

The goals of eclectic therapy are mixed in that behavior change and insight, as well as support of adaptive functioning, may all be relevant. Thus, the eclectic therapist using self-hypnosis may intermittently shift focus from one goal to another, depending on the patient's needs and the situational context.

The broad range of induction techniques serves eclectic therapy well. Particularly, imagery and deep breathing provide a nondirective approach to self-hypnosis, although when more direction is necessary, any of the induction techniques are appropriate. Eclectic therapy permits free association, guided imagery, partly unguided imagery, dream interpretation, and problem-solving techniques to be used among other techniques. Self-hypnosis is well suited to the inclusion of these tasks. The self-hypnotic phenomena derive from a complex interaction among the situation, the patient's response to trance, and the patient's needs and cognitive style. According to Fromm and Kahn (1990d), the interaction between structural and content variables is critical.

The eclectic therapist may teach the patient self-hypnosis during the first 2 weeks of therapy. Practice may be spaced; that is, the patient may be asked to practice for short periods, three or four times per day as is the case with many behavioral approaches. Or, in contrast, the practice may be massed, that is, one 30-to-60 minute or longer practice session per day, as seen in hypnoanalysis and uncovering therapy. The frequency of practice depends not only on goals and strategies used, but also on the integrity of the patient and his or her ability to tolerate long periods of imagery without outside contact. Although patients without significant ego dysfunction can do well with massed practice, the more vulnerable patient may panic under prolonged massed practice. Fromm et al. (1981) found that highly hypnotizable and normal subjects adapted to the self-hypnotic state over time.

Generally, eclectic self-hypnosis is a combination approach that integrates behavioral, physiological, uncovering, and naturalistic techniques that can be used with a wide variety of problems. Indeed, the permutation possibilities are great. Thus, diverse problems such as anxiety reactions, identity crises, certain types of narcissistic disorders, phobias, pain, habits, and severe disturbances can all be treated with an eclectic approach.

Paul Sacerdote describes an example of eclectic hypnotherapy that utilizes and combines psychodynamic principles, dissociative phenomena, projectic techniques, behavioral methodologies, perceptual alterations, and suggestive and supportive interventions. He forewarns the reader that the hypnotherapist must be prepared to face specific difficulties and challenging opportunities that arise out of the intensity and uniqueness of the hypnotic relationship (Sacerdote, 1972).

The following case example was taken from Paul Sacerdote's work with a pain patient. The presentation comprises a very eclectic approach, encompassing ideas from physiology, behavioral conditioning, hypnoanalysis, and naturalistic techniques.

In preparation for future trances, and setting the ground for self-hypnosis and independence, I explained to her, as I objectively observed the onset of catalepsy, that I had simply given her the proper opportunity for her brain to activate preexisting neural circuits, leading to the development of hypnosis. She was learning now to reactivate those circuits for whenever she would need hypnosis in the future. Then . . . I explained to her that the hand would begin to imperceptibly move downwards, so slowly that it would be like trying to notice the movement of the minute hand on the face of a clock. At the same time, I indicated that she would start to feel a very comfortable relaxation starting in the muscles of her eyes and gradually extending down to all the rest of her body. When her eyes would begin to close, her head would spontaneously begin to rotate to the left, while the hand would gradually come to rest in her lap. These suggestions were given as statements of fact. Your brain is connected to every part of your body through many intermediate switchboards; therefore, you can send messages down the line to stop pain that arises from many areas, even before the pain messages can reach your brain.

Your brain continues to monitor your body, protecting many areas where bones have been weakened but without your having to feel pain. (Sacerdote, 1972, pp. 511–520)

Sacerdote trained the patient to develop further her talent for formal and informal hypnosis, and he used her figurative language to feed back her ideas and images of telegraphing herself messages for switching off the unnecessary pain, nausea, retching, and sadness. The patient learned to use her simplified version of the nervous system for preventing pain signals from reaching her brain. In addition, she learned to reinterpret pain signals as pleasant musical vibrations. Dissociative experiences were used to achieve positive hallucinations that permitted her to experience herself in a healthy way. Also, she used dreams to achieve better understanding. Thus, with this patient, Sacerdote creatively combined physiology, free association, and imagery that were then reinforced by self-hypnosis.

PSYCHOANALYTIC ORIENTATION

Psychoanalytic hypnotherapy combines hypnosis with psychoanalysis (Fromm, 1977; Gill & Brenman, 1959; Gruenewald, 1982b; Schneck, 1965). This merger is a powerful technique that can bring about or facilitate adaptive ego functioning. This new personality integration increases productivity, coping, and personal growth.

Essentially, hypnoanalysis is a relatively long-term treatment. Including self-hypnosis enables the patient to access the unconscious more easily. In addition, whereas hypnosis intensifies the transference, self-hypnosis minimizes dependency. According to Fromm, because of the easier access to the unconscious from heightened ego receptivity, hypnoanalysis requires half the time that would be spent in traditional psychoanalysis (Fromm, 1984; Brown & Fromm, 1986).

The goals of hypnoanalysis are: (1) the uncovering of underlying drives, instincts, and defenses, (2) working through, and (3) a new personality integration. This process is one of maturation and self-growth.

As in psychoanalysis, the hypnoanalyst interprets the transferences and the defenses. The resistances may not need interpretation but may be utilized or bypassed. If this is not possible, they can be interpreted (Brown & Fromm, 1986). The techniques involved are also psychoanalytic. The use of free association is enhanced by free-floating imagery. Analysis of dreams and analysis of the transferences are carried out in a manner similar to psychoanalysis, that is, via interpretation.

According to Fromm (1980) and Fromm and Kahn (1990a), in self-hypnosis with normal, highly hypnotizable subjects, there is greater ego-receptivity to the unconscious drives, affects, and creative potentials. The ego is active in its receptivity; that is, it is adaptive rather than passive or overwhelmed. The attention is more free-flowing and unfocused than in heterohypnosis, although it is possible for the patient to achieve some degree of concentrative attention. The thought processes are to a greater extent unconscious and imaginal rather than realistic or logical. That is, primary process thought is "fluid, mobile, free-flowing psychic energy" (Fromm, 1978-1979, 1981, p. 36) as opposed to secondary-process, sequential, rational, logical thinking. The two processes coexist and interact. Finally, in self-hypnosis, the ego can function on a continuum of automatized behavior by which the person performs automatically without conscious input. Deautomatized behavior, on the other hand, consists of hypervigilance of hyper-self-monitoring, which leads to self-consciousness and distraction from the task. Self-hypnosis can maximize the ego's receptivity to the unconscious, encourage more free-flowing psychic energy in free association and free-floating imagery, decrease self-monitoring and self-consciousness, and generate more creative adaptation, thus facilitating the analysis.

In addition to the traditional tools of psychoanalysis, the hypnoanalyst has access to hypnotic tools that can enhance the analysis. The hypnoanalyst, for example, can encourage imagery, a representative hypnotic technique, in order to tap into the ego ideal, which sets goals. According to Fromm, the ego ideal is important in motivation and planning because it represents what one hopes to be or strives to be. The hypnotherapist can induce dreams in the session, suggesting to the patient that he or she dream about a particular problem that the patient is struggling with. The patient can be asked to redream the dream in a different manner. And the therapist may also suggest that the patient will be able to understand the symbolism and meaning of dreams more easily. In addition, the hypnoanalyst can use posthypnotic suggestions that the patient will have some further insights during the week. And the therapist can suggest that the patient rehearse solutions to problems in imagery and in dreams.

Through self-hypnosis, the patient is introduced to a new world of inner being, which can challenge him or her to move toward goals and to achieve mastery and integration.

According to Fromm (1977), in self-hypnosis the patient is ego-receptive; that is, the patient has greater access to primary process thoughts and images. The barriers between consciousness and awareness and unconscious experience and the preconscious are lowered, leading to greater availability of unconscious material (Fromm, 1972a).

Erika Fromm illustrates the use of the ego ideal technique by describing Kate, a female medical student who had a fear of blood; she fainted whenever she saw it. However, she wanted to become a physician.

Fromm described to her an ego ideal "Melissa" who had come in as a competent young woman physician able to bandage a child's bleeding wound or to perform surgery when needed. She let "Melissa" tell Kate that she had scheduled surgery for a patient and that she must now go over to talk to the patient for a while and see to it that he was wheeled into the operating room. Then she suggested to Kate that she felt an urge that could not be overcome to move into the body of "Melissa" and that, safely encased in "Melissa," she was going to watch the surgery that "Melissa" would perform on the patient. In the next therapy hour, Dr. Fromm let her feel that she had become so accustomed to seeing blood and had remained so relaxed about it while watching from within "Melissa's" body that she now could step out of "Melissa" in the imaginary operating room and assist her with the surgery (Fromm, 1984, pp. 142–154).

The patient can experience this ego ideal technique in self-hypnosis. The effortless experience of such imagery may lead to desensitization carried out in a self-hypnotic psychoanalytic orientation.

According to Wolberg, it is best to teach hypnosis early before the full development of the transference. Thus, teaching the patient hypnosis within the first few weeks of treatment is advised (Wolberg, 1945). Self-hypnosis practice can also begin as the patient feels more comfortable with it. Practice sessions for self-hypnosis are generally longer than those for more structured hypnotherapy practice, as, for example, 30 to 60 minutes of self-hypnosis practice once a day. This massed practice facilitates ego receptivity to unconscious ideation and heightens the drive to self-mastery. The patient may maintain a journal describing the self-hypnosis experiences to be discussed in the therapy.

Hypnoanalysis can be used with a wide range of problems, among them psychoneuroses, narcissistic disorders, and personality disorders. The use of long-massed practice sessions may need modification in those patients who cannot tolerate long periods of trance. These patients may do better with short practice sessions.

BEHAVIORAL ORIENTATION

The underlying basis for behavioral orientation is that of classical conditioning (Kroger & Fezler, 1976; Pavlov, 1941; Wolpe, 1958; Dengrove, 1973). In hypnosis, fantasy rehearsal permits covert conditioning to occur. In imagination, the patient may initiate relaxation as a way of desensitizing him- or herself to a given fear, such as an airplane phobia.

One patient, Susie, had an airplane phobia for 3 years. It had occurred rather suddenly during her flight home from a hectic "crash course" in accounting. She felt herself panic on the plane, fearing that nothing was holding the airplane up in the air. Since the termination of that flight, she had been unable to get on a plane again. In hypnotherapy, she recognized the need to expose herself in a gradually progressive manner to airplanes. With self-hypnosis practice, she recognized that she could counteract any anxiety she experienced. Finally, she was able to develop a number of positive attention distracters to occupy herself in the airplane.

In heterohypnosis with me, Susie pictured herself in a safe, comfortable place where she felt warm and relaxed. She described her home. Then she stated that she liked to ride on buses. I asked her to imagine that she was on a wide bus, with me, feeling very comfortable and very relaxed. After she nodded, I asked her to imagine that she had a cassette tape player and a number of tapes of music that she liked and was listening to her favorite music. The suggestion elicited a smile. I asked her to think of something else she might like to have on the bus. She said that she liked to crochet. I asked her to imagine that she was crocheting a woolen shawl. As she settled in to picture this scene, I mentioned that the bus was now arriving in Charlotte. How did she feel about this short trip? She was amazed at just how quickly the trip was finished.

I instructed her to practice self-hypnosis by taking 10 long, slow, deep breaths. Then she could begin to relax by relaxing every muscle in her body, just as we had done here in the office. Once she had relaxed all of her muscles, she could imagine that she was on a bus going from Raleigh to Charlotte. On the trip she was to take as many distractions as she liked: crocheting materials, books, cassette player and tapes, cards, or anything else she preferred. She was to practice imagining herself on this bus trip, enjoying the materials that she had with her. She would be surprised at how comfortable and brief the bus ride was.

The second week, Susie spontaneously transformed the big bus to a comfortable airplane that remained at the gate. We were both comfortable. She brought into her imagery as many distraction materials as possible. Her task was to get on the airplane, sit down, and get involved with her distractions, effortlessly. On the third week she transformed the plane so that it was no longer stationary. She allowed herself to experience it as moving, as it taxied to the runway but remained on the ground like a bus. She continued to experience getting involved with her distraction materials. The fourth week, she experienced the airplane moving to the runway, rolling down the runway, and taking off. She was so absorbed, however, in her distractions that she did not notice the takeoff. Rather, she was amazed to find herself at the Charlotte airport.

The underlying assumption in a behavioral orientation is that problem behaviors are learned, persistent, and unadaptive. Because these behaviors are learned behaviors, they can be unlearned or eliminated through unlearning.

Anxiety is viewed as a part of the original learning situation that produced the problem behavior. The therapeutic task is to alter the learned connections between previously neutral situational or response events and these anxiety responses. This goal is achieved by presenting the anxiety-eliciting events or symbolic representations of them in temporal contiguity to responses that are antagonistic to anxiety, for example, relaxation. In this way, anxiety is prevented from occurring, and the bond between the eliciting event and the anxiety is weakened. For this patient, the bond between the airplane and anxiety was weakened, and the patient was able to fly.

Hypnosis and self-hypnosis provide a natural environment in which to facilitate relaxation, desensitization, and new learning. In hypnotherapy, the bridge from heterohypnosis to self-hypnosis permits the patient to explore independently, knowing that he or she can return to the safety of heterohypnosis during the session, should the need occur, much like the early stage of rapprochement in early development, when the child first ventures away from the parent, only to return for reassurance.

PHYSIOLOGICAL SELF-HYPNOSIS

A physiological orientation to self-hypnosis is based on the assumption that mind and body interact and that self-hypnosis is a way of affecting that interaction. Current research in pain and in psychoneuroimmunology reflects the growing conviction that self-hypnosis will serve a useful purpose in the holistic treatment of disease (Black, Humphrey, & Niven, 1963; Hall, 1983; Olness & Culbert, 1989; Stein, Schleifer & Keller, 1982; Barber, 1984; Persinger & De Sano, 1986; Risenberg, 1986).

Of particular relevance to the voluntary control of immune processes is the interaction between the cerebral cortex and the hippocampus. The hippocampus incorporates a type of indexing system that provides access to the imagery of memory (Teyler & Discenna, 1984). These patterns are assumed to be stored within the modules of the cortex. Specific patterns of modules recruit a variety of biochemical responses that are under the control of the hippocampus and the amygdala.

The basic techniques require the patient to image certain organs and/or metaphors or specific suggestions in which ideas are associated with meanings related to increasing recruitment of immune processes (Persinger & De Sano, 1986) or to focus on ideas that represent organs, or to achieve a deep hypnotic state that will impact on the physiological functioning of the body (Barber, 1984; Meares, 1978). It is hypothesized that imagery will trigger physiological reactions, much as the image of eating a lemon triggers saliva.

The goals of physiological self-hypnosis are to access the physiological level of functioning, thus reducing physical tension, lowering blood pressure, decreasing heart rate, decreasing digestive juices, increasing the production of certain natural pain-reducing substances, and increasing the effectiveness of the immune system. Certainly some of these responses are easily monitored, for example, relaxation, heart rate, and blood pressure. Others are more difficult to track, and still others are in a hypothetical format requiring more controlled and replicable research. Nonetheless, impressive anecdotal studies are reported (Crasilneck & Hall, 1985; Olness & Gardner, 1989).

Hypnotic imagery of calm scenes induces relaxation and a lessening of body tension. It is the changed perception of body observation that reflects the effect of interaction between physiology and self-hypnosis. Physiological metaphors may be used, such as rubber bands to represent headache pain that can be loosened in imagination to make the patient feel more comfortable. Deep breathing seems to lead to more parasympathetic system activity and to reduce sympathetic activity. The mind–body interface cannot be denied.

Physiological therapists may teach the patient self-hypnosis within the first few weeks of therapy. They may ask for frequent but brief practice sessions such as Schultz and Luthe's autogenic training (1959) and Jacobson's progressive relaxation (1929). Relevant work with cancer patients has been reported by Margolis (1982–1983). Brown and Fromm (1987) review the current hypnotic work in behavioral medicine. Gardner and Olness (1981) present pertinent self-hypnotic work in pediatrics. Gardner and Olness (1988) and Sarbin and Slagel (1979) report on germane work in neurology, as do Meszaros, Banyai, and Greguss (1985).

Psychophysiological disorders, neurological problems, especially those involving loss of motivation, pain, anxiety secondary to deficits, management problems, and control of emotion related to illness as well as psychophysiological disorders are all relevant to a physiological orientation. Even cancer patients and AIDS patients can work to improve their quality of life, that is, decrease pain perception, increase alertness, and decrease pain medication. With self-hypnosis the patient can learn to control or reduce pain without drugs or on reduced amounts of drugs: he or she can stay more alert, thus be able to interact with friends and family members. Emotionally, also, terminally ill patients are more centered and less frightened when practicing self-hypnosis. Thus the quality of the time remaining to them is much improved.

According to Rossi, the neurobiological approach focuses on the relevance and importance of biological factors in the development of psychological disorders. This biological perspective emphasizes what individuals bring—genetic, chromosomal, biochemical, neurological, and physiological characteristics and predispositions that directly and indirectly affect behavior and development. One's biological clock, energy level, extraversion, overall health and stamina, and presence or absence of physical or neurological abnormality or handicap are all genetic factors that contribute to behavior.

Nugent, Carden, and Montgomery describe a therapeutic approach to a phobia for needles in one college subject that used the natural ultradian rhythm unique to that person as the key to change (Nugent, Carden, & Montgomery, 1984, pp. 202–203). Many people find that the rest phase of their ultradian rhythm is the best time to meditate or do self-hypnosis. An ultradian approach to self-hypnosis uses natural psychobiological rhythms that are more deeply rooted in the storage of state-dependent learning experiences. According to Rossi (1986), "allow your unconscious to do its own work in its own way. Avoid any form of verbal self-suggestion that might distort the self-healing needs of the total personality" (p. 278).

Using words and images to affect the body's ultradian rhythm cycles points to the use of words and images to affect other body processes. The patient learns to affect his or her own body processes at home, at work, and away from the therapist's office by practicing self-hypnosis. The patient using self-hypnosis takes control of physiological responses paradoxically, in an effortless manner.

Naturalistic

Milton Erickson used naturalistic patterns of behavior to develop posthypnotic suggestions. That is, he used the behavior he observed in the patient as the content of hypnotic suggestion and posthypnotic suggestion. For example, he gave a series of posthypnotic suggestions about how the subject's natural pupillary behavior can be used in the future, both by his or her own unconscious and by his or her therapist. After hypnosis had been induced, Erickson gave the following suggestions:

> In future work with you, your unconscious is going to resort to that pupillary dilation at times to let Dr. H. know that your unconscious is really talking, is really listening; so that he, in watching your pupils, will recognize that he is talking to both your conscious mind and your unconscious mind; [so that he will know] that your unconscious mind has thereby invited him to say something. Now whether or not he says the right thing is not important. The mere fact that he says something, because your unconscious invited him to, and that tells your unconscious that he is being responsive, and therefore it can be responsive, too. (Rossi & Ryan, 1985, p. 278)

The ingredients of the naturalistic orientation include a positive double bind where, no matter what happens, the patient's unconscious will be receptive. That is, whether or not the therapist says the right thing is not important. Rossi interprets this as a fail-safe posthypnotic suggestion. In addition, the way the posthypnotic suggestion is presented highlights the fact that the patient's unconscious has requested a response and can also respond to a suggestion. According to Rossi, "all that is required of the hypnotherapist is a sincere, therapeutic dialogue wherein the patient's unconscious is given the freedom to respond, and, if necessary, to correct and even guide the therapist, who is able to recognize the voice of the unconscious via its minimal cues" (Rossi & Ryan, 1985, p. 278).

Reframing and reinterpreting the significance and meaning in a person's life experience can allow potentials and behavior to be tapped and expressed. By reframing, understandings are reorganized so that the problems can be resolved. The change in meaning affects feelings, understandings, and perceptions; it also conveys meanings.

Accessing the unconscious and its storehouse of positive experience is an important goal of naturalistic hypnotherapy. The techniques to access the unconscious are similar to other types of hypnotherapy. Therapist questions, sharing of thoughts, and telling stories that are related to the patient's problems, are all ways to access the unconscious. The uses of analogy and metaphor are very important. In addition, focusing on the positive memories stored in the unconscious to create a positive mind-set is important for therapeutic use of self-hypnosis.

The use of analogy and metaphor can serve to illustrate this. "Just as a horribly traumatic experience can condition a person with tremendous force and rigidity, so can a pleasant experience" (Erickson, 1985, p. 55). According to Rossi and Ryan, the manner in which appeals are made to the unconscious mind establishes a foundation for the patient's future thinking and feeling about hypnosis, about dentistry, medicine, their bodies, and about how they react to physical and mental distress (Erickson, 1985).

Erickson described a person who was blocked in creating art work. He blanked out every time he started to think about artistic creation. However, he did not want to be hypnotized. Erickson proposed a technique whereby the patient was to sit down for 20 minutes in his chair after his day's work and relax. He was told to just slump in the chair with his head down, enjoy the relaxation, and let his unconscious do as it pleased. Two months later, the artist reported back that he had relaxed for 20 minutes or so each day, and that this activity had increased his creativity. According to Erickson, "In autohypnosis you merely give yourself the opportunity of doing things with your unconscious" (Erickson & Rossi, 1977, pp. 50–51). Notice that Erickson did not ask the patient to falsify his own understanding: rather, he provided other understandings that nullify, contradict, absorb, and hold the patient's focus so that he cannot give all his attention to what is distressing him. Distraction can lead to mastery and new levels of adaptation. Erickson frequently gave homework assignments to his patients. Some were behavioral, in which patients were asked to carry out some behavior; others required going into self-hypnosis. Thus, he provided different requirements for different patients.

CONCLUSION

Now that we have perused the major orientations, what have we learned? We have learned that all the orientations have access to all the hypnotic phenomena. However, they will be used in a variety of ways to reach specific goals that will differ in emphasis, in content, and in rationale. The complex interactions within the individual contribute to the idiosyncratic response of the patient.

The therapist orientations will differ in three dimensions. One dimension is concerned with permissive or authoritarian styles of interacting with the patient. The second dimension is concerned with directive or nondirective styles of making suggestions. Finally, the therapist may be active or passive vis-à-vis the patient. The theory underlying the therapist's orientation to psychotherapy dictates this aspect of the therapeutic interaction. All of the orientations may use any hypnotic induction that works with a given patient and that the therapist is comfortable using.

Although there is a great diversity of self-hypnotic methodology, some common self-hypnotic techniques include free-floating imagery, guided imagery, hypnotic dreams, relaxation, hypnoanesthesia, metaphoric imagery, ego ideal, self-desensitization, self-cognitive restructuring; self-interpretation may be used by therapists practicing any orientation. However, the way a suggestion is presented and the manner in which it is used will reflect, in part, a specific therapeutic orientation interacting both with a general effect of hypnosis or self-hypnosis along with all the many other complex variables contributing to the response. The possibilities are manifold. We see the similarities between orientations as well as the diversity of ways that hypnotic and self-hypnotic experience may be used.

In all the orientations, the notion of experiential awareness is important. However, this awareness may be explicitly suggested as in a direct approach or implicitly assumed as a response to a suggestion that elicits such a response (a nondirective strategy).

And in all the orientations, the power of words and images to generate actions and reactions via specific meanings in the patient is self-evident. With the speed of a word, a patient may transform him- or herself from a person in panic to a person at ease. With the speed of an image, a person in pain can transform him- or herself into a person in comfort. With the speed of a thought, 1/18th of a second or 7,560 bits per minute (Rossi, 1986), the human consciousness is prepared to act.

Our consciousness presents a clearinghouse for a multitude of sensations, perceptions, memories, and images, which we differentiate, focus on, and keep in awareness. Our conscious experience is a private experience, apparent only to ourselves. It is by nature subjective. In a phenomenological framework, the very subjectivity is immediate. The individual knows that he or she knows, and that what he or she knows is unique. The therapist validates the patient's unique experience.

All these theories jointly maintain the power of words and images to bring about transformation. The stated goals may be diverse, but the means to those goals are through the powerful meanings given to words and images by the patient. The therapist encourages the tools of communication, word pictures and sensory images, to transform pain into comfort, unawareness into awareness, and problem into solution. The crucial studies delineating self-hypnosis are only just beginning. And crucial studies of self-hypnosis as a clinical tool can only be determined by clinical judgment and patient judgment. However, I have found that self-hypnosis has been described as a useful tool by patients, and I have observed positive effects of daily practice of self-hypnosis. These anecdotal observations, nonetheless, according to Orne and McConkey (1981), do not comprise systematic data clarifying the frequency with which self-hypnosis is used clinically, the benefits derived from it, and the few attempts to assess the kinds of changes brought about by an individual's use of self-hypnosis.

Observing how the patient uses self-hypnosis and the ways that self-hypnosis affects him or her is critical to hypnotherapeutic intervention. I believe that a more phenomenological approach to observation and description of the patient in relation to his or her use of self-hypnosis would lead to a greater understanding of self-hypnosis within a convergent model using other measures.

The purpose of theory is to postulate how hypnosis works. It presents some ground rules. However, these rules may change over time, as is customary when scientific research tests out the hypotheses generated by theory. In the next chapter we look at research in self-hypnosis and related research in hypnosis.

For those interested in a more in-depth discussion of theory and research, the reader is directed to read *Self-Hypnosis: The Chicago Paradigm* (Fromm & Kahn, 1990a).

CHAPTER 5

Research in Self-hypnosis

For knowledge, too, is itself a power.
—Francis Bacon

This chapter focuses on relevant research in the area of self-hypnosis. Although research is not the major thrust of this book, it is important to recognize the need for basic comparative research and theory. Only recently has this research come of age. As mentioned in Chapter 2, until the 20th century, most reports of self-hypnosis were in fact therapist observations of patients using self-hypnosis by themselves. The initial descriptions were of self-hypnosis conceived of as an automatic, nondirected state. However, as more careful observations were made, therapists began to report teaching patients self-hypnosis for specific effects. And the therapists began to include some mention of this teaching in their anecdotal case examples. However, case reports are ideographic, and the scientific times demand a more nomothetic approach to the understanding of self-hypnosis.

The questions raised about self-hypnosis involve many of the same issues raised in heterohypnosis. Objectivity requires clarification of those characteristics that are specific for self-hypnosis. Additionally, theorists are interested in clarifying those personality characteristics that may interact with self-hypnosis. Theorists wish to tap susceptibility to self-hypnosis. They wish to identify those phenomena that characterize self-hypnosis. In addition to differentiating the phenomena, they wish to identify those factors that interact and produce influential effects such as changes in cognition, affect, and control functions operative in self-hypnosis. Because controlled research is really just beginning in the laboratory, the sorting and differentiating process is exciting to watch. Clinical studies have not clearly differentiated self-hypnosis and heterohypnosis and have more frequently assumed them to be similar (Kroger, 1977).

One problem affecting research in self-hypnosis is the problem of comparing laboratory-defined self-hypnosis with clinically defined self-hypnosis. Erika Fromm et al. (1981) have made important strides in the definition process, as discussed in Chapter 4. However, these definitions have focused on self-hypnosis with normal subjects in the laboratory. Clinical patients may have more vulnerability in the operation of ego functions and may not be able to use self-hypnosis in the strictest sense, but may need more time to adapt. Some evidence for this is found in the work of Baker (1983a, 1983b) and Scagnelli (1980). Another level of complexity exists in the clinical situation in that the hypnotherapist holds both a theory of hypnosis as well as a theory of psychotherapy. The resulting interactions may mask the relevant variables. Clinical reports of patients who have been treated with some form of hypnotherapy and self-hypnosis imply that therapeutic change occurs because of hypnosis and self-hypnosis. According to Gruenewald (1982a, 1982b), changes that occur during hypnotic intervention may or may not be directly linked to hypnosis. She goes on to discuss the various influences that may occur in association with hypnotherapy. From a scientific point of view, it is desirable to gain a clearer treatment mode (Gruenewald, 1982a).

According to Wain (1980), it is a foregone conclusion that the clinical application of hypnotic-related phenomena is far ahead of its scientific elucidation. Many clinicians believe that the variables present in the clinical setting are minimized or absent in the laboratory. For example, issues related to the therapist–patient relationship may either be minimized or exaggerated in the laboratory. Contextual variables are quite different in the two situations (Gruenewald, 1982a; Wain, 1980).

McConkey and Sheehan (1982) recommend careful analysis to determine precise strategies employed by the subject (patient) in order to experience his or her imagination. It is important to determine what he or she believes to be the source of his or her experiences. Finally, it is necessary to discover whether the patient is willfully expending effort or if the response is effortless.

Specific and nonspecific effects of heterohypnosis as an adjunct to behavior therapy have not been convincingly demonstrated by controlled outcome studies (Spinhoven, 1987). Spinhoven recommends that the context of therapy, type of disorder, patient characteristics, and hypnotic interventions under which type of hypnosis (i.e.,

self-hypnosis) be studied in relation to each other. Spinhoven further
states that in the absence of confirming data, the most parsimonious
position is to state that hypnotherapy is procedurally similar to certain
(cognitive) behavior therapy procedures but that it is labeled otherwise (Spinhoven, 1987).

Another problem in studying self-hypnosis concerns patients' subjective reporting of multiple observations. Subjects or patients must
observe themselves, direct themselves, as well as respond to their own
self-suggestions. This task is complicated. The subject without training
may be unable to maintain scientific objectivity. According to Tart, the
subject must be trained in techniques of observation, direction, and
response (Tart, 1975). Self-observation is a complicated process. In
addition, the observer needs some criteria against which to evaluate
the outcome of the self-hypnosis process (Johnson, 1979). Thus, specific goals need to be defined. Not only is this goal definition important in the laboratory, it is important in the clinical situation.

Basic research in self-hypnosis has been difficult in the past because traditional ways of data-gathering were not sensitive to the
measurement of self-hypnosis (Shor, 1979a, 1979b; Tart, 1970, 1975,
1978–1979). Much of the response to self-hypnosis is subjective. That
is, the focus is on inner experience rather than external manipulation
(Johnson, 1979). Johnson describes self-hypnosis as a paradox because
of the implications underlying simultaneous internal self-experience
and external hypnosis control. To capture the subjective response and
subjective experiences, a more descriptive method of observation is
necessary. Ron Shor developed a descriptive or quasi-phenomenological method[1] of observation and measurement (Shor, 1979) that permits
comparisons between qualitative observations as well as quantitative
ones. He combined therapist observations, clinical interviews, and
therapist ratings of subject involvement on rating scales of hypnotic
depth. He believed that this combined approach permits comparisons
between self-hypnosis and heterohypnosis (Shor, 1979b). Nonetheless,
other methods also need to be developed.

As in other hypnotic research, the influence of demand characteristics biases observations in such a way as to augment those phenomena unique to self-hypnosis. Aspects of the experimental situation, expectations, hypotheses, and anticipations all affect the outcome
of the research. This influence must be taken seriously (Johnson, 1981).

[1]Shor's method in my opinion is actually a quasi-phenomenological method, integrating
empirical measurement with clinical observation. A pure phenomenological exploration
would not include measurement.

REVIEW OF LITERATURE

The term "hypnotherapy" signifies such a wide array of theoretical formulations and practical techniques that the word has almost lost its descriptive value (Wadden & Anderson, 1982). According to Spinhovan (1987), hypnosis may be defined in two different ways: as an antecedent variable (the therapist defines the criteria) and as a subject variable (hypnotic susceptibility). Clinical self-hypnosis also covers a wide array of theoretical formulations and practical techniques.

The last few years have yielded increasing amounts of research in the following areas:

1. Theoretical basic research.
2. Research on psychopathology and the facilitation of self-hypnosis on treatment. This research is not yet clear about the specific contributions of self-hypnosis. Most frequently, clinical studies confound these two variables.
3. Research on creativity, sports facilitation, and skill building. While this research is interesting, most of it has been on heterohypnosis and has yet to mature in the area of self-hypnosis.

While this chapter focuses on research relevent to self-hypnosis, such research is not the main thrust of the book, which is to focus on the use of words and images empowered by the patient to change or transform. For a more comprehensive discussion of theory and research in self-hypnosis, the reader is directed to Erika Fromm and Stephen Kahn's new book *Self-Hypnosis: The Chicago Paradigm* (Fromm & Kahn, 1990a) and Fromm and Shor's book *Hypnosis: Developments in Research and New Perspectives* (Fromm & Shor, 1979).

BASIC RESEARCH

The questions raised about self-hypnosis involve a variety of questions. The lines of interest extend from the basic task of differentiating heterohypnosis from autohypnosis and self-hypnosis to defining the phenomenal characteristics that may be related to self-hypnosis. Currently, the questions raised in the headings below are reported in the literature.

What Research Methodologies Are Used to Study Self-Hypnosis?

Research methodologies used in self-hypnosis studies follow traditional heterohypnosis as a conceptual and empirical baseline (Fromm et al., 1981). There is a wide range of approaches to self-hypnosis. In terms of this range of approaches, no one approach can be considered to be the correct method of application or investigation (Orne & McConkey, 1981). In some studies, considerable training is given (Fromm et al., 1981). In others, naive subjects are used, and structure is minimized (Ruch, 1972, 1975). Standard scales of heterohypnosis may be used (Orne & McConkey, 1981; Fromm et al., 1981). Phenomenological differences or similarities were first demonstrated by Johnson, who used an inventory of the self-hypnotic experience (Johnson, 1979).

According to Orne and McConkey (1981), behavioral and experiential paradigms predominate the literature. They recommend for clinical studies that convergent measures based on clinical tasks and consequences be used. They believe that the clinical use of heterohypnosis generally sets the protocols for the use of self-hypnosis by patients as a way of refreshing or reinforcing the suggestions given to them by the clinician (Gardner, 1981; Sacerdote, 1981). Fromm et al. (1981) suggest that experiential measures be used in addition to more standardized behavioral measures.

Utilizing Shor's quasiphenomenological approach (Shor, 1979b) to study descriptive or phenomenal characteristics of self-hypnosis, and using Tart's self-rating measures of hypnotic depth (Tart, 1970), Erika Fromm et al. (1981) combined the experiential and behavioral observations of self-hypnosis. They screened 425 subjects for hypnotizability on the Stanford and Harvard scales. Subjects attaining a score of 9 or more were given the Rorschach to screen out serious personality disorders. They were also given the Minnesota Multiphasic Personality Inventory (MMPI; Hathaway & McKinnon, 1956), and the Personality Orientation Inventory. Out of 58 highly hypnotizable subjects, 33 completed all aspects of the study. This research followed the subjects over 4 weeks of practice of self-hypnosis, thus providing a longitudinal perspective.

After the screening, which involved all the subjects learning heterohypnosis, the remaining subjects were given the following instructions.

> You are now going to begin your 4 weeks of self-hypnosis. During three preexperimental standardized hypnotic experiences with the experimenters, you have become familiar with a good number of hypnotic procedures. You may use these as an example of what you can do in your hour of self-hypnosis each day. However, do not feel

that you need limit yourself to these. You may wish to think up suggestions for some other experiences and then experiment with them. You may also wish at times just to remain in trance but not do anything specific. We want you to experience self-hypnosis for about 60 minutes every day for four weeks. (Fromm et al., 1981, p. 205)

The experimenters monitored the self-hypnosis in the following ways:

1. *Journals.* Subjects kept daily journals in which they detailed the contents of their experiences, including date, time duration, self-suggestions attempted, outcome, and critical reflections on each aspect of the self-hypnotic experience. Monitoring during the 4-week period was limited to weekly telephone calls and biweekly meetings. No suggestions were given during these meetings as to the content of the journals. Thus, according to the authors, the self-hypnotic experiences were essentially self-directed, oral, phenomenological, and clinical methods that provide considerable information. Fromm stresses the need for multiple research strategies along with valid measures of change and improvement (Fromm et al., 1981).

2. *Depth.* Subjective judgment of depth was made based on a slightly revised version of the Tart Self-Report Scale. Previously, this scale has been used only with heterohypnotic subjects. The self-reports of depth correlated highly with hypnotizability and with imagery measures described below (Fromm & Kahn, 1990d).

3. *Questionnaires.* Three questionnaires were used for rating on a 5-point Likert scale to provide information about depth, reality orientation, and content of the hypnotic phenomena experienced. Also included was the analysis of the self-hypnosis journal, which was coded for imagery production by scoring for both reality-oriented and primary process imagery. Rather than behavioral comparisons, Fromm was interested in the phenomena of self-hypnosis. To obtain these self-hypnotic phenomena, the subject was required to initiate his or her own self-suggestions and was not given tasks (Fromm et al., 1981).

The results of this pioneering study demonstrate that the Tart depth scores are a valid indicator of self-hypnotic depth among highly hypnotizable subjects. Furthermore, they show that both heterohypnotic susceptibility and imagery production are related to self-hypnotic depth. The authors found that the association between imagery and hypnotic susceptibility results from the relationship of each of them to self-hypnotic depth. These convergent results support the notion that self-hypnotic depth is multidimensional and that this combined experiential–behavioral approach permits the study of self-hypnotic phenomena (Fromm & Kahn, 1990d). Additional results from this study will be discussed later.

Some researchers have discussed the method of functionalism (Hilgard, 1969), which permits the identification and classification of behaviors and responses without enlisting the hypothesis of unusual causal properties, for example, the notion of a different state of awareness. In his work with the neodissociation theory, Hilgard emphasized convergent operations. The results focus on the functional relationships between variables in terms of a key operation, for instance, the relationship between hypnotic susceptibility and memory. In this manner, states of awareness can be studied without reference to unusual causal properties. Although this work was not directed at self-hypnosis specifically, the paradigm is an interesting one.

The "hidden-observer" method described by Hilgard (1979a) is another method that appears promising for the study of self-hypnosis, although it has not been used in self-hypnosis research. Hilgard found that, while in hypnosis, highly hypnotizable subjects would report two different pain ratings when one hand was immersed in circulating water. The subject would report pain as being completely absent; simultaneously the subject would rate pain with increasing intensity during an automatic writing task. These reports were more than zero but less than the pain reported when unhypnotized. Hilgard called this hidden reporter "the hidden observer" that can be accessed through automatic writing and through automatic talking or even through finger signals that may be a way to access the self-hypnotic experience. The hidden observer reports on experiences of which the unhypnotized person may be unaware and of which the deeply hypnotized person may also not be aware. The hidden observer appears to monitor what is happening at all times and appears to characterize a split within the cognitive monitoring system. Although no studies of clinical self-hypnosis have used the hidden-observer paradigm, it would seem interesting to access the hidden observer during self-hypnotic experience. However, this technique is appropriate only for the highly susceptible subject and is not useful for low-susceptibility subjects. It would be necessary first to select subjects who are highly hypnotizable before using the approach. Although some therapists may be fearful of confounding the effects of high hypnotic susceptibility with the responses to the hidden observer, others have favored working with highly susceptible subjects to obtain a pure response sample (Weitzenhoffer, 1989).

The most traditional paradigm in hypnotic research has been the behavioral paradigm. A behavioral paradigm presents a set of standardized items that are administered verbatim and scored in terms of precise and objective criteria. The use of a susceptibility scale is an example of taking observations in a standardized manner and providing a comparative measurement of overall depth of hypnosis as defined by success in hypnotic behavior of variable difficulty. It permits comparisons between variables under standardized conditions. However, it may limit the emergence of more spontaneous self-hypnotic responses. Some compromises are needed to study the phenomena of self-hypnosis in the clinical situation. As mentioned, this study could take place in session with the hypnotherapist present, asking questions or giving modified suggestions. This follows the recommendation that the clinical use of heterohypnosis generally sets the protocol for the use of self-hypnosis by patients as a way of refreshing or reinforcing the suggestions given to them by the clinician (Gardner, 1981; Sacerdote, 1981).

The only published scale to measure self-hypnotic susceptibility is the Inventory of Self-Hypnosis—Form A (Shor, 1962a). This inventory is an adaptation of the Harvard Group Scale of Hypnotic Susceptibility, Form A (Shor, Orne, & Orne, 1962). The Harvard Group Scale is an adaptation for group administration and self-scoring of the individually administered and self-scored Stanford Hypnotic Susceptibility Scale, Form A (Shor & Orne, 1962b). The 12-item inventory includes items on relaxation and drowsiness, eye closure, suggested body movements, vivid imagery, muscular inhibition, and temporary controlled forgetting. Administration time required is 1½ hours. This scale uses a fractionation approach to self-hypnotic suggestion, requiring that the subject read the item instructions, enter self-hypnosis, carry out the task, then exit self-hypnosis to prepare for the next item. Fromm is not convinced that this measure actually taps self-hypnosis susceptibility (Fromm & Kahn, 1990a).

The clinical interview provides a way of accessing self-hypnotic phenomena. Such an interpretive diagnostic evaluation of the hypnotic response as experienced by the patient can reflect the experience of the patient. In the clinical method, the patient is asked to rate how deeply hypnotized he or she feels him- or herself to be, then is asked to describe his or her experiences. Subjective experiences such as hypnotic dreams, hypnotic hallucinations, and age regression can all be studied. The demand characteristics of the situation and the wish to please the hypnotherapist are important aspects of subjective experience. In the clinical situation these can be monitored as they can in the laboratory. A limitation of this approach is its focus on specific self-hypnotic phenomena, suggesting a bias toward maximizing the difference between self-hypnosis and heterohypnosis (Johnson, 1981; Johnson, Dawson, Clark, & Sikorsky, 1983).

The method of phenomenology is concerned with the description of consciousness. Measurements of hypnotic depth are made by the observer in terms of rating scales applied to the subject's descriptions. Shor has designed a rating scale for the measurement of trance, the measurement of archaic involvement, and the measurement of non-conscious involvement (Shor, 1979b). It is the latter that appears most relevant for measurement of self-hypnosis, although to my knowledge it has not yet been used in such a study. Nonconscious involvement (dissociation) may be approximated by the ratings made by the interviewer from the subject's descriptions during an interview.

Self-Hypnosis as an Altered State

The literature consistently supports the theory that self-hypnosis is an altered state of consciousness in that it reflects those phenomena characteristic of altered states of consciousness. Johnson (1979) found that self-hypnosis and heterohypnosis were comparable in that each facilitated access to the unconscious. Fromm et al. (1981) demonstrated that self-hypnosis is an altered state of consciousness, characterized by absorption as well as by the fading of the general reality orientation. Tart includes self-hypnosis as an altered state of consciousness or dasc (discrete altered state of consciousness) (1969, 1975). The consensus appears to support the theory that self-hypnosis is an altered state.

WHAT ARE THE CHARACTERISTICS
OF SELF-HYPNOSIS?

Those characteristics that are state specific to self-hypnosis are attention and ego receptivity. Attention is expansive and free-floating; ego receptivity to stimuli coming from within the unconscious comprises a second discriminator (Fromm, 1977; Rappaport, 1967). Johnson and Weight (1976) found that self-hypnosis generated more vivid and frequent experiences of time distortion, disorientation, active direction, and trance variability than heterohypnosis.

Imagery is richer in self-hypnosis than in heterohypnosis. The subject experiences the vivid imagery and the uniqueness of directing and experiencing simultaneously (Fromm et al., 1981; Singer & Pope, 1981; Hilgard, 1970, 1979). According to Fromm and Kahn (1990d), self-hypnotic imagery is a multidimensional pheonomenon and must be investigated as such. They found both reality-oriented imagery and primary process imagery.

Since these measures were carried out with essentially normal subjects, there is at this time no way of knowing how patients seeking hypnotherapy may look on this dimension. Do patients have more primary process imagery? Is there less intertwining of these two types of imagery? Is there a dissociation between the two? There is much to be studied with the patient population. Another question arises about attention. In self-hypnosis, is it possible for the patient to focus his or her attention more narrowly but more deeply, rather than to expand it as an ego-active coping mechanism? Clinicians have been aware that patients vary greatly with respect to attention: some have a too diffuse attention span and require a more narrow focus; others have a narrow focus and require an expansion. Viewing attention as a continuum as described by Fromm et al. (1981) would suggest that self-hypnosis can be used to both expand attention as well as to focus it. Whereas in self-hypnosis it may be more difficult to focus than in heterohypnosis, it would still be possible. In the clinical situation patients are able to focus their attention in an effortless way after adaptation to self-hypnosis.

Time Perception

Much more research is necessary to compare the perception of time in heterohypnosis and self-hypnosis. Johnson found that deeply hypnotized self-hypnotic subjects experienced more time distortion than those in heterohypnosis (Johnson, 1979).

The subject in self-hypnosis experiences time in a distorted way (Fromm et al., 1981; Kroger, 1977; Crasilneck & Hall, 1985; Erickson & Cooper, 1959). With a reduction in self-monitoring and a division of executive functioning, the subject has greater difficulty monitoring the passage of time (Schwartz, 1978). Initially, this experience may be disorienting. We know in the clinical situation that time distortions are frequent in the hypnotherapy hour (Brown & Fromm, 1986) and in self-hypnosis practice. In my own teaching, I have found even in workshop experiences that the perception of time is altered. In dissociative disorders of various types, time distortion in the form of flashbacks, confusion of the past with the present, and an inability to project into the future are important frequent experiences. Yet little has been reported about ways to alter these distortions of experienced time. Most reports in this area have been by Milton Erickson (1980b, pp. 192–195). Studies of interaction of time distortion and self-hypnosis in the clinical situation are necessary as of now, since so little formal evidence is available.

The patient may learn to desensitize him- or herself in self-hypnosis and to become more comfortable in the altered state, freeing him- or herself to explore his or her own experience. Gradually increasing time spent in self-hypnosis can be helpful. Fromm et al. (1981) found that subjects did adapt to the self-hypnotic state. With practice, they could enter self-hypnosis more easily and more quickly.

The research evidence to date clearly supports the notion that self-hypnosis has state-specific characteristics. Heightened ego receptivity and expanded attention are state-specific for self-hypnosis. Additionally, experiences of time distortion, disorientation, active self-direction, and trance variability are heightened during self-hypnosis. These experiences can maximize hypnotherapy if the patient can adapt to the experience.

Are Self-Hypnosis and Relaxation the Same?

The training of relaxation and hypnotic induction procedures of both self-hypnosis and heterohypnosis share similarities. Benson, Arns, and Hoffman (1981) compared these three conditions. They found that neutral hypnosis (the state initiated by a traditional induction before the time of suggestion) and the relaxation response are associated with a similar physiological state characterized by changes in autonomic functioning: decreased heart rate, respiratory rate, and blood pressure. These researchers hypothesized that before experiencing hypnotic phenomena, an individual first experiences the relaxation response. After the physiological changes of the relaxation response occur, the individual may proceed to experience other, more exclusively hypnotic phenomena such as perceptual distortions, age regression, post-hypnotic suggestions, and amnesia (p. 267).

I believe that the purpose of suggesting relaxation would in part define the subject's experience: relaxation only or hypnosis. That is to say, if suggestions are given to use relaxation imagery or to focus on specific goals such as relaxation, then the subject would most likely experience relaxation. On the other hand, if suggestions are given to experience cognitive distortion of some type, then the subject goes beyond the relaxation response to experience hypnotic phenomena. The relaxation response becomes a pathway to hypnosis if suggestions are given to use imagery or to focus on specific goals beyond relaxation.

The hypnotic response also depends on the way that the therapist interacts with the patient. If instructions are given for relaxation and no other suggestions are given, the patient and the therapist may be unaware of hypnotic responses. Such responses would not be utilized. The seasoned hypnotherapist who teaches the patient relaxation may go beyond relaxation training and make use of hypnotic suggestion to enhance the effects of relaxation. Clearly the interaction between therapist and patient provides a powerful effect on the patient's response. More research is needed in this area. Viewed in this light, it appears that although relaxation and hypnotic induction may share common characteristics, the two are not identical.

According to Orne and McConkey (1981), the clinical use of heterohypnosis generally sets the protocol for the use of self-hypnosis by patients as a way of refreshing or reinforcing the suggestions given to them by the clinician (Gardner, 1981; Sacerdote, 1981).

Personality Characteristics

The question of which personality characteristics are associated with self-hypnosis is an intriguing one, but one that is not easily answered. Since research regarding self-hypnosis is still in its infancy, relatively little data are available. Fromm's research is looking into interactions among personality variables, structure variables, and content variables of deeply involved self-hypnotic subjects. The self-hypnosis sample scored substantially lower than medical patients on the following MMPI scales: Hypochondriasis, Psychopathic Deviate, Psychesthenia, and Social Isolation, suggesting that the subjects were less likely to be in conflict with their environment, more emotionally stable, and reported fewer unusual thoughts and experiences than the comparison group. Whereas this finding may be characteristic of normal, highly hypnotic susceptible subjects, these findings cannot be generalized to the patient population.

Meaningful but tentative relationships appeared between self-hypnosis and spontaneity, feeling reactivity, understanding, and sentience. Self-hypnosis does not appear to be an unitary phenomenon but varies to some extent according to personal style. Personality factors interact with structure (trance) and imagery content. No clinical studies of self-hypnosis have as yet focused on this complicated interaction. Tellegan and Atkinson (1974) have argued for the need to consider interacting variables on resulting hypnotic responsiveness. Kumar and Pekala (1987), for example, found interactions between trait and state situational variables in hypnotic response. In addition, phenomenological differences appeared augmented during hypnosis, presumably by state and induction interactions, situational cues, and the contextual environment.

There are no systematic data clarifying the frequency with which self-hypnosis is used clinically and the benefits derived from it. Also, few attempts have been made to assess the kinds of changes effected by an individual's regular use of self-hypnosis (Orne & McConkey, 1981).

In my view, clinical self-hypnosis presents yet another level of interaction that contributes to the quite complicated equation, and that level of interaction derives from the therapist–patient relationship. The therapist as teacher, guide, and monitor contributes to the overall outcome.

The variety of methods now available for the study of self-hypnosis permits exploration of executive and monitoring functions in hypnosis as well as examination of dissociated experience. New paradigms are needed to study the complex multidimensional aspects of self-hypnosis.

IMAGERY

Imagery,[2] a phenomenon that occurs in our everyday waking consciousness, is affected by self-hypnosis. Singer and Pope (1981) describe the similarity of skills needed to experience daydreams and to experience hypnosis. These skills are internal absorption in imagery and adaptation to imagery. In self-hypnosis, imagery does not occur in sequential processes. Rather, the imagery in self-hypnosis is similar to fantasy, hypnosis, and night dreaming.

According to Lusebrink (1986–1987), images as mental phenomena have differential patterns of their psychophysiological components. He believes that imagery can involve several levels of information processing; depending on the meaning of the image, it is associated with a different pattern of activity in different areas of the brain and body.

Shor and Easton (1973) reported initial comparisons of imagery between self- and heterohypnosis. However, the Chicago group have shown quite clearly that self-hypnosis generates enhanced imagery (Fromm et al., 1981). Coe, St. John, and Burger (1980), on the other hand, found that heterohypnosis enhances imagery.

According to Fromm and Kahn (1990d), self-hypnotic imagery is multidimensional. It consists of both reality-oriented fantasy and primary process fantasy (Fromm & Kahn, 1990d). Since their data are based on normal subjects, we have no way of knowing how patients seeking hypnotherapy would experience such fantasy. Do they expe-

---

[2]The term imagery encompasses more than visual images. It embraces all sensory experience, that is, visual, auditory, kinesthetic, olfactory, size, and weight experiences.

rience more primary process fantasy? Do they experience less fantasy in general? We need more studies of patient populations.

The question of personality characteristics that are associated with self-hypnosis is an intriguing one, but one that is not easily answered. Since research regarding self-hypnosis is still in its infancy, relatively little data are available. The emerging data are exciting and point to the need for more experiential studies taking into consideration interaction between variables. A first interactional study by Fromm and Kahn (1990d) found that both reality and fantasy images were obtained by subjects. Clinically, there is a need to obtain primary process material but also a need to integrate it with secondary process thought. Clinical self-hypnosis requires flexibility between primary process and ego activity to lead from insight to change.

SELF-INDUCTION OF INEXPERIENCED SUBJECTS

One question regarding self-hypnosis is that of learning self-hypnosis: Does the subject have to experience a heterohypnotic induction first? Ruch (1972, 1975) found that self-hypnosis seemed to be related to heterohypnosis. He developed qualitative measures of self-hypnosis and used them with 88 undergraduates to investigate how effective self-hypnosis is both without initial training and following heterohypnosis. The subjects first received group adaptations of the Harvard Group Hypnotic Susceptibility Scale, Form A and the Stanford Hypnotic Susceptibility Scale, Form C. The conventional group received the usual standardized inductions. The first-person group received rephrased inductions, and the self-instructed group supplied their own inductions. All subjects then received a self-instructed Form C and a conventional Form A. The results showed that self-instructed scales yielded satisfactory measurements, both objective and subjective. Untrained subjects in self-hypnosis were as effective as subjects who were given heterohypnosis instructions. Untrained self-hypnosis was as effective as heterohypnosis. Conventional heterohypnosis inhibited later self-hypnosis, but first-person inductions did not. This latter finding seemed related to order and contextual effects (Johnson, 1979) in the induction of hypnosis. In the clinical situation, I have found the majority of patients I have seen need some prior heterohypnotic training. Nonetheless, over the years, I have seen some patients who already knew how to enter self-hypnosis due to other experiences. These individuals need to be accommodated.

SURVEY

Changing perspective now to the hypnotherapist, an important part of the equation, in a survey of clinicians using self-hypnosis with patients and with themselves, Sanders (1987) found that self-hypnosis is taught to patients in a selective manner and that some patients are excluded from such training. In addition, the survey suggested that hypnotherapists tend to use a variety of techniques, but how they label them, explain them, teach them to others, and use them for themselves are somehow all different and appear to be related to a variety of interactions including disciplinary training, goals, personality styles, types of theories of hypnosis and training adhered to, as well as their orientation to psychotherapy in general.

Ninety-two percent of the 233 respondents endorsed the personal use of self-hypnosis in their own lives. This high percentage may reflect either a bias in the respondents sampled or the fact that the hypnotherapist who uses self-hypnosis with patients may be an individual who is comfortable and successful with self-hypnosis experience. This is an empirical question that can be answered in the laboratory.

The respondents tended to endorse the following psychotherapy orientations: behavioral, 28.6%; eclectic, 34.8%; analytic, 22.9%; physiological, 7.02%; and naturalistic, 6.6%. The teaching of self-hypnosis appears to proceed across all orientations.

Therapists were asked to rate their perception of the role of the hypnotherapist vis-à-vis the patient, based on ratings from 1 (strongly disagree) to 6 (strongly agree). The mean ratings are seen as trends rather than as absolute differences between respondents.

Role perception	Mean rating
Teacher	5.1
Prescriber	3.8
Guide	3.5
Healer	3.1

Most respondents viewed themselves as teachers, reflecting the attitude that self-hypnosis is a skill that can be taught by the therapist. The role of the teacher is both active and permissive. The patient, too, is viewed as an active partner, the student. Fewer therapists viewed themselves as prescribers. This trend may reflect a more directive and authoritarian approach in which the patient is viewed as being more passive. The psychotherapists who viewed themselves as guides suggest a permissive and nondirective function in which the patient is viewed as more active, being the fulcrum of change and holding the key to the solving of his or her own problem.

Some psychotherapists saw themselves as healers. Healing is a term used to describe medical practices in helping clients to master their problems, thereby restoring the mental health of the client. The term healer was not intended to denote psychic healing but rather to ascribe the activity of the therapist as active vis-à-vis the patient, restoring the health of the client. The role of the therapist is active and directive.

As with other hypnotic research, the influence of demand characteristics biases observations in such a way as to emphasize those phenomena unique to self-hypnosis. Aspects of the experimental situation, expectations, hypotheses, and anticipations all affect the outcome of the research. This influence must be taken seriously (Johnson, 1981).

In order for self-hypnosis to occur, it is necessary to consider the division of cognitive functions into a directing and an experiencing mode, the paradox of self-hypnosis. The notion of nonconscious involvement or dissociation as an explanatory process underlying the self-hypnotic process is an appealing one. Lynn, Nash, Rhue, Frauman, and Stanley (1983) have observed nonvolitional behavior in heterohypnosis. This construct may be studied in one of the formats described earlier. In the not-too-distant future, it may be assessed in part by a paper-and-pencil measure of dissociation. Both Bernstein and Putnam (1986) with the Dissociative Experiences Scale (DES) and Sanders (1986) with the Perceptual Alteration Scale (PAS) (see Appendix A) have developed scales to measure the construct of dissociation as one measure in a convergent series of measures. Other studies of cognition demonstrate that hypnosis and self-hypnosis are affected by cognitive processes. These need to be clarified (Crawford, 1981, 1982; Diamond, 1983).

SELF-HYPNOSIS AND CREATIVITY

The hypothesized link between self-hypnosis and creativity is of ever-increasing interest. Creativity has been defined in a variety of ways. I prefer Carl Rogers's definition of creativity: "The mainspring of creativity appears to be man's tendency to actualize himself, to become his potentialities, whether it be to solve problems in life, in therapy, or to produce symbolic works of art" (Rogers, 1959, p. 153). In this view, everyone has creative potential that can be elicited under the proper conditions (Sanders, 1976).

Most ego psychologists refer to regression in the service of the ego when discussing creativity (Eisen & Fromm, 1983; Fromm, 1977). Ken Bowers found in a preliminary study of creativity that hypnotic susceptibility interacts with role-playing instructions to generate more regressive modes of thinking (K. Bowers, 1968). Bowers went on to report (K. Bowers, 1971) that creative persons perceive the world somewhat differently than others. He studied the anecdotal, clinical, and experimental literature on hypnotism, dreams, and drugs as they related to the creative person, products, and process. He believes that the natural development of conscious awareness will enhance an individual's creative potential.

Gur and Reyher (1976) found, in a study of 36 male highly susceptible subjects divided into hypnosis, simulation, and waking groups, that the hypnotic group scored higher than all controls on overall creativity and on global creativity but not on verbal creativity. The results seem to support the application of the ego-analytic concept of adaptive regression to both hypnosis and creativity. In addition, this study supports the association between hypnosis and the activation of the nonverbal cerebral hemisphere.

Pat Bowers (1979) studied the experience of storytelling and writing under hypnosis with students and writers. The relationship between individual differences in styles of creativity and hypnotizability was explored. The review of the students suggests that allowing the structure of a problem to affect associational processes without the interference of volitional selection strategies contributes to the discovery of creative solutions. Given this finding, self-hypnosis apparently would provide an excellent medium to generate creativity. Of course, replication studies are necessary before generalizations can be made to other populations.

In the Soviet Union, Raikov (1977) found that subjects using an imagined identification with a famous person led to new or hidden potentialities in the subject that may have been unknown to him or her. Raikov concludes tentatively that the hypnotic state brings about a functional alteration of nervous system activity that is accompanied by a reprogramming of control and analytic systems that adapt and treat information of a hypnotic nature. This is one view.

Sanders (1976) found that creativity scores increased, both on a standardized test of creativity and on solutions to life problems, when subjects practiced group hypnosis and self-hypnosis. The evidence suggests that hypnosis and self-hypnosis may enhance creativity, but much more validation is needed. One problem in this study is the confounding of hypnosis and self-hypnosis.

The role of self-hypnosis in facilitating creativity is based more on inference from studies of heterohypnosis and creativity. It is a heuristic hypothesis.

TAPES AND SCRIPTS

There is much controversy in the literature regarding the effectiveness of tapes and scripts in treatment. The use of tapes is sometimes related to self-hypnosis, at other times to hypnosis, and still at other times to a teaching situation. In addition, the literature revolves around poorly controlled clinical studies reflecting a diversity of problems, subjects, and techniques. At the present state of knowledge, it is not known how tapes or scripts affect the person or why. They may appear to work because of repetition, time, and attention or a placebo effect. For some people, they provide a structure to follow. Clearly they do not work for everyone.

I do not believe that a tape leads to a self-hypnotic experience. For some persons, it may trigger an archetypal self-hypnotic state. For others, it is simply a cognitive exercise. However, cognitive exercises may be quite effective. Thus, with caution, some individuals may find that a tape reinforces the learning obtained in the heterohypnotic session.

Lieberman, Fishers, Thomas, and King (1968) used tape-recorded suggestions as an aid to probationary students. Thirty-five pairs of probationary students matched for curriculum, predicted grades, sex, marital status, and age were randomly assigned to control and experimental conditions. The experimental group reported four daily 10-minute sessions for 3 weeks. Three different tapes were used, one each week. Final grades showed no differences, but more experimental subjects were removed from probation at the end of the quarter. Susceptibility made no difference. They conclude that the use of taped suggestions is an inexpensive and effective way of helping students.

Paul and Trimble (1970) evaluated recorded versus live relaxation training and hypnotic suggestion tapes for comparative effectiveness for reducing physiological arousal and inhibiting stress response. Relaxation training and hypnotically suggested relaxation by means of prerecorded tapes were evaluated against the same procedures conducted in the usual live manner regarding effectiveness for reducing tension. Results indicated that recorded relaxation was significantly inferior to live induction on all counts except self-report. The difference was attributed to the loss of response-contingent progression that was not possible from a prerecorded tape.

J.M. Kaye (1987) used tapes along with hypnosis in the treatment of cancer patients. Symptoms included nausea, anxiety, depression, anorexia, and pain. Hypnotherapy included induction, relaxation, visualization, and suggestion. The authors concluded in the study of 12 patients that brief hypnotherapy can be helpful with terminally ill patients.

Summers (1982) used tapes with adolescents with emotional and behavioral problems. The groups met weekly for 1 hour of training. Two practice sessions of 15 minutes were used for tapes. Group members were trained in muscle relaxation, self-awareness, and ego building. The adolescents displayed a readiness to learn. The author concluded that adolescents have the ability to learn and to use self-hypnosis to improve their self-concept.

Walker, Collins, and Krass (1982) developed four hypnosis scripts to evaluate the effectiveness of imaginative rehearsal, direct suggestion, and aversive suggestion. Nonchallenge modification of the eye fixation technique served as the induction. The scripts cover new habits related to food, exercise, increased inner control and self-esteem, coping with tension, and compulsions related to eating.

Hammond (1987) studied the hypothesis that depth of hypnosis and subjective quality of tape-assisted self-hypnotic experience would be greater when fractionalization was used in contrast to another deepening technique. The results showed no differences between conditions. In the clinical situation, for selected patients, a tape may provide a reassuring experience for a frightened patient during home practice of self-hypnosis. However, a tape is not a substitute for *in vivo* therapy. Rather, a tape may be introduced to the patient as a reinforcement to be used sparingly. It may function in part as a transitional phenomenon in providing a safe inner space (Winnicott, 1953).

The results are not clear-cut as to just how efficient tapes and scripts are. Their operation is frequently confounded by the use of a variety of other techniques and procedures. A cautious use of tapes and scripts may be helpful, but there is no evidence that these techniques are effective on their own, separate from the methods of hypnotherapy and psychotherapy.

WHERE ARE WE?

The future of self-hypnosis is very promising. However, many questions remain to be answered, many differentiations to be made, and a need exists for more clarity in describing the way that self-hypnosis is taught within the therapist–patient interaction as well as how it interacts with other aspects of the treatment situation. The investigation of self-hypnosis offers a wealth of possibilities. We are on the horizon of very challenging questions and experiences. It is time to look carefully at the use of clinical self-hypnosis with patients. One question regards the manner in which patients attribute meaning to words and images. Let us consider what processes are involved. Obviously, several interacting processes are important. As we have seen, self-hypnosis is an altered state of consciousness; that involves changes in cognition. For example, the cognitive distortions described by eating-disordered patients can be corrected during the practice of self-hypnosis (Gross, 1983a, 1983b).

In addition, further studies teasing out personality correlates of self-hypnotic susceptibility are needed, similar to the one carried out by Kihlstrom on heterohypnotic subjects (Kihlstrom, 1980), as well as studies that clarify how self-hypnosis can mediate or effect changes in affect. For example, Brown described how he used self-hypnosis with a borderline patient to teach recognition and control over strong affects (Brown, 1985). Gruber (1983) presented several hypnotherapeutic techniques for use with patients who demonstrated affective instability. Similar descriptions of self-hypnotic techniques geared to stabilize affect should be forthcoming.

Self-hypnotic research should also look at those factors that predispose a person to enter self-hypnosis, for example, fantasy proneness (see Lynn & Rhue, 1985), as well as at the interaction of goal-directed fantasy with self-hypnosis (Lynn et al., 1987).

Furthermore, studies need to go beyond experiential and behavioral comparisons (Johnson and Weight, 1976) to include comparisons at a physiological level. They should explore the physiological concomitants of self-hypnosis, as did the heterohypnotic study by Tebecis and Provins, (1976) and the investigation of brain functioning utilizing the EEG by Tebecis, Provins, Farnbach, and Petony (1975). More formal evaluation needs to be done of self-hypnosis as a self-protective mechanism in the face of trauma (Stutman & Bliss, 1985), as well as an alterater of physiological processes. Rossi, for example, hypothesized that self-hypnosis could be maximized by tapping into the individual's ultradian cycles (Rossi, personal communication, March 1990). This warrants further study. In addition, research on the brain and hemispheric preferences may be a fruitful source of study.

Studies of defense mechanisms, particularly of dissociation and how dissociation may be used as a defense against coercion, should also be conducted. Dissociation appears to be an effective defense when the external environment is threatening (Spiegel, 1986a; Ludwig, 1983; Stutman & Bliss, 1985). In addition, Balsam, Depster, and Brooks

(1984) and Frankenthal (1969) consider autohypnosis as an effective defense against coercive persuasion.

Borrowing from Banyai and Hilgard (1976) it would be of interest to observe active alert self-hypnosis.

From this bird's-eye view of the work that needs to be done to clarify, to understand, and to use clinical self-hypnosis meaningfully, we will now look at applications of clinical self-hypnosis.

PART III

Diagnosis, Intake, and Applications

CHAPTER 6

Evaluation

For there is nothing either good or bad but thinking
makes it so.
                                   —Shakespeare, *Hamlet* (II,ii)

Evaluation of the patient is crucial to optimize the use of hypnotherapy and self-hypnosis as part of that hypnotherapy. As with any therapeutic plan, good intake procedures will streamline the therapy prescribed, including hypnotherapy. Although there are many ways to evaluate the patient, given the wide diversity practiced by clinicians using self-hypnosis, there is no one preferred method. This chapter describes a sampling of relevant intake procedures to clarify the patient's history, description of the problem, and expectations for treatment.[1] Positive outcome of treatment requires a therapeutic plan that taps the inner potentials of the patient to transform, master, and overcome the problem. Generally, the evaluation consists of a clinical interview, possible diagnostic questionnaires, and a hypnotic screening to assess these potentials. Whereas heterohypnotic susceptibility does not guarantee self-hypnotic susceptibility, relevant research has demonstrated that high susceptibles appear responsive to self-hypnosis (Fromm et al., 1981). In the consulting room, highly motivated patients, even though they may not be high susceptibles, can also use self-hypnosis. The focus on the bridge between heterohypnosis and self-hypnosis is particularly important during the evaluation and first hypnotic induction.

---

[1]I believe in a thorough evaluation.

I first describe eight specific areas of inquiry that can be satisfied via careful questioning and interviewing. According to Fromm, the personality is revealed by the manner in which the patient organizes and orders his or her world, life, and being (Fromm et al., 1981). The evaluator simply needs to listen, observe, and differentiate his or her perceptions of the patient. Second, I present some specific questions that can generate relevant information about the patient's ability to self-reflect.

1. *Clinical history.* The clinical history focuses on obtaining a verbal description of the problem, when it first occurred, and how frequently the problem recurs, for example, whether it is acute or chronic. An acute problem is defined as existing for less than a year. The problem is chronic if it is manifested for longer than a year. In addition, it is important to determine what other types of emotional, behavioral, or physical problems exist. The clinical history reveals a baseline to which the patient can be compared when treatment is terminated. In addition, the clinical history discloses important behavioral and motivational characteristics. It helps the therapist to decide on strategies, approaches, and techniques. Response to self-hypnosis is to a variable extent a very personal experience in the arousal of meaningful associations, memories, problems, and fantasies (Fromm et al., 1981). The clinical history reveals the manner in which the patient organizes and orders his or her world.

2. *Physical health.* Has the patient had a physical examination during the past year or two? This information is particularly relevant when the patient has a psychophysiological problem or eating disorder. If the patient has not been examined, I require the patient to have a physical exam administered by his or her physician.

3. *Exploration of the patient's diet.* Is the patient eating in a balanced manner, or does the patient eat irregularly? A diet history in the form of a food diary is useful in evaluating depression, eating disorder, and/or self-care skills. Improper diet contributes to the patient's sense of disease.

4. *Exploration of social history.* What is the nature of the patient's interpersonal relationships? Does the patient relate well to people, including the therapist? Does the patient feel intimidated by others? Does the patient have a history of good friendships? Knowing the patient's responses to others is helpful in predicting the nature of the therapist–patient interaction or transference.

5. *Activity history.* Does the patient exercise? What leisure activities does the patient have? Do leisure activities and work activities

balance out? Is the patient inactive and without avenues of tension release or sublimation? Activities can bind tension and alleviate reactions to stress. They may also contribute to the overall stress. A verbal description of activities is quite revealing.

6. *Educational history.* How much schooling has the patient completed? At what level does he communicate? Matching the patient's level of communication enhances the doctor–patient relationship. The observer should note the manner in which the patient communicates. Does the patient rely on words or body language. Both verbal (speech, tone of voice, flow) as well as nonverbal (posture, facial expressions, eye movements, motor activity, and mannerisms) are of equal importance. Do the client's verbal and nonverbal behaviors match, or do they contradict each other? Finally, the client's philosophy of life and characteristic attitudes are important. Is the client literal or metaphoric? Concrete or abstract? Action-oriented or thought-oriented? The patient's communication style helps individualize the manner in which self-hypnosis is taught by tapping into the patient's motivation and curiosity. The evaluator needs to listen, observe, and differentiate these characteristics.

7. *Intelligence.* Assessment of intellectual functions is important. Verbal style, vocabulary, education, and occupation all reflect intellectual achievement. Underachievement and overachievement can be noted. Attention span and ability to concentrate are helpful indicators of hypnotic responsiveness. Limited attention span and frequent shifts in concentration highlight the need to use short inductions and fractionation techniques that may be lengthened over time. In the absence of formal intellectual testing, asking the patient to describe his or her education and performance over time can be revealing.

8. *Thought content.* In addition, recognition of the spontaneous stream of consciousness reflects both quality and spontaneity of thought, blocking of thought, and/or flight of ideas. Rambling, unfocused associations require a narrowing of attention. Fromm et al. (1981) define personality as the tendency of an individual to order experience in characteristic ways across situations. They found that the self-hypnosis sample tended to be spontaneous and to show feeling reactivity, understanding, and sentience. Although more research is needed, this study suggests that self-hypnosis is a multidimensional phenomenon that varies to some extent according to personal style. Through basic behavioral observations the evaluator can check for presence or absence of these characteristics.

Specific questions can generate specific information about the patient. These questions can be asked directly, or the information can be gleaned from a more descriptive, open-ended type of interview. I simply list some direct questions.

Is the patient psychologically minded? Can the patient describe him- or herself dynamically? Does the patient reflect on his or her contribution to the problem, or does he or she blame others? Is the patient capable of tolerating insight? How does the patient make decisions and choices? Is his or her judgment good or weak? Reviewing the patient's important choices over time is helpful. Answers to these queries help to determine the manner that hypnosis is taught and the type of suggestions that will be most useful. For example, if a patient is psychologically minded and able to recognize dynamics and reflect, then he or she is a good candidate for hypnoanalysis.

MYTHS AND MISCONCEPTIONS OF HYPNOSIS

This section presents a discussion of expectations possibly held by the patient about the nature of hypnosis in general. To prepare the patient to learn hypnosis and self-hypnosis, the patient's expectations need to be discussed and clarified.

Patients may be reluctant to enter hypnosis for a variety of reasons, generally related to something that they have heard about from someone else, something they may have read about in a novel or spy story, or something they may have seen on the stage or television. Some patients may even have experienced a negative induction sometime in the past. The following is a list of the most common misconceptions.

1. *The patient fears that he or she will be out of control of self and that the therapist will be in control of him or her.* The popular myth exists that when an individual is hypnotized, he or she is unaware of what is going on and therefore not in control of his or her own thoughts, feelings, and emotions. The patient needs to understand that in hypnosis, he or she remains in control although the perceptions, affects, and behaviors may seem different. In effect, the patient is able to assume even more control.

2. *The patient may believe that only very stupid and very gullible people can be hypnotized.* Entering a hypnotic state and maintaining it require concentration and vigilance. Intelligent and imaginative people are able to maintain these behaviors more easily.

3. *The patient may believe that only dependent people can be hypnotized.* Hypnosis may be used in such a way as to foster independence of thought and action. Because of the versatility of hypnosis,

dependency can be minimized, particularly when the patient is taught self-hypnosis.

4. *The patient may be afraid that he or she will say something that he or she had not meant to say.* Even in hypnosis, the person has a choice about what is said or done. The patient has veto power over any suggestion and can choose whether or not to respond, to speak, or to remain silent.

5. *The patient may be afraid that he or she will remain "stuck" in hypnosis.* Because hypnosis is such a pleasant state and the patient is so comfortable, he or she may not wish to terminate hypnosis. Nonetheless, while in hypnosis, through discussion about the need to come out now, the patient can terminate the hypnotic state easily and naturally, just as easily and naturally as when awaking from sleep or reverie.

6. *The patient may be afraid that he or she will do something that he or she might otherwise not do.* In hypnosis, the patient still holds the same ethical code as ever and will not engage in behavior that runs counter to his or her ethical code. In addition, the therapist will not ask the patient to do anything that is unrelated to his or her goals.

7. *The patient may be fearful of not remembering what happened in hypnosis.* Most people remember everything that happens in hypnosis. Those people who typically do not remember are those who generally have difficulty remembering even in their usual state. We can tape record the session so as to have an ongoing account of what happened so that we can compare experiences.

The purpose of reviewing the myths and misconceptions held by the patient is to establish the patient's need to be in control and to educate the patient about hypnosis. Defusing misconceptions can make the difference between successful hypnosis and resistant hypnosis.

The hypnotherapist, by sharpening his or her own keen sense of observation, can tease out of the patient's responses his or her characteristic use of sensory impressions. The patient's verbal language and body language contain the description of his or her sensory preferences (Bandler & Grinder, 1975).

The patient's ability to use sensory impressions appropriately is especially important when considering hypnotherapy. Is the patient visually oriented? Is the patient more auditory in orientation? Is he or she more kinesthetic? Does the patient make appropriate use of sensory input? Is the patient presenting self-stimulating behaviors such as visual images, illusions, or hallucinations? Sensory–motor functioning is an important indicator of hypnotic potential. Although this focus may not apply to all patients, for some patients it is useful.

The therapist needs to determine what motivates the patient—what rewards are meaningful to the patient and what absence of rewards might be meaningful. Rewards are important in any learning situation, for they increase the likelihood of occurrence of newly learned behaviors. Absence of reward decreases the occurrence of behaviors. In addition, rewards are vital to the maintenance of self-esteem. The patient may be asked, for example, to compose a list of possible rewards that can then be used to reinforce progress when appropriate.

NEGOTIATION OF GOALS

The patient comes to see the therapist ostensibly for a purpose. According to Orne and McConkey (1981), the outcome of hypnotherapy needs to be measured in relation to reaching some criterion or expected goal(s). Therefore, the patient and therapist must come to some common agreement about goals that can be realistically met.

Thus, the patient may want to lose weight, stop smoking, become less anxious, or relieve a disturbing symptom. However, he or she may be realistic or unrealistic in his or her expectations about how this change can be accomplished. The patient may want to stop smoking, for example, automatically, with no knowledge or conscious participation in the act. The patient is unaware of the fact that he or she is already functioning automatically as he or she chain smokes one cigarette after another and is unaware of exactly how many cigarettes were smoked. The initial goals may be to teach the patient to monitor him- or herself so as to make change more meaningful and lasting. The self-monitoring can be achieved by a smoking diary. Graded goals permit ongoing evaluation of the patient's progress in hypnotherapy.

Another patient may want to lose 50 pounds at once, an impossibility. This patient needs to learn to recognize small steps and small successes. Following a weight control plan can be measured day by day, rather than in terms of pounds, and by reviewing healthy eating habits and problems that appear. There are multitudinous possible goals that need to be identified, depending on the patient and the problems that the patient brings.

Presenting hypnosis and self-hypnosis to the patient as a way to learn to be more in control of the body is one useful rationale, among others, and one that reinforces the notion of experience and improvement. The 3,000 years of medical history also graphically portray the importance of experience and gradual improvement toward a goal. Goals may be multiply layered, starting with small steps and gradually becoming more complex. The important point is that the patient experiences mastery/success within the session. There are manifold possibilities.

HYPNOTIC INDUCTION

The first induction in the office is viewed as a learning experience for both the therapist and the patient.[2] It is a learning experience for the therapist because he or she has the opportunity to observe and learn about the patient via the patient's approach to the induction. It is a learning experience for the patient because it represents a new experience complete with fears generated by past exposures to the new and novel. Although many hypnotic inductions exist and may be used, space does not permit the listing of all of these. Therefore, I list a few very common, traditional inductions (Sanders, 1987). These inductions may be used individually or in combination for deepening, or used along with other inductions: relaxation, deep breathing, Spiegel eye roll, imagery, naturalistic, and arm levitation. The basic goal in administering a hypnotic induction is to provide the opportunity for the patient to alter his or her consciousness, cognitively, affectively, and behaviorally. To achieve this goal, the therapist needs to be precise in providing instructions and suggestions. Precision is generated by using those words and images that match the experience of the patient.

Methodology

A variety of induction styles exist. There is no one best methodology. The important guideline is that the therapist and patient be comfortable with the procedure. The following procedure is one I follow, flexibly.

The therapist follows the rule of parsimony: keep the induction simple. I realize that there are exceptions to this rule, but I have found, generally, that the simple induction is the most direct. In those exceptional situations where the patient is nonresponsive, knowledge of and skill in the application of indirect techniques are essential. However, in the majority of patients that I have worked with in my office, the

---

[2]I believe in starting with a successful heterohypnotic induction since most patients learn self-hypnosis as a posthypnotic suggestion once they have entered heterohypnosis. At the same time, I realize that some individuals do not need a formal induction. The experienced hypnotherapist who conducts a thorough evaluation will recognize these individuals.

direct induction takes less time and has been quite efficient in working with pain patients. There is no clear-cut evidence that direct or indirect techniques are better (Lyn, Neufeld, & Matyi, 1987; Woolson, 1986). More important is the need to individualize, to use what works with a given patient. When appropriate, indirect inductions can be used. They can be combined. It is a matter of selecting techniques that match the patient's natural style.

The therapist, like Aesculapius, needs to develop and maintain rapport with the patient. To meet this goal, the therapist needs to be sensitive to the responses of the patient and, when in doubt, to request feedback from him or her. In recognizing the needs of the patient, whose eyes are most probably closed, the therapist needs to provide accurate information to him or her and present accurate feedback about what is happening. In a real sense, the therapist and patient are engaging in dialogue.

The therapist provides suggestions during the induction, such as asking the patient to take a deep breath. The behavioral response of the patient is important. If the patient in fact takes a deep breath, then the therapist can reinforce the positive response to suggestion by providing positive feedback, as, for example, the famous Milton Erickson response "That's right." Positive feedback to the patient decreases anxiety and heightens rapport and motivation.

Sometimes the patient does not respond positively to the suggestion. Rather, the response may be contradictory or oppositional. For example, if the patient does not take a deep breath, it is best to accept this omission and instead make positive use of the patient's spontaneous response. The use of usch naturalistic techniques was described by Erickson and others (Erickson, 1958a; Barber, 1982a). Such naturalistic techniques, using the patient's spontaneous behavior as a suggestion, are critical in maintaining rapport and motivation. The therapist benefits the patient by the use of mirroring and following the spontaneous response of the patient.

It may be useful to embed suggestions within the descriptions and instructions of the induction. For example, "As you take a deep breath, you begin to relax and to feel more comfortable, just as comfortable as you would like." The embedding of suggestions within the induction frequently leads to a positive response.

During the induction, it may become necessary to contradict oneself. The patient is less critical with eyes closed and confronted with a new experience. Under these conditions, replete with primary process thought, logic does not apply. If the patient is not becoming lighter, for example, but describes feeling heavier, the therapist moves in the direction of validation because the subjective experience is most important.

The therapist includes as a revealing tool his or her own reactions. In watching his or her reactions, the therapist may feel a sense of synchrony with the moment or else feel a sense of disparity. The therapist's reactions at this critical time are important.

In addition, the therapist needs to be ready and willing to discuss with the patient any aspect of the induction. The discussion can be held both in and out of trance. Because the induction is a form of dialogue between two people, the therapist needs to provide feedback when appropriate, such as "that's right. Your arm is going down. You are taking a deep breath." Any response from the patient gives the therapist information and feedback. Even a nonresponse discloses a block in the communication. If the patient spontaneously terminates the induction, it is important to discuss the induction in an effort to determine what interfered with the process and to establish what else could be done.

The levels of experience that operate in an induction are intricate. Much like the onion, experience, too, has numerous overlapping layers that operate simultaneously in a complicated fashion. In fact, there are several levels of communication.

1. The conscious here and now is the first level of experience. The patient is aware of being in the office for a specific reason now. This awareness colors the patient's reactions in a cloak of feeling. The patient may be relieved to receive help. Or the patient may be resentful that he or she needs help. He or she may view him- or herself as a passive, helpless individual and, at the same time, may see him- or herself in a more ideal way. Simultaneous self-perceptions are the rule rather than the exception. These concurrent self-perceptions and feelings wage a civil war within the patient.

2. The conscious past is also carried in part into the present moment. The life difficulties from the past that have led to the patient's decision to seek treatment interact with the anxieties of the present. Feelings of being overwhelmed by a history of life's vicissitudes victimizing him or her merge with self-perceptions darkening the present moment. In addition to the historical review, it is also important to review any other induction experienced by the patient. A prior induction that has been successful can set the stage for success in this treatment. In a like manner, an unsuccessful induction experience can fix negative expectations to a self-fulfilling prophecy of failure.

3. The unconscious here and now is operative at the moment. Although nonverbal, the patient's reactions, movements, emotions, and gestures, even his or her words, may reflect the autonomy of the unconscious in the here and now. This aspect of experience affects the patient's response, even though he or she may not recognize or be aware of this connection. Consonance of conscious and unconscious experience predicts unity of motivation. Dissonance of conscious and unconscious experience reveals the conflict between the two. The patient who verbally describes his or her willingness to work fully and completely is nullified by the simultaneous postural backing away.

4. The conscious future expectations color the patient's response. For example, if the patient expects that being in hypnosis will be an indication of dependence on the therapist, then he or she is less likely to go into hypnosis. On the other hand, if he or she values mastery and expects that going into hypnosis will strengthen mastery, then he or she will be more likely to enter hypnosis. The expectations of what will happen in the future will bias the patient's response.

5. Unconscious future expectations based on fear, whether it be fear of loss, humiliation, shame, or embarrassment, will color the patient's response negatively. On the other hand, if he or she unconsciously expects that the hypnosis sessions will provide a useful buffer for anxiety, these positive expectations endow the present with positive motivation and facilitate hypnosis.

The practice of self-hypnosis can provide the patient with an opportunity to differentiate the different levels of experience and help him or her to move toward compromise and integration, that is, a meaningful unified experience.

Instructions for administering a hypnotic induction are provided here because many theorists, although not all, are in agreement that self-hypnosis in the clinical situation is best learned as a consequence of heterohypnotic induction with a trained professional. The induction that I use most frequently is one that combines relaxation, deep breathing, and imagery. In my practice, this type of induction works well in teaching the patient to enter hypnosis.

The following induction is but one version of a relaxation induction:

Just sit quietly and take long, slow, deep breaths. That's right. And again. Take another long, slow, deep breath, breathing in relaxation, breathing out tension. And again, breathing in relaxation, breathing out tension. Now, continuing to take long, slow, deep breaths, begin to let the tension go. Just relax the muscles of the toes. Good. Just relax at the muscles of your feet. Fine. Just relax the ankles and the calf. Just let those muscles become comfortable. Continuing to breathe deeply and slowly, relax the thighs. Just let those muscles relax. Now relax the hips and the abdomen. Just let those muscles become comfortable. Relax the back and the chest. Good. Now relax the fingers and the hands. Relax the arms and the upper arms. Relax the shoulders. Relax the neck. And even the muscles of the face. Good.

Now taking another long, slow, deep breath, allow yourself to think of a place that you have been, a place where you have felt comfortable. Just nod your head if you are thinking of that place. Good. Now just allow yourself to be there, to see how it looks, how it sounds, how it feels, just as if you were there. Just experience it . . . Good.

Yes, you are in your comfortable place and you feel very, very comfortable.

And whenever you feel tense as you do now, it is perfectly all right for you to relax, just as relaxed as you are now. You can begin by taking long, slow, deep breaths, relaxing every muscle in your body, and going to your comfortable place. You will find that you can relax, on your own, more and more deeply, as you practice more. So that the exercise of relaxation becomes a daily part of your day. This practice will permit you to enter self-hypnosis easily when you want, where you want, and how you want.

Now, just count back from 5 to 1 and open your eyes to the here and now.

As you can see, this first induction paves the way for self-hypnosis practice. Expectations are focused on using self-hypnosis. The rationale given after the induction focuses on the task of learning self-hypnosis. By practicing the relaxation exercise, the patient will learn self-hypnosis. However, the patient is expected to practice four times a day, 7 days a week, so that when he or she returns for his or her appointment, he or she will be able to enter hypnosis more quickly and more easily.

The patient is asked to describe his or her experience, a debriefing task. In particular, he or she is asked to rate how vividly he or she imaged on a scale from 1 to 10, where 1 is not vivid and 10 is very vivid. Also, he or she is asked to rate what images were most helpful and what images were least helpful on a scale of 1 to 10. Description of imagery deepens the patient's involvement in the experience.

As we have seen in the long history of hypnosis, the therapist needs to have confidence in him- or herself and his or her strategy. This need is important even today. The reactions the therapist experiences during the session are important communications. Feelings of synchrony with the patient or feelings of disharmony may reflect the strength of the rapport. The therapist's gut reactions at this critical time are vital.

Strategies for Transformation

We have defined self-hypnosis as a self-induced state in which the patient gives him- or herself suggestions (in the form of words and images) to transform, for example, to change tension into relaxation, or to change from a negative habit to a more helpful habit. Because of the creative diversity of hypnotherapists, there are many possible strategies to foster transformation, but space only permits a few examples. I use positive suggestion, reduced self-monitoring, imagery, and effortlessness with my patients. Controlled research to document the clinical effectiveness of these strategies is beginning in the laboratory, but such group data do not always pinpoint or identify the highly motivated patient who might compensate. With a given patient who is motivated in the clinical situation, these techniques have been found useful; it is, however, important to keep in mind that many strategies exist, and new ones are being created in the cooperative endeavor of hypnotherapy. The following techniques are among those that have been reported in the literature.

1. The patient learns to saturate him- or herself with positive suggestions. A skew to the positive heightens self-esteem and hope. Positive words are words of power. They bring hope, increase motivation, and enable one to construct new possibilities.

2. In self-hypnosis, the patient can put the censor aside. Reducing his or her usual level of self-monitoring, the patient is able to try out new behaviors and new ways of experiencing. In self-hypnosis, too much criticism can inhibit exploration of the self-induced trance. However, in self-hypnosis, it is probably more difficult to achieve this reduction than in heterohypnosis (Fromm et al., 1981).

3. The patient can generate imagery that is relevant and helpful as well as imagery that may lead to feeling overwhelmed. The therapist assists the patient in selecting helpful images. In order to maximize success, the therapist may suggest or fine-tune those images that are most helpful by reinforcing them by way of posthypnotic suggestions. The images become attached to the meanings inherent in the posthypnotic suggestion. The patient is asked to experience the self-hypnosis at home.

The provision of feedback from the therapist, when appropriate, maintains the hypnotic trance. The feedback reassures the patient and validates his or her experience.

If the patient spontaneously terminates the induction, it is necessary to discuss what the patient has experienced in an effort to determine what interfered with the process and to establish what else can be done. The therapist must be ready to discuss with the patient any aspect of the induction. The discussion can be held both in and out of trance.

ASSOCIATING IMAGES WITH GOALS

The patient's spontaneous imagery may reflect possible goals, or the patient may self-suggest that his or her own unconscious is participating in reaching a specific goal through the effortless flow of unconscious ideation into conscious awareness. Possible goals might include:

- to release tension
- to gain insight
- to find a new solution
- to restructure an idea
- to heighten positive feelings
- to reduce negative feelings
- to enhance a sense of self-control
- to develop healthy habits
- to transform a sensation from unpleasant to pleasant
- to remove or reduce a symptom
- to substitute a less disabling symptom for a more disabling one

Of course this list is not exhaustive. The goals for any particular patient will be dependent on the nature of the patient's problem and the resources available.

Each of the goals listed above is illustrated with a description of spontaneous imagery, described by a patient who was asked to wonder what words, feelings, sensations, and images come to mind when focusing briefly on a specific goal. The responses are taken from a variety of patients, all very verbal and insightful. The "I" repesents a composite patient.

1. *To release tension.* A young woman with high performance anxiety experienced sailboat imagery as a representation of the tension she experienced, and wished for release:

"I see a sailboat, with its sail being tight, filled by the wind. As the sail is released, the tension of the wind is released. When I feel taut with tension, I find myself releasing the tension by taking a long, slow, deep breath and slowly exhaling."

2. *To gain insight.* A graduate student working on his dissertation experienced the following spontaneous imagery:

"Reading a book and understanding it is similar to the process of gaining insight. Both have boundaries, but the true meanings are deep within. I see myself with a book, looking deep within and suddenly I understand."

3. *To find a new solution.* A businessman experiencing blocking used problem-oriented imagery to become more flexible in his thinking and more expansive:

"I look at the problem from a new perspective. Rather than looking at it as unsolvable, I assume that a solution is available. I see myself making a list of possible solutions."

4. *To restructure an idea.* Cognitive restructuring starting at a volitional conscious level can lead to a bridge to more receptive imagery:

"I find myself focusing on function. Feelings have faded. Rather than feeling, I become curious. What function does this anxiety serve? It is an alerting response that motivates me to prepare."

5. *To heighten positive feelings.* Expanding cognition and memory can lead to the heightening of positive imagery in some patients:

"I remember just how good it felt when I did something just for me. I find myself feeling the same way right now. It is just happening, those good feelings all around me right now."

6. *To reduce negative feelings.* One patient spontaneously constricted her attention by focusing on a distant place:

"As I take deep breaths and return to my comfortable place, I am less and less aware of painful feelings. I see. . . ."

7. *To enhance a sense of self-control.* One patient who experienced panic attacks imagined what it would be like to feel a sense of control:

"I allow myself to feel a sense of control, much like the way I feel when I am driving my car. I control the direction, the speed, and I can brake and bring the car to a stop. I am in control."

8. *To develop healthy habits.* A woman who wanted to develop healthy eating habits experienced an image of eating slowly and eating like a thin person:

"I experience self-hypnosis every day. I can go into hypnosis every day, 7 days a week. Before long, the self-hypnosis exercise becomes a habit, an automatic part of my life, effortless, comfortable, automatic, and I am beginning to feel thin."

9. *To transform a sensation from unpleasant to pleasant.* One patient experienced pain changing in quality to a more neutral experience:

"The sensation of discomfort is changing to a neutral pressure."

These examples are only a sampling of the many possible ways to image and experience goals in self-hypnosis. Each person will respond in his or her own unique way.

HYPNOTIC SUSCEPTIBILITY

Since persons differ in their susceptibility to hypnosis, as noted by the Abbé de Faria, it is useful to evaluate the patient's susceptibility. However, some patients have difficulty with this observation, since they may view the challenges given as a demand to be resisted. Frankel et al. (1979) report that it is a matter of clinical judgment. He recommends testing the patient, if possible, but not to do so if the testing interferes with rapport.

The following measures have been used to evaluate hypnotic susceptibility in heterohypnosis. Few formal studies of trance depth have been reported for self-hypnotic subjects. Nonetheless, good heterohypnotic subjects generally can become good self-hypnotic subjects. Indeed, most self-hypnotic subjects have learned self-hypnosis via heterohypnotic experience.

Various tests exist, however, to evaluate hypnotic susceptibility. Hypnosis, according to Shor, has several characteristics, and the tests can measure one or more aspects of these characteristics (Shor, 1979b). The following is a list of tests that may be used to measure susceptibility to heterohypnosis:

1. Group scales
   Harvard Group Scale
   Barber Group Scale

2. Individual tests of hypnotic susceptibility
   Stanford Hypnotic Susceptibility Scale, Forms A, B, C
   Stanford Clinical Scale of Hypnotic Susceptibility
   Creative Imagination Scale (CIS)
   Hypnotic Induction Profile (HIP)

3. Phenomenological scale
   The subject's description of consciousness is rated by the
     experimenter in terms of rating scales
   Nonconscious involvement
   Archaic involvement
   Absorption

4. Self-rating scale
   LeCron Scale
   The Carolina Scale

5. Absorption
   The Absorption Scale

6. Dissociation
   The Perceptual Alteration Scale
   Dissociative Experience Scale

7. Children
   Stanford Hypnotic Susceptibility Scale for Children

Individual Tests

The Stanford Hypnotic Susceptibility Scales (Weitzenhoffer & Hilgard, 1962) consist of three 12-item tests. Form A evaluates responses to motor suggestion. Form B is an alternate form also evaluating responses to motor suggestion. Form C is a 12-item test that includes fantasy and cognitive distortion. Each of these tests requires 45 minutes to administer, and they contain a standardized induction that is read verbatim from the manual.

The Stanford Hypnotic Clinical Scale for Adults (SHCS-Adult) is a brief form of the original Stanford Hypnotic Susceptibility Scale (Hilgard & Hilgard, 1975). The clinical scale consists of five items and takes 20 minutes to administer.

The Creative Imagination Scale (Barber & Wilson, 1978) is a 10-item scale that taps fantasy and imagination. This test requires 20 minutes of administration time, and it can be given in groups or to the individual. This 10-item scale can be used in clinical or experimental sessions. In addition, it can be used individually or with groups. The items consist of arm heaviness, hand levitation, finger anesthesia, water hallucination, olfactory gustatory hallucination, music hallucination, temperature hallucination, time distortion, age regression, and mind–body relaxation. Each task is self-scored by the subject on a scale from 0 to 4. Administration time required is 20 minutes. Test–retest reliability reported was 0.82, and split half 0.89. The scale correlates with absorption and with the Stanford scales.

The Hypnotic Induction Profile (Spiegel, 1972) is a six-item test of hypnotizability. This scale was developed on 4,621 private psychiatric patients. It can be administered in 5 to 10 minutes and appears useful in predicting treatment outcome. Instructions include looking up, looking toward the top of the head and closing eyes (the eye-roll sign), and an arm levitation induction procedure.

Self-Rating Scales

Self-rating scales are described by Charles Tart (1970, 1978/79). He suggests that hypnotized subjects can frequently rate themselves using a subjective rating scale that goes from 0 to 10 or 1 to 100.

Le Cron (1953) reported that he was able to measure hypnotic depth by simply instructing his subjects that they would be able to scale their hypnotic depth on a 100-point scale. He instructed that subconscious minds always know how deeply hypnotized they are and that whenever he asked the subjects what their depth was, a number would flash into consciousness. These self-reports of hypnotic depth correlated with clinical estimates of subject's depths (Cheek & Le Cron, 1968).

The North Carolina Scale requires frequent reports and instructions to subjects that the reports would just flash into their minds instantly. State reports were obtained immediately following the induction and at various times during the trance (Tart, 1970). The instructions given are the following:

> During your experience of hypnosis, I will be interested in knowing just how hypnotized you are. You will be able to tell me this by calling out a number from 0 to 10, depending on how hypnotized you feel yourself to be. Zero will mean that you are awake and as alert as you normally are. One will mean a kind of borderline state between sleeping and waking. Two will mean that you are lightly hypnotized. If you call out the number 5, it will mean that you feel quite strongly and deeply hypnotized. If you feel really very hypnotized, you would call out 8 or 9. Ten will mean that you are very deeply hypnotized and can do just about anything I suggest to you. Naturally, hypnosis can increase and decrease individually from time to time, and that is the kind of thing I'd be interested in finding out from you. Let me explain how you will report your state of hypnotic depth. When I ask "State?" you are to tell me the first number that pops into your mind, and this will represent your state at that time. We've found that this first impression is more accurate than if you stop to think about just what the number should be. This may seem a little hard at first, but it will get easy as you go along. Just call out the first number that pops into your mind when I ask "State?" Remember the number 0 means your normal waking state,

5 means quite strongly hypnotized, and 10 means you are deep
enough to experience just about anything I suggest. Just say the first
number from 0 to 10 that comes into your mind when I ask "State?"
Let's try it now. "State?" At various times during your experience, I'll
ask for your state, and you'll call out the first number that pops into
your mind. (Tart, 1978/1979, pp. 198–199)

Because subject reports of depth vary significantly in session
when examined over short time intervals, they are averaged together
over the session to provide a stable rating.

Children's Scale

The Children's Hypnotic Susceptibility Scale (CHSS; London, 1963)
consists of an individually administered scale based on The Stanford
Hypnotic Susceptibility Scale, Form A, reworded for children. The
first part uses the same 12 items as the Stanford Hypnotizability Scale,
Form A, focusing on motor response. The second part uses 10 items
and is based on items in the Stanford Hypnotic Susceptibility Scale,
Form C, focusing on cognition, hallucination, age regression, and
dreaming within hypnosis. This scale requires an hour for full administration.

Many clinicians feel that the patient's response to a hypnotic
induction itself is the best measure of hypnotic susceptibility. Of
course, clinically, this approach may be true. However, such an approach does not make it possible to compare individuals on the variable of hypnotic susceptibility. The fragile patient, the patient who
feels undermined by challenges, is best not challenged by the threat of
testing and possible failure (Tart, 1970).

The evaluation process and the induction process permit the patient and the therapist to determine what types of strategies, images,
and suggestions are most helpful for the patient. The successful induction enables the therapist to provide posthypnotic suggestions that
facilitate the patient's use of self-hypnosis. In this sense, the induction
process is also part of the evaluation, showing the patient's natural use
of defense, dissociation, and trance tolerance. The patient's response
to self-hypnosis is a very complicated interaction between very complex variables yet to be defined. The resulting words and images
described by the patient are filled with meaning reflected from within
that enable the patient to change.

CHAPTER 7

A Multiplicity of Applications: A Uniqueness of Response

Every man is more than just himself; he also
represents the unique, the very special and always
significant and remarkable point at which the world's
phenomena intersect, only once in this way and
never again.
—Herman Hesse, Prologue to *Demian*

The applications of self-hypnosis are manifold. The broad range of problems at which self-hypnosis can be directed encompasses a continuum of possible behaviors ranging from normal skills and talents to many kinds of emotional problems. Virtually anything that one can think about can also be a possible application of self-hypnosis, providing that the patient is motivated to use self-hypnosis. In addition, it is important that the self-hypnosis be used in concert with appropriate treatment techniques. Hypnosis and self-hypnosis are not a panacea.

Indications for using self-hypnosis include the following:

1. Patient motivation, that is, an interest in using self-hypnosis to master the problem (von Dedenroth, 1962; Estabrooks & May, 1965).
2. Therapist availability, for instance, an opportunity for the patient to discuss questions, concerns, words, and images

generated in self-hypnosis (Carrington, 1977). Therapist monitoring is important to insure that helpful suggestions, words, and images are used. The patient is in treatment precisely because he or she has not been able to take command and feels out of control. The therapist must help the patient to regain control by providing a safe, comfortable, therapeutic environment in which he or she oversees the productions generated by the patient.[1]

3. The self-hypnosis experience reinforces the posthypnotic suggestions and forward movement of the psychotherapy. It provides opportunities for the patient to gain mastery and self-confidence (Crasilneck & Hall, 1985).

4. Of course, hypnosis and self-hypnosis must be beneficial to the resolution of the problem (Gardner & Olness, 1981).

Clinical self-hypnosis, rather than being the sole treatment modality, is an adjunct to ongoing treatment. The experience of taking control and successfully altering perception is a vital experience of self-mastery. The self-hypnotic environment provides a special self-therapeutic opportunity. This occasion is characterized by relaxation, an increase of imagery, sensory involvement, and broadening concentration (Fromm et al., 1981). These characteristics are all consonant with facilitation of healing.

Contraindications for using self-hypnosis include the following:

1. Lack of patient motivation. The patient implicitly or explicitly does not want to use self-hypnosis. To include it leads only to an unnecessary power struggle between the patient and therapist.

2. Self-hypnosis is used negatively in the service of resistance. Rather than reinforcing helpful suggestions and forward movement, it leads to negative therapeutic reactions (Bliss, 1983; Shengold, 1978). Or it may lead to the patient escaping from the work of the therapy (Bliss, 1986).

3. Hypnosis and self-hypnosis provide no therapeutic advantage in the treatment of the patient's problem.

4. The patient lacks susceptibility to hypnosis and self-hypnosis. Not everyone is capable of using self-hypnosis in a self-directed yet free-flowing manner.

[1]Clinical self-hypnosis as an adjunct to hypnotherapy requires professional guidance.

Thus, the therapist needs to consider both the advantages and disadvantages of teaching a specific patient self-hypnosis.

This section focuses on using self-hypnosis with anxiety problems, psychogenic amnesia, stereotyped movement disorders, stuttering, and depressive episode. The purpose of this section is to illustrate how self-hypnosis can be used in the therapy and home practice of the patient, by giving both descriptions of techniques and descriptions of the patient. To date, the clinical research has tended to confound hypnosis and self-hypnosis. For this reason, it is perhaps premature to theorize. However, with the new structural research as a background, it is hoped that clinical research will begin to sort through the intricate maze of the interacting aspects of the clinical use of self-hypnosis.

ANXIETY, EMOTIONAL, AND HABIT PROBLEMS

Anxiety is a common problem that leads the individual to seek hypnotherapy. Generally, treatment of anxiety disorders focuses on both the reduction of tension and insight into those intrapsychic, interpersonal, and performance situations that generate anxiety. The goals of such treatment are for the patient to observe and revise self-expectations and expectations of others and to accept both his or her strengths and weaknesses, when appropriate. The great diversity of ways to use self-hypnosis with anxiety problems provides the opportunity for creativity. Whether one follows a hypnobehavioral or hypnoanalytic orientation (Brown & Fromm, 1986), I have found the following four-step program useful.

The therapist initially teaches self-control strategies such as meditation, biofeedback, and/or self-hypnosis. By learning and doing "exercises" such as self-relaxation, deep breathing, and hand warming, the patient gains control of physiological responses. These self-control techniques have been found useful in studies of meditation, biofeedback, and hypnosis (Brown, 1977; Van Nuys, 1973; Glucksman, 1981; Holroyd, Nuechterlein, Shapiro, & Ward, 1982).

Step 1 involves learning to enter hypnosis and to use imagery and self-suggestion to bring about physiological alteration.

Step 2 involves imagery rehearsal of experiencing comfort. Imagery has been found by a variety of theorists to be effective in fostering relaxation and comfort (Cautela, 1967, 1975; Leuner, 1969). Self-hypnosis generates more imagery than heterohypnosis, and in a more vivid manner (Fromm et al., 1981). By engaging in the self-hypnosis practice, the patient becomes familiar with the experience and begins to enjoy his or her experience of comfort and relaxation. He or she achieves this end by means of words and images, which for him or her trigger comfort and relaxation. These might conjure up the beach, the mountains, a room at home, or even some activity. The trigger image brings, at the speed of a thought, the associated experience in the patient who is absorbed in the experience. An important structural variable in self-hypnosis is absorption (Fromm et al., 1981). According to Fromm, the patient in self-hypnosis experiences the imagery as real (Fromm, 1977, pp. 372–387). Nonetheless, Soskis, Orne, Orne, and Dinges found that self-hypnosis practice tended to drop off after several months.

Step 3 involves corrective imagery of a realistic self-image and successful experiences (Fromm, 1965a, 1965b). The imagery in this self-hypnotic task requires both ego activity so as to make use of intellectual learning as well as ego receptivity to generate the words and images that are emotionally and realistically appropriate to bring about change. The imagery is not willed but experienced. It seems to happen as described by Fromm (1977), as an example of automaticity. Rossi also views corrective imagery as automatic in the sense that the solution happens in the imagery automatically. The patient may think the word "comfortable," but how the comfortable image occurs is beyond awareness (Rossi, 1990).

Step 4 requires validation in real life (Sanders, 1976, p. 63). After living through the experience in self-hypnosis and reviewing it with the therapist at the session, when the patient is ready, he or she can experience him- or herself in this new way in the real-life situation. These four components provide an open-ended way of using self-hypnosis in the clinical situation while permitting the patient to use his or her own spontaneous images and goals in a systematic manner.

Case Example

John was a college student who experienced high levels of anxiety in social situations. He had a persistent irrational fear of situations in which he was exposed to possible judgment by others. Thus, he avoided going with others even though he felt lonely and abandoned. In hypnotherapy, he needed to learn relaxation, feeling comfortable when alone, and gradually to increase this sense of comfort from one person to the inclusion of several persons. Imaginally, this expands the patient's horizons, although it also permits an increasing tolerance of others.

In self-hypnosis, John imaged himself in a vast supermarket where there were many delicacies to be sampled. This image was unbidden and automatic but contained the vital ingredients. Each new food area comprised the possibility of meeting different types of people. He wondered about the experience of sampling the artist group. He feared that his creativity was too mediocre. He wondered about the experience of sampling the foreign foods group, but he feared his grasp of languages was too limited. He wondered about the experience of sampling the sports arena. He believed that he swam well and could participate in this area. He practiced in his imagination the pleasure of swimming and sharing his experience with others. This experience enabled him to join the swim team and to begin to develop new friendships.

Whereas the overall treatment included desensitization, reframing, and free association to develop insights, his powerful image of swimming and pleasure served an important function in motivating him to move toward mastery in real life. Both the meaning and the accompanying affect of the images provided psychological fuel for adaptive movement.

PSYCHOGENIC AMNESIA

In psychogenic amnesia, the patient displays a sudden inability to recall important personal information. The degree of amnesia goes beyond ordinary forgetting (APA, 1980). Marlene Eisen reported the hypnoanalytic treatment of a patient with functional amnesia (Eisen, 1989).

The treatment naturally divided into three phases. In the first phase, the therapist introduced hypnosis, providing induction and deepening suggestions and metaphors on which the later work could build. During this phase, the therapist was quite active and the patient more reactive. This might be called the novice phase, or setting the stage. In the second phase, the patient directed her own hypnotic work. Once trance was induced, usually by the therapist but at times by the patient herself, the patient took over the process, describing her images and the feelings they evoked as she went along. The therapist took a much less active role, serving to facilitate and encourage the patient's self-guided experience. This might be described as the seeking-the-self phase. In the third phase, hypnosis was used primarily for relaxation and reinforcement of positive feelings as the patient and therapist worked together in dynamic psychotherapy to integrate and organize the patient's recollections into a cohesive life history. This might be referred to as the consolidation phase.

Case Example

In this example, Sharon was provided with visual representations of her self-structure that provided her with a foundation on which to build. The therapist suggested that deep within her mind there was a special room. In the center was a strong column on which rested a large book with a golden lock. Over the book was an everlasting light that shone brightly and never went out. She was told that the book contained the story of her life. Only she could unlock the lock, read whatever she chose, and then relock it.

The everlasting light, she was told, was the light of her own spirit, which never went out despite the assaults made against it. The strong column represented the strong core of her own self. It was reiterated often in trance. The ability to look back would give her the strength to move forward, and the ability to confront what was painful and ugly in her life. Such confrontation would help her appreciate what was beautiful and satisfying. When she first began to look into the book, she saw only dimly lit pictures. After a while, the pictures became clearer, and eventually words appeared.

In a journal, Sharon described brief, concrete descriptions of daily occurrences. She wrote about the sensation of water on her skin as she showered, a sensation she had not allowed into consciousness before. After 6 months of therapy, she wrote that she felt she was coming together inside. The journal became an important element in the therapy, a time for sharing with the therapist her day-to-day life. Through a torrent of words so intense at times, they set her trembling, Sharon began to make sense out of the chaotic images and feelings that had disabled her (adapted from Eisen, 1989, pp. 107–115).

Role of Self-Hypnosis with Amnesia

In the above example, the patient was unable to initiate helpful images, but with helpful guided images from the therapist she was able to begin to relax and gradually to assume a more self-directive stance in the hypnotherapy. As she recognized her strengths and her identity, she could begin to integrate and organize her new self-perceptions. The imagery was a powerful transitional phenomenon for her. Self-hypnosis alters the affects, perceptions, and cognitions of the individual. During such alterations, the person may be able to retrieve memories, feelings, perceptions, and cognitions as well as to become aware of why the amnesia was triggered. Self-hypnosis opens a window to the unconscious, bringing to awareness meanings in the form of words and images.

Case Example

A 34-year-old married woman, during the prolonged absence of her husband who was on a tour of duty, drove to a motel where she met another man and had sexual relations with him. She reported no memory of the event, although several people who knew her recognized her, and she was shown the motel registration form on which she had signed her name.

Following an eye-fixation induction and descending stairs imagery for deepening, the patient spontaneously was able to remember the event she had previously forgotten. She had experienced such memory losses before, also coinciding with the absence of her husband. She was seen for hypnotherapy and marriage counseling to recognize and to integrate her feelings of desertion during her husband's absences and her need to be "loved" as well as her need to get revenge on her husband.

The self-hypnosis was an adjunct to ongoing therapy as a cognitive tool to help the patient cope with her feelings of aloneness. In addition, using imagery rehearsal, she was better able to integrate her angry feelings and to translate them into words rather than deeds. The images initially were guided images from the therapist, but as treatment progressed, the patient was able to allow herself to become more open to her own unconscious. She became more ego-receptive to the meanings transmitted by feelings and perceptions.

The power of words and images is immediate. It cannot be denied. The patient reports that he knows that something is different. He knows that he feels different. It is as though things are in place. Whether words and images are used for insight or for cognitive restructuring or problem solving, when they work, they work comprehensively, efficiently, and holistically. Of course, the need for therapist self-monitoring continues to insure that the patient uses effective images rather than negative ones that interfere.

STEREOTYPED MOVEMENT DISORDERS

A tic is an involuntary rapid movement of a functionally related group of skeletal muscles. The patient generally feels uncontrolled and is self-conscious about the occurrence of a tic. Frequently the patient will avoid situations such as social situations where the tic may become more obvious. In a chronic motor tic disorder, recurrent, involuntary, repetitive, rapid, and purposeless movements occur. The intensity of the tic continues over weeks or months or even years. The patient may have the ability to suppress the movements voluntarily for minutes or even hours.

The use of self-hypnosis provides general therapeutic effects as well as a situation for practice, success, and reinforcement. By practice, I am referring to using self-hypnosis effortlessly, allowing imagery that is helpful to surface and to stimulate further successes. Finally, repeated exploration in self-hypnosis frequently leads to insight, understanding, and increased receptivity to the unconscious.

Tourette's Disorder

Tourette's disorder is characterized by recurrent, involuntary, repetitive rapid movements including multiple vocal tics. While the movements can be voluntarily suppressed for minutes or even hours, they tend to recur, and the intensity, frequency, and location of the symptoms vary over weeks or months.

The head and the neck generally are involved in the tics. The patient may have an irresistible urge to utter obscenities. The symptoms appear to be exacerbated by stress. However, during sleep, the symptoms do not occur. An important goal in the management of tics is to take control effortlessly, to inhibit the tic actively by using imagery to restructure the perception of the situation or to reinterpret the meanings inherent in the situation.

Case Example

A 16-year-old male who had facial grimaces, eye twitching, chirping sounds, and inappropriate laughter for 8 years was otherwise in good health, of average intelligence, and performed at an average level in school. Since the patient refused medication, hypnotherapy was instituted by Dr. Fran Culbertson following a three-pronged model: (1) awareness of feelings of a tense, stressed body alternating with feelings of a relaxed body; (2) awareness that control of body and functions is available via finger temperature readings; and (3) learning self-hypnosis strategies using Spiegel's three-step procedure (Spiegel & Spiegel, 1978). The first session primarily involved history taking and developing rapport. In the second session, the patient was taught progressive relaxation, enabling him or her to differentiate a relaxed body from a tense body. The third session included progressive relaxation and thermal biofeedback. Progressive relaxation was considered successful when the patient was able to raise finger temperature 4° and to describe verbally the difference between relaxation and tension.

During the fourth session, the patient was taught Spiegel's three-step procedure (Spiegel & Spiegel, 1978), which the patient was to practice every 2 hours. On Step 3, with eyes closed, body relaxed, and arm floating upward to touch his face, the patient was asked to develop an image of calmness, peace, and quiet—one that was particularly pleasant for him. He described a lake frozen over, without a ripple and very still air. The patient was asked to transfer this image to his face and body while keeping his face and body as still and quiet as the lake. He could remain with this image for as long as he wished and then count back from 3 to 1, bringing these quiet feelings back with him. The patient was seen for a total of eight sessions, with significant improvement (adapted from Culbertson, 1989, pp. 252–256).

In this example, the patient learned to access physiological change through relaxation and control of finger temperature. Spontaneous imagery was permitted in the third session, during which the patient imaged a frozen lake, an image that permitted him to contain his body as still and quiet as the lake. His unconscious created the image that led to actual self-control. The paradox of active, but effortless imaging leading to quieting of physical responsivity is a major characteristic of self-hypnosis.

STUTTERING

Frequent repetitions of sounds, syllables, words, or unusual hesitations and pauses that disrupt the rhythmic flow of speech are characteristics of stuttering. Speech may be rapid or slow. There may be inappropriate inflection or lack of variation in pitch. A fearful anticipation of stuttering leads to both a self-fulfilling prophecy and an avoidance of particular sounds or words.

Case Example

David was a 25-year-old musician who had difficulty initiating conversation or answering questions because of a stuttering problem he had always had. At times, when he was in a safe place with friends, the stuttering abated. However, the stuttering at times was so intense that no one could understand him. He tended to stutter in the office when talking about his early development and, in particular, when talking about his mother.

In hypnosis, while comfortable, he spoke in a clear, distinct manner without stuttering at all. He generated spontaneous imagery that enabled him to begin to work on understanding his feelings, particularly anger, and how that anger affected his speech. Self-hypnosis was assigned to help him reduce tension and to increase his sense of mastery over his speech. He could relax and watch his thoughts through imagery. According to Schneck, free association and visual imagery are useful self-hypnotic methods to accompany hypnoanalysis (Schneck, 1965, p. 133). Using deep breathing as the signal to enter hypnosis, David rapidly relaxed. He initiated imagery rehearsal to see himself with his friends, relaxing and speaking easily. At the first sign of anger, David learned to deepen the relaxation and then experienced the transformation of anger into clear speech. This experience was not willful but automatic. It happened effortlessly.

SELF-HYPNOSIS WITH BORDERLINE AND PSYCHOTIC PATIENTS[2]

Patients who are interested in and receptive to hypnosis are introduced to the concept of auto-hypnosis and the potential of this technique to enhance their own self-mastery, control, and independence. Autohypnosis is taught after the patient has experienced a standard relaxation technique, allowing the patient to operate either with or without eye closure. Various combinations of breathing, progressive body relaxation, imagining counting down a staircase, imaging a safe and relaxing place, and reverse arm levitation are used according to the needs and abilities of the patient. Patients are encouraged by posthypnotic suggestion and direct suggestion to practice their own trance relaxation. It is stressed that their ability to develop trance is not really new, that they have been going into trance all their lives, and that now they can learn some ways of controlling when and how they go into trance and what they want to do with their trance.

A patient learning autohypnosis can use it formally or informally with the therapist and can also use it independently of the therapy session. The patient learns that he or she has the right and the power to create dreams and images as well as to change them any time they become too frightening or too overwhelming. According to Joan Murray-Jöbsis, once the patient understands his ability to control images, his sense of power, mastery, and security is greatly enhanced (adapted from Murray-Jöbsis, 1984, pp. 368–402).

[2]This section is adapted from Murray-Jöbsis (1984).

Working with the severely disturbed is complex, requiring the building of a relationship with them, trust in that relationship, understanding, and insight into negative self-concept and its unreal origins, and appreciation of the lack of correlation between negative self-concept and current functional abilities (adapted from Murray-Jöbsis, 1984).

Baker selects hypnotic techniques to be used early in treatment to manage the intense, changeable, and negative quality of the transference with borderline patients. These techniques use circumscribed trance experiences and directed imagery to establish a positive internal representation of the therapist and to evoke and support the affect availability necessary for the development of rapport in psychotherapy. Baker lists as goals: ego support, mastery, management of disturbances in boundary integrity and identity, modulation and abreaction of disruptive affect, and support of the therapeutic alliance (Baker, 1983b, 1985).

With such severely disturbed patients, it is important to include ego-building skills as well as skills leading to affect modulation. Moving towards free access to the unconscious too quickly can lead to retraumatization and the overwhelming of the ego (Baker, 1985). One new approach to moderating and controlling affect is described by Brown (1985). Gruber (1983) also discusses ways to use hypnosis and self-hypnosis to control affect.

DEPRESSIVE EPISODE

The depressed patient manifests dysphoric mood and/or loss of interest in activities. He or she experiences feelings of depression, hopelessness, and irritability. Physically, he or she exhibits poor appetite, insomnia, psychomotor agitation or retardation, and loss of energy. The depressed patient has little energy, tends to feel tremendous guilt, and is socially withdrawn. Self-hypnosis can help in a number of ways: (1) by teaching the patient relaxation; (2) by helping the patient to carry out busy life tasks such as cleaning the house; (3) by helping the patient to moderate expression by talking rather than turning the patient against him- or herself.

Crasilneck warns that symptom removal is inappropriate with depressed patients because they may act out their anger through suicidal tendencies (Crasilneck & Hall, 1985). Rather than suggesting changed affect, helpful hypnotic techniques include ego-strengthening techniques, for example, "Each and every day you will feel more in control, more able to do tasks." Another useful technique centers around the experience of calmness and relaxation while working through the sad feelings with the therapist, for example, "As you take deep breaths you feel calmer and more relaxed."

Torem describes a multiplicity of techniques drawing on the work of others (Torem, 1987).

1. *The affect bridge.* This technique links similar affects from the present to the past. In my opinion, this technique is best practiced during the therapy hour. The patient may or may not be able to cope with the feelings and memories self-generated (Watkins, 1971).

2. *Movie or TV screen.* The patient is asked to imagine a movie or TV screen and to watch a movie of his or her life that focuses on situations that have led to helplessness, hopelessness, and present-day depression. Because of the nature of the affect, helplessness, it is a matter of clinical judgment whether to permit the patient to use this technique at home alone or to reserve it for the therapy hour.

3. *Age regression.* The technique of reliving experiences from an earlier time also involves a matter of clinical judgment as to whether to permit the patient to use this technique at home alone. Of course, it is possible for the patient to experience a spontaneous age regression when alone, or even when dreaming (Fromm, 1965b). For this reason, therapist availability, if only over the phone, is essential.

4. *Personal diary.* The patient is asked to keep a running record of feelings, dreams, occurrences of feelings, and behaviors. The diary can generate imagery, affect, and dreams as well as insight.

The treatment of depression appears to require a multidimensional approach with self-hypnosis reinforcing appropriate cognitive functioning, providing support during abreaction, and helping the patient to modulate feelings.

PATIENT EXAMPLES OF SELF-HYPNOSIS PRACTICE

The following examples are descriptions of spontaneous self-hypnotic experiences the patients had when alone. The imagery is vivid.

One patient experienced inexplicable panic attacks. In self-hypnosis she viewed one such attack and did not permit her ego to be overwhelmed but rather remained active and receptive:

> I sat down to pay the bills and found that I was suddenly hit with a feeling of panic and desperation. I experienced a rapid drop in mood—from 80° to about 32°. One of the triggers seems to have

been the notice from the insurance company stating that further reimbursements for therapy were discontinued through the end of the fiscal year. I felt abandoned, alone, and helpless. The cat jumped on my lap, and I remembered that as a child I had believed that the family cat was the only creature that cared about me or loved me. As I reviewed this, I realized that I had dissociated my anger and was aware only of panic and helplessness.

The patient had obtained some perspective to help her in the future.

Imagery and Perspective

One professional woman who wished to make some positive changes in her life experienced this imagery and change in perspective:

A visual image of a plateau may lead to nowhere. Better to think of the mesa as a break in the hike, a time to catch my breath, a chance to look at how far I've come, to appreciate how much further that is than I thought when starting. The trick is enjoying the climb and looking forward to the next stage. An emotional growth plateau requires breaking through boundaries, getting out of the cage, refusing to stay in a role or mode of thinking that's too constricting or limiting. I am the only one who really notices my changing. My own appreciation and recognition are what count. I am coming into my own.

What comes ahead will be thrilling. There might be some moments of danger and indecision. I might even feel like turning back. I will like the physical feelings of being thinner; I will feel more powerful. So it will be with my continuing emotional growth. It will bring me freedom and peace. When I'm ready for it, I can choose to become thinner. I can begin to risk and to relax with self-hypnosis.

Shortly after this experience, she changed her eating habits and also began getting regular exercise.

Changing Mental Attitudes

Cognitive restructuring appears to involve transformation of expectations about oneself, about other things and events, and about other people. The following examples of self-hypnotic cognitive restructuring, reframing, or transformation are home practice experiences a professional woman described.

When a particular incident of failure or inadequacy seems to dominate my thinking, I can turn my attitude around. Settling down into relaxation, I can think, first, of the positive side of the experience. Was it all bad, or were there good ingredients? How can I experience it in positive terms? How many positive factors can I list? If I had to choose one positive aspect of the experience to emphasize, what would I choose? Can I accept the fact that the positive aspects may outweigh the negative and that my initial evaluation may be biased? If one of my friends had been in the same situation, what would I tell her to help her see the positive side of the experience?

She combined problem-solving techniques such as brainstorming with a focus on the generation of positive factors and personal choice. Her next description begins as she entered an affirmative mind set. "Now that I am in an affirmative mood, how many things that are positive or enjoyable can I list that have happened this week? What sources of pleasure or accomplishment would be on the list? Can I imagine myself accomplishing something that gives me great satisfaction or pleasure?"

She needed more time to become receptive to her own choices and decisions as well as to permit herself to become open to satisfaction. Each question presented an opportunity for imagery experience. The example illustrates the requirement for therapist monitoring. Without such monitoring, the patient might have become discouraged or overwhelmed.

Self-Hypnosis Exercises

Sometimes patients become stuck with the alien, the foreign, and therefore the frightening experience. Using imagery as a way of achieving familiarity is another example of cognitive restructuring or transformation of meaning. The patient is a career woman who feels stuck and bored. Her imagery permitted her to make the familiar unfamiliar. It transformed boredom into curiosity.

Sometimes I feel in a rut. What I know has become too familiar. It has lost its novelty. I become bored. How can I access novelty—the new, the unfamiliar. Maybe by thinking about something I don't know very much about, something unfamiliar, such as being in a space ship. I am in a space ship. It is confining; the space is not large. Yet it frees. Being in a space ship is exciting. I can contact Mission Control in Houston. I am not alone. My trusty computer "Aristotle" is with me. I can contact Mission Control. I am on a journey. I don't know what to expect. I am energized by my curiosity. Boredom has been displaced by curiosity. The thrill of space travel has replaced my boredom, and everything seems fresh, alive, exciting.

This example captures the excitement of change.

Sometimes the task is just the opposite type of reframing: the unfamiliar must become familiar. A graduate student working on her dissertation needed to reframe or restructure the unfamiliarity of writing a dissertation, and to make the unfamiliar familiar, experienced the following:

Sometimes when I am in a new situation, I become frightened because I do not know what to expect. My anxiety overwhelms my curiosity. Maybe I can begin to decrease the anxiety attached to the unfamiliar situation by focusing on something familiar, something safe and predictable, that stabilizes. I am thinking of the safe, warm predictability of my favorite pair of shoes. These shoes feel good. They mold to my feet. They feel right so that I have a feeling of being centered—on balance—even though I am in a new situation. Just as the shoes mold to my feet, this new situation begins to be more safe, more predictable. Just as these shoes stabilize and provide comfort, so the newness becomes less frightening and more comfortable. A figure–ground reversal has occurred. I am aware of comfort and of being centered. I am less concerned about anxiety.

The student feels more in control, on balance, and able to work.

SUMMARY

Self-hypnosis is an uniquely personal and subjective experience. The characteristics of focusing attention within while focusing less on the external world permit the patient to experience helpful self-suggestions and imagery effortlessly at home. This self-directed practice is based in part on imagery that was generated in the heterohypnotic session or on imagery that was spontaneously generated. The goals of such practice may be simply to permit the experience of mastery and comfort to occur automatically. According to Fromm et al. (1981) self-hypnosis at least possesses the capacity to alter one's orientation so that internal events are attended to in new ways. The notion of transformation of meaning through words and images is consistent with this interpretation.

I believe that the creative work of the patient is to transform the words and images into explicitly and implicitly meaningful experience related to mastery and comfort. This transformation, however, cannot be willed. Rather, it occurs as part of an effortless, but meaningful experience in imagery, in affect, and in cognition.

Whereas self-initiated responses may be the essence of laboratory-initiated self-hypnosis, according to Johnson (1981), self-directed responses may be more in keeping with traditional clinical self-hypnosis, which consists of self-directed performance of therapist-taught tasks (Johnson, 1981, p. 249). According to Johnson, there will always be some compromise with heterohypnosis influence unless the research is limited to spontaneous self-induced trance. "The heterohypnosis input inevitably comes, if not through explicit suggestions, or wording, for self-hypnosis practice, then through giving heterohypnosis training and a mind-set for self-hypnosis technique" (Johnson, 1981, p. 249). In the clinical situation, I would expand this set to include open-ended suggestions, guided imagery, and goal orientation. The patient has come to therapy for a reason, and the self-hypnosis is explained or framed as a way to reach that goal.

I have found that the following questions and imagery experiences are helpful to access personal words and images in heterohypnosis as a path to self-hypnotic words and images.

1. Ask the patient to describe a comfortable place.

2. Ask the patient to amplify the quiet and calm and the feeling of becoming more in control.

3. Ask the patient to describe how he or she felt before becoming blocked.

4. Associate positive imagery in the present to positive imagery in the past. The words and images the patient develops may become ego-guiding self-suggestions, a blend of conscious and unconscious processes. Eisen and Fromm (1983) have described the interweaving process of patient suggestions and therapist suggestions.

5. Ask the patient to have a hypnotic dream related to positive associations, for example, "Just allow yourself to have a dream about feeling more comfortable."

I do not assign abreaction as a goal of self-hypnosis, since the experience of strong affects while the patient is alone may be overwhelming. Although such abreactions may occur spontaneously, abreactions are generally dealt with in the hypnotherapy session itself.

6. Words and images associated with positive values may be used to reframe negative meanings.

There are a multiplicity of ways to teach the patient self-hypnosis, but prediction of every possible patient response is not possible, for we enter the realm of individual creativity; the interaction among constitution, experience, and opportunity; and the complex interactions among structural, content, and idiosyncratic variables.

One patient may need to see him- or herself on a ship in a rocky sea coming safely to port, whereas another will see him- or herself climbing Mt. Everest or else sitting royally on the beach under an umbrella. Even the very same image will hold dramatically different meanings for different patients. What works rests within the patient, and needs only to be excavated.

The power of words and images to transform is an unique power within the particular patient. The power can be accessed through the patient's involvement in the personal meanings he or she unconsciously assigns to words and images.

Clinical self-hypnosis leads to a variety of phenomena such as relaxation, imagery, rehearsal in fantasy, age regression and progression, hypnotic dreams, and metaphors. The key to success lies not in the hypnotic phenomena that are used; rather, the key to success lies in the integrated meaning the words and images hold for the patient. Clinical self-hypnosis enables the patient to open the doors to the unconscious, to open up new ways of experiencing, new possibilities of being in the world. The self-hypnotic experience can build a new awareness of the self. The self-hypnosis experience can access a new perception, feeling, and behavior that reinforces mastery in this way only for this patient at this time.

CHAPTER 8

Pain Management

For they can conquer who believe they can.
—Vergil

Pain management or reduction is an important therapeutic goal. As we have seen throughout our sampling of hypnotherapeutic approaches, the ways of using hypnosis show wide diversity. Pain control also, as in other areas of clinical use of hypnosis and self-hypnosis, shows a similar heterogeneity. Formal clinical research has yet to tease out the many layers of complicated interactions between variables. In this chapter, beginning from heterohypnosis as the starting point, we review how some hypnotherapists teach self-hypnosis for pain control to their patients. It is too early in the development of this area to cite definitive research about which techniques are best. The emphasis continues at the state-of-the-art level in that the techniques are matched to individual patients. The future may give rise to different interpretations.

Pain reduction requires alteration of both affect (suffering) and alteration of cognition (ways of thinking about pain). In effect, the patient learns to take control of body perception by altering the cognitions and feelings that generally invade awareness. The experience of taking control and successfully altering pain perception is a vital experience of self-mastery (Barber, 1982; Chaisson, 1981; Crasilneck, 1982; Ewin, 1978; Spiegel & Spiegel, 1978; Erickson, 1966; Hilgard & Hilgard, 1975).

Self-hypnosis is a useful adjunct to psychotherapy and hypnotherapy because it enables the patient to alter selectively his or her perception of pain when necessary. Initially, the patient learns how to alter perceptions cognitively, affectively, and physiologically in hetero-hypnosis. By doing so, he or she feels more in control of self. Rather than feeling helplessly overwhelmed, the patient experiences mastery. The bridge to self-hypnosis is frequently a posthypnotic suggestion by the therapist that the patient can do these things for him- or herself whenever necessary, whenever he or she would like. This post-hypnotic suggestion often is the major instruction for self-hypnosis. According to Hilgard and Hilgard (1975), once a person has been hypnotized, he or she can follow the same routines used by the hypnotherapist both to enter hypnosis and to emerge from it.

According to Hilgard, "the hypnotized person has at least two ego fractions operative at once: a hypnotized part, doing what the hyp-notherapist suggests; and an observing part, monitoring what is going on and quite capable of interrupting if anything untoward is sug-gested." Thus, according to Hilgard, "some fraction of self-monitoring operates synchronously with the hypnotized part" (Hilgard, 1979, p. 19).

The phenomenon of pain presents an enigma to clinicians because of the unpredictable treatment outcomes of the patient with chronic pain (Melzack, 1973). More recently, holistic programs of treatment have been offered on an inpatient basis that address all aspects of patient care and changes in lifestyle, exercise, nutrition, and psycho-logical coping techniques (Fordyce, 1978; Finer, 1982). These pro-grams appear quite promising. Frequently, relaxation and self-hypnosis are included as important strategies for coping with the psychological aspects of pain, especially the suffering component.

Pain is both an intrinsic biological signal that something is wrong in our body and an adaptive response. In this respect, the perception of pain arises as a simple, urgent, and primitive message (Melzack, 1973). However, pain is not always perceived after injury, especially when we are engaged in a fully competitive activity. At other times, the signal value of pain is superfluous because it provides misleading information, as, for example, in the case of phantom limb pain in which perception of pain only interferes with one's energy and quality of life. Superfluous, misleading pain is both dreaded and depressing.

The phenomenon of pain perception oscillates. Pain perception, like other perceptual experience, can be transformed; it ebbs and flows. It differs from person to person and from culture to culture, reflecting cultural expectations as well (Hardy, Wolff, & Goodell, 1952; Sternbach & Tursky, 1965). Pain that seems intolerable in one person may be tolerated silently by another. Another person may even seek out pain-producing stimuli, for example, the masochist who de-

lights in pain. Because of these contradictory responses, pain perception cannot be defined simply in terms of response to particular kinds
of stimuli. Rather, it is a highly personal experience, depending on
cultural learning, the meaning of the specific situation, and other
unique factors (Sacerdote, 1982).

One key to pain control then is to modify the learnings, meanings,
and memories associated with the pain (Erickson, 1966). According to
Haley (1967), hypnotic techniques induce a favorable setting in which
to instruct the patient in a more advantageous use of his or her own
potentials to control pain.

The experience of altering attention, suggestion, and cognitive
strategies apparently modifies the pain threshold. For example, when
the attention of an athlete is diverted by the competitiveness of a
football game, he or she may not experience pain from a severe kick
on the shin, whereas an overanxious tense individual may report that
he or she feels severe pain when he or she accidentally brushes up
against an unexpected object.

Although pain traditionally has been described as a sensory experience, the accompanying affect sharply differentiates pain from sensory experience per se. Clearly pain becomes overwhelming, demands
immediate attention, and disrupts ongoing behavior and thought. The
affect aroused may be panic, anxiety, depression, fear, and helplessness, all of which augment the perception of pain.

I believe that the interruption or dissociation of perception of
sensory pain from overwhelming affect is an integral part of mastering
pain and fostering comfort. In the heterohypnotic situation, the patient
learns to tap his or her dissociative abilities. Because the heterohypnotic experience of hypnoanesthesia sets the stage for the patient's self-
directed use of self-hypnosis to reinforce the hypnoanesthesia, I present the hypnotherapist's verbalization.

The self-hypnotic environment provides a special self-therapeutic
opportunity. This occasion is characterized by relaxation, an increase
of imagery, sensory involvement, and heightened concentration
(Fromm, 1981). Relaxation alone has been demonstrated to reduce
pain perception by 40% (Hilgard & Hilgard, 1975). These authors
believe that if the patient is also motivated to learn specific techniques
that will help him or her to control the subjective perception of pain,
then the pain perception can be diminished even further. Their research demonstrated that in highly hypnotizable subjects, the reduction in pain can approach 100%. In addition, self-hypnosis can be used
on demand by the patient to reinforce the hypnoanesthetic effects
(Crasilneck & Hall, 1985; Sacerdote, 1982).

TECHNIQUES

Techniques first learned in heterohypnosis in the hospital or office can be adapted for effortless self-hypnosis practice. These techniques include, among others, hypnoanesthesia, glove anesthesia, dissociation, distraction, age regression, time distortion, substitution, and displacement.

Hypnoanesthesia consists of suggesting that the perception of pain is changing, diminishing, becoming numb. An experience of total hypnoanesthesia would diminish responses to both touch and pain. An experience of analgesia would diminish pain but not touch. In self-hypnosis, the patient may repeat these suggestions to him- or herself or simply reexperience the sensory alterations via imagery or in response to a predetermined signal as, for example, a deep breath or a finger levitation.

Glove anesthesia entails suggesting to the patient that the fingers and hand are becoming numb and insensitive. The hypnotic phenomenon is explored initially in a neutral area, the hand, and, once achieved, the experience of anesthesia can be transferred to some other part of the body, for example, the hip. Transfer is accomplished by suggesting to the patient that the numbness in the hand is moving to another part of the body, the hip. Soon the hip becomes numb and insensitive, just as insensitive as the hand. In self-hypnosis, the patient can experience the numbness and insensitivity very quickly.

Dissociation consists of suggesting to the patient that he or she experience him- or herself in another place or experience an out-of-body state. The patient, by effortlessly focusing his or her attention, for example, can psychologically experience him- or herself as being in another time, place, state, or in a different way: "Just imagine that you are on the beach in Bermuda, and you are enjoying the healing warmth of the sun." In self-hypnosis, this type of dissociation is similar to spontaneous reverie and daydreams that transport one to distant places.

Distraction involves a suggestion to automatically focus attention on something that is unrelated to the pain, for instance, focus on the wall. The patient finds that by focusing on the wall, he or she may become so distracted that, for a time, he or she is unaware of the pain. In the clinical situation, some patients are able to use distraction easily, whereas for others, this technique may be difficult.

Age regression entails the suggestion to revert in time to before the accident, illness, or injury when the patient felt fine. Simply going back in memory to a time before the illness or injury, the patient reexperiences the feelings of well-being. One patient in a group for pain management experienced himself at Fenway Park when the Red Sox won the pennant. He felt wonderful. With repetition, chronic pain patients can learn to use this technique as easily as imagery (Toomey & Sanders, 1983).

Time distortion consists of suggesting to the patient that time is passing so quickly that the perception of pain is short-lived or that the painfree times seem to last longer and longer. The creative ways of distorting time are manifold (Erickson & Cooper, 1959).

Once the patient has learned these techniques in heterohypnosis, with repetition, the patient can effortlessly self-suggest and reexperience these phenomena on his or her own, a self-hypnotic experience. Natural imaginative abilities, integrity of ego functions, and flexibility of thought capacity will shape the patient's response to pain reduction.

Some patients are more able to implement these techniques on their own without a prior heterosuggestion. One professional woman, for example, wanting to use hypnoanestheia for impending dental surgery, was unable to transfer numbness from the hand to the jaw with heterohypnotic suggestion, but when left to her own self-suggestion, she was able to achieve this transfer dramatically: Her jaw drooped, and she spoke heavily as though she had been injected with novocain.[1] For this patient, self-hypnotic suggestion was more effective than heterohypnotic suggestion. She was a self-mover, not in a deliberate sense but rather in an automatic, involuntary manner.

Self-hypnosis is useful in reinforcing treatment for the pain patient in part because of the general effects of self-hypnosis: a reduction of the generalized reality orientation and absorption in the inner experience (Fromm et al., 1981). Through the use of guided imagery stimulated previously by the therapist and of spontaneous imagery, the patient transforms perceptions, meanings, and sensations. The transformation of perception is not "willful." Rather, it is intentional: The patient is motivated to help him- or herself. The complicated interactions among structural variables, personality variables, practice goals, and expectancies all contribute to the remarkable experience of clinical self-hypnosis and pain management.

SPECIFIC HYPNOTHERAPISTS

This section focuses on the techniques used by specific hypnotherapists. Included are brief excerpts from Joseph Barber, Harold Crasilneck, Milton Erickson, and Paul Sacerdote, among others.

[1]Seminar on hypnosis, University of North Carolina School of Medicine.

Whereas many theorists report that hypnotic susceptibility is the crucial factor in response to hypnotic control of pain (Hilgard & Hilgard, 1975), others believe that the crucial factor is the particular approach used with the patient (Barber, 1982a, 1982b). I believe that the interaction among the patient's experience of self-hypnosis, critical goals, and expectations facilitates the transformation from intolerable pain to increasing comfort and self-control; the change lies in the meaning of the experience to the patient, which is reflected in the richness of words and images.

Joseph Barber uses indirect suggestions with pain patients. Indirect suggestion in his view is an invitation for the patient to respond in a certain kind of way. He teaches his patients self-hypnosis via posthypnotic suggestion and a tape they can listen to for practice purposes. He teaches the patient hypnoanesthesia in the heterohypnotic situation, which is reinforced by self-hypnosis. The following examples are taken from his book (Barber, 1982a, 1982b):

1. Analgesia: "I really cannot say when . . . but maybe it would be interesting to you . . . to just suddenly notice how much more comfortable you feel . . ." (Barber, 1982a, p. 53).
2. Substitution: "Experience can change. Any part of your experience can become a part of your comfort" (Barber, 1982b, p. 177). This technique involves replacing a particular, painful sensation with a less uncomfortable sensation. The change is one of quality.
3. Displacement: "Just notice the movement of the feeling . . . be curious as you notice how the feeling can continue to move in an ever-increasing spiral, moving round and round your abdomen, and notice which leg it begins to move into . . . " (Barber, 1982, pp. 47–48). This technique involves changing the location of pain from one area to a different, less involved area.
4. Substitution of a painful sensation by a different, less painful stimulus: "I notice how my perceptions can change. The throbbing pain is leaving and I am becoming aware of a light pressure, which can be increasingly comfortable" (p. 47). The new perception of pressure and comfort substitutes for the discomfort of pain (Barber, 1982a).

According to Barber, the patient in acute pain first must shift attention from pain perception to auditory perception to hear the therapist. Once trusting attention has been established, the therapist administers suggestions to prepare the patient for painful and frightening medical procedures. The patient can be led gently from suffering to increasing comfort. The alteration of perception involves sensory, physiological, and affective change leading to increased comfort (Barber, 1982a).

Barber recommends self-monitoring the sensory perceptual aspects of pain. Self-monitoring brings the recognition that pain can wax and wane, change, and become more tolerable. The receptivity to the inconstancy of pain is a demonstration that change is possible (Barber, 1982).

According to Sacerdote (1982), hypnosis in the management of pain involves multiple methodologies aimed at achieving neurophysiological alterations, changes, and reorganizations in cognitive-emotional understanding, improved behavioral patterns, and new useful perceptions of time and space. Sacerdote feels it is important to use diverse methods that alter not only neurophysiological functioning but cognitive and emotional contents of the illness, disability, and pain experience as well. His approach to pain control is holistic.

Sacerdote also teaches the patient self-hypnosis in the heterohypnotic situation and provides the posthypnotic suggestion that the patient can do these techniques on his or her own. Sacerdote uses a simile of electric wiring based on the gate-control theory of Melzack and Wall (Melzack, 1973). "Under hypnosis the patient is asked to demonstrate his or her potential ability to switch on or off, or turn down certain electrical circuits or radio receivers or television sets, or to plug in certain lines in preference to others" (Sacerdote, 1982, p. 69). Other techniques used by Sacerdote are reinterpretation of signals (observation of pain and discovering ways to control it); association and conditioning (combining comfort with imagery and relaxation); dissociation (separating pain from relaxation); amnesia (forgetting the pain); positive and negative hallucination (seeing connections); dream induction (dreaming about a solution); time and space distortion (decreasing time spent in pain); relaxation; glove anesthesia; and control of autonomic functions. Self-hypnosis can be used by the patient to relieve pain on repeated occasions.

Sacerdote suggests associating the pain with a pleasant memory. He also recommends reinterpretation of the meaning of pain, calls for instead a focus on the teleological usefulness of pain. The purpose, meaning, and function of the pain must be addressed.

Milton Erickson used a combination of direct and indirect approaches to hypnosis and self-hypnosis. He cleverly embedded suggestions within an almost conversational induction and dialogue: "Now as I talk, and I can do so comfortably, I wish that you will listen to me comfortably as I talk about a tomato plant. That is an odd thing to talk about. It makes one curious . . ." (Erickson, 1966, pp. 198–209).

Milton Erickson, in this example, essentially embedded meaningful, critical suggestions within a conversational dialogue of specific interest to the patient, in this case, a farmer. For some patients the demonstration that things can be different effortlessly enables the patient to restructure his or her pain. For others, the meaning that change is difficult is an important aspect of the transformation process.

Crasilneck uses a direct suggestion approach, focusing on symptom amelioration and symptom substitution (Crasilneck, 1979). He reports the value of hypnosis in lower back pain. Frequently the treatment outcome is positive in that there is a decrease in pain medication and an increase in comfort. He describes the beginning of hypnotherapy as intensive, daily or more frequently, gradually decreasing the frequency of hypnotherapy as the patient's pain lessens (Crasilneck & Hall, 1985). Self-hypnosis lengthens the effectiveness of posthypnotic suggestions for pain relief (Crasilneck, 1979).

The self-hypnotic induction taught at the second session consists of raising the finger in precisely the same manner as if the patient were signaling the therapist. The suggestions cited were:

> As I lie in my bed I am going to do all in my power to help myself recover . . . I can control most of my discomfort . . . and as I am concentrating my thoughts on the fingertips of the right hand, I slowly raise the forefinger . . . I am becoming free from muscular tension and free from stress and strain . . . I am becoming aware of some heaviness in my right leg . . . and I know I can consume all the foods given to me that will give me strength . . . I will follow the treatment prescribed, knowing that I can improve and benefit maximally from the treatments . . . I will sleep well because of the power of my unconscious, and the majority of discomfort will be controlled, and I will gain in strength, free from tension, free from tightness, free from the majority of the discomfort. (Crasilneck & Hall, 1985, p. 431)

Crasilneck recommends that in the control of organic pain, reinforcement of pain control should occur before the pain exacerbates. This reinforcement may be necessary at 3-to-5-hour intervals in the first 24 hours. The frequency of reinforcement of self-hypnosis decreases as the patient progresses.

Clarke and Jackson (1983) taught their patients self-hypnosis for security and reinforcement. They told the patient, "When you do this at home and get this nice relaxed feeling, I want you then to think of some of the ways that you are learning to get rid of your problem."

Elkins describes the patient's ability to take control of his bodily functions, such as becoming warmer or cooler, as a way of controlling pain. Such control involves an initial denial of reality because the created image was opposed to immediate experience. The patient compensates for helplessness by making the passive active, that is, creating a positive change (Elkins, 1987, p. 19).

Despite the diversity of approaches—indirect, direct, metaphoric, and symbolic—each hypnotherapist creates a mental set for self-hypnosis and the possibility that the patient can help him- or herself by doing something, allowing things to happen, by becoming absorbed in images and words that are both a stimulus to the patient to experience as well as a response from the patient that is replete with a unique meaning for him or her.

In my practice, I use the same four-step approach to pain management as described for anxiety, only the suggestions are aimed at the management of pain: body control, comfortable imagery, rehearsal in imagery, and validation, that is, recognition of comfort.

Case Examples

A 18-year-old college undergraduate had injured her back 9 months prior to the visit. She had always been exceedingly active, running 5 miles per day, dancing 2 hours per day, and engaging in a variety of aerobic exercises. She was fearful that her back would hinder her from her activities. She claimed that she was doing very little currently. She rode her bike 1 hour per day and still jogged 5 miles, but she was not doing any other exercise because of her back.

In hypnosis, she learned that it was okay to relax and to reduce tension. At home, in self-hypnosis practice, she was able to achieve effortlessly a comfortable state of relaxation.

Her comfortable image was seeing herself and experiencing herself running along the beach by the water. In her self-hypnosis practice, she experienced this image more deeply and more comfortably. As she engaged in this comfortable imagery, she simultaneously realized that she did not have to do as many physical exercises each day. She established pain control in this way through this effortless self-hypnosis practice.

During the experience, unbidden understandings emerged such as the realization that she was active and that she could use her energies to improve her studies and see her boyfriend, in effect to lead a fuller life. She could now perceive herself as being more comfortable, and wanted to get on with her life. In effect, she became remotivated.

She began to enrich her self-hypnotic experiences in an ego-active manner with pacing, combining some running activities, some quiet activities, and found that this proper balance did indeed increase her comfort. She could perceive herself in a more realistic light, not as

Wonder Woman but as a human being with physical limitations. She became ego-receptive to her humanness.

We also discussed the dynamics involving her upcoming graduation from college, her impending separation from her boyfriend, and her having to face getting a job and supporting herself. She realized that there was considerable secondary gain in having back pain. This pain provided the opportunity for her to be dependent and taken care of. With this combined insight and her increased level of comfort, she could validate her more realistic self-image and get on with her life.

Hilgard and Hilgard report the case of Louise, a research subject in their laboratory, who learned to control pain through hypnosis. She learned autohypnosis and self-suggestion 2 months before giving birth. In self-hypnosis, she used counting as an opportunity to find herself in a relaxed hypnotic state; she then concentrated on the idea that any pain would be perceived as a light tingling sensation, as when one's arm has fallen asleep and come to just a little (Hilgard & Hilgard, 1975, pp. 108–109). From reading this example, one senses that the power of altering perception via self-hypnosis was evident in this experience.

Hilgard and Lebaron (1984) describe the self-hypnosis induction as repeating the words and imitating the approach used in heterohypnosis. Self-hypnosis as a self-mastery experience is reflected in the different examples. Each style of teaching the patient self-hypnosis and each hypnotic technique used presents an occasion for the patient to access personal meanings that enable him or her to conquer the pain, partly because he or she believes it possible. His or her success of course reinforces a belief in his or her ability to access personal power. The access is automatic—it happens. The images and words that the patient creates at an unconscious level may be different from the ones the therapist provides. Nonetheless, the therapist's words and images frequently become the stimulus for the patient's creativity. Clinical self-hypnosis is a cooperative effort.

Spontaneous Self-Hypnosis during an Accident

A 52-year-old woman was in an automobile accident in which she had crashed into a car sitting at the bottom of a hill. On impact, she momentarily felt extreme ischemic pain in her right foot. She found the pain disappearing as she dissociated her foot. It was as though the foot were no longer attached. The woman subjectively felt far away, as though she had retreated from the highway into a cave. She simply sat in the cave quietly, feeling no discomfort whatever. She briefly wondered if her foot was all right after all but decided wisely not to test this hypothesis. Rather, she would continue to stay in the cave, quiet, safe, and without physical distress. Until the ambulance came, she did not move a muscle. Interestingly, when asked about this, she replied: "I feel comfortable and do not wish to move."

As she was helped out of the car, she saw her foot, swollen and grotesque, and wondered why it did not hurt. Then she reinforced the dissociation, disowning ownership of that foot. Her powerful dissociation or nonownership of her foot combined with no thoughts about the injury enabled her to feel comfortable during the initial stages of treatment.

ANESTHESIOLOGY

David Spiegel describes how some anesthesiologists teach simple self-hypnosis as a routine part of their preoperative visit. They show the patient how to enter self-hypnosis. They then instruct him or her to associate the routine preparations for surgery as a cue to enter self-hypnosis. For example, the patient may be told that the transfer from bed to gurney is a signal to close eyes, take a deep breath, feel body floating, and concentrate on the motion as a pleasant experience. As the patient enters the elevator and feels the elevator moving, this movement is a signal to relax even more.

The operating room is associated with being on the beach. The bright light is related to being in the sun, resting comfortably on the beach. The training in self-hypnosis provides a natural bridge to post-operative care (Spiegel, 1983).

EXAMPLES OF SELF-HYPNOSIS PRACTICE

One 56-year-old woman with chronic pain associated with lupus was seen in the rehabilitation unit of the UNC Memorial Hospital for pain control. She responded well to guided imagery experiences of distraction, refocusing attention, and restructuring of thought to positive perceptual experiences. In a self-hypnotic trance she refocused her attention on the following imagery, which was stimulated by the sounds of springtime in North Carolina, that is, the singing of a bird, the warmth of the sun. The image suddenly came into her awareness:

I look, feel, hear,
I feel the beauty of autumn, the cool fresh air,
I hear the song of the birds,
This is my experience to enjoy.

This brief description can only scratch the surface of the deeply entranced self-hypnotic patient who is caught up and involved in an engaging sensory experience. The words are merely communication symbols translating the powerful experience into a redirection of what she heard, saw, and felt.

Although this image is not one reflecting direct suggestion of hypnoanesthesia, it does reflect the absorption of pleasant, distracting imagery that is very real to the patient.

COMFORT PRACTICE

A 60-year-old woman postoperatively felt frightened and uncomfortable. She was referred for self-hypnosis in order to reduce her discomfort in terms of both pain and suffering. She was able to focus her images on feeling comfort and storing negative thoughts and expectations until the next visit with the therapist. Her self-hypnotic experience was described by these spontaneous experiences of perceptions, feelings, and thoughts:

I feel increasingly comfortable.
I experience pleasant things—how they look, feel, sound, are.
For now, because of time, I put all negative thoughts and ideas in a storage box until a later time, a time that is appropriate.
Now is the time to be more comfortable.
I allow myself to drift, to float without thoughts for a while.
I feel myself in a warm, soothing situation.
A wall of comfort surrounds me.
I can see this wall of comfort, feel it; I am captivated by its colors.

These words are only pale reflections of the patient's inner experience of comfort and pleasure. The inner microcosm is beyond words. The imagery here is the absorbing factor, not the words, which are simply a way to communicate to the hypnotist what the subject experienced.

COGNITIVE PROBLEM SOLVING

Some patients handle pain reduction in a more cognitive manner, focusing on brainstorming, rehearsal in imagery, and self-affirmation. A problem-solving approach can be useful to an individual who may be more cognitively oriented and goal directed. Some patients are simply more in the intellectual or active ego mode and less likely to go deeply into more primary process experience (Toomey & Sanders, 1983).

A young man who was a manager tended to obsess about his recuperation in the hospital following surgery. He responded well to a focus on using his cognitive abilities to reach his goal of achieving pain control and mastering boredom. He described the following imagery:

> I make a list of pleasant ways to occupy my time.
> I engage in each activity, one at a time, in my mind's eye as if I were really doing it.
> I feel the sense of pleasure and accomplishment.

It is precisely the mental engagement that involves the patient. At the moment, the activity seems so very real. The affect of pleasure and accomplishment is synonymous with actual feelings of pleasure and accomplishment. In the deeply hypnotized patient's experience, there is no difference. In the less susceptible patient, high motivation can blur the differences.

OBSTETRICAL USE

The indications for the use of self-hypnosis in obstetrics are to increase relaxation, decrease pain, and diminish capillary blood loss. Self-hypnosis is taught to the patient to practice and to increase an anesthetic effect (August, 1961; Davenport-Slack; 1975; Kroger, 1977; Crasilneck & Hall, 1985).

Another example of teaching self-hypnosis for pain control is:

> You can practice producing anesthesia by yourself at home. It will only take a few minutes each day . . . Seat yourself comfortably . . . Look at a spot on the wall . . . After the trance has been induced she will find that when the allotted time has expired or when her attention is needed elsewhere, she can end the trance voluntarily. The patient who has accomplished this learning is the one who controls the sensation or lack of it. She can induce trance to alleviate discomfort. She learns to accomplish all her new learnings as a post-hypnotic suggestion without the need for a formal hypnotic induction. (Erickson, Hershman, & Sector, 1981, p. 68)

I have worked with the following images with obstetrical patients. The images focus on having a normal delivery, the wisdom of the body, relaxation, and the journey of the baby to meet the patient. The verbalization is presented in the first person as though the patient were describing the image. Ruch (1975) found in his research that inductions and instructions worded in the first person were more effective in leading to self-hypnosis than those worded in the second person. (See the following for an example of this.)

> I am aware that labor is normal. I know that my body knows what to do. I can help most by going to my comfortable place. A contraction is a message from my body that the baby is on its way. I recognize the pleasant sensations of movement, bringing the baby closer. I look forward to seeing my baby. The contraction is a signal for me to go to my comfortable place . . . going deeper.

CONCLUSIONS

Control of pain is a particularly potent use of self-hypnosis. It draws on the creativity and motivation inherent in the patient. In my view, the core of pain control lies in dissociation and amnesia, the separation of sensation, affect, and concept. By such alterations, the patient can master pain and magnify his or her cooperative efforts to become more comfortable. They who believe it is possible can master their pain by using self-hypnosis to reinforce a hypnotherapeutic approach to pain management.

Although it would be interesting to compare different uses of and styles of hypnoanesthesia across the variety of hypnotherapists working with different types of patients, it is not yet possible to determine which techniques are best or most useful. In the clinical situation, the therapist often will use a variety of techniques and, in discussion with the patient, identify those techniques that work best for that patient. If the patient maintains a diary of self-hypnosis experiences, these experiences can be reviewed to determine what experiences are most useful for that patient. When patients are taught hypnoanesthesia it is best to associate the technique with a specific goal or condition that has been diagnosed to insure that the patient does not use hypnoanesthesia inappropriately.

Another area that is lacking in the reviews of hypnoanesthesia is a greater emphasis on the subjective experience of the patient as he or she engages in self-hypnosis to conquer pain. The growing literature on self-hypnosis (Fromm et al., 1981) focuses on the interaction between personality variables such as imagery and structural variables such as absorption in the laboratory. Primarily clinical studies have yet to be done using a similar framework. According to Wain, the clinical application of hypnotic-related phenomena is far ahead of its scientific explication (Wain, 1980, p. 2).

The variety of techniques and ways of explaining self-hypnosis and hypnoanesthesia work are manifold. The need for controlled, comparative studies is ripe. As the body of knowledge emerges clarifying self-hypnosis and how self-hypnosis interacts with clinical goals, clinical orientations, and clinical methodologies, the answers will be found. Until such a time, I believe in the effectiveness of self-hypnosis experience to generate playful activity of self-hypnotic imagery that permits transformation: The patient consoles self, feels support and security, and strengthens his or her ability to comfort and soothe him- or herself. Like the wonder of the reflective mind that can both think and experience, in self-hypnosis the words and images can be interactive. They can be generated as guided imagery from the therapist or from the patient's own unconscious primary process thought, but they are transformed by the unconscious into powerful meanings that do affect him or her. This new mastery over discomfort results in the integration and reintegration of body parts into the totality of the body image. The self-hypnotic experience fits the conceptual description offered by Fromm and Kahn (1990a): The complex interactions among the altered state of consciousness (structural variables), content variables (imagery, both realistic and primary process), and therapeutic goals and orientations (expectancies) generate the unique, powerful responses of the patient. The patient's unconscious choice of words and images leads to transformation of meaning and perception. The patient uses self-hypnosis for stimulation, but he or she also responds to that stimulation, reflecting the double-edged paradox of self-hypnosis that parallels the two sides of conscious awareness: the self as subject and the self as object.

CHAPTER 9

Psychophysiological Disorders

Prevention is better than cure.
—Erasmus, *Adagio*

Because of the close link between mind and body, hypnosis and self-hypnosis are applicable in the total management of psychosomatic problems. Influences of the autonomic nervous system interact with emotional arousal. It is not surprising that a wide range of such psychosomatic problems are influenced by hypnotherapy (Crasilneck & Hall; 1985; Wright, 1960; Collison, 1970; Frankel, 1976). Cannon (1953) described the relationship of bodily changes to specific emotional states such as pain, hunger, fear, and rage.

Clinical reports of hypnosis influencing the parasympathetic nervous system have been cited by Erickson (1943), Wolberg (1948), and Raginsky (1963), among others. Benson (1975) described the positive effects of the relaxation response on physiological functioning. Because of the recognition that psychological factors can contribute to physical problems, a diagnosis code was agreed on and is currently listed in the DSM-III.

This DSM-III diagnosis code 316.00 (Psychological Factors affecting Physical Condition) reflects the important contribution of psychological factors that initiate or worsen a physical condition (APA, 1980). Common examples include but are not limited to obesity, headaches, low back pain, neurodermatitis, asthma, and ulcer. The patient frequently appears nonpsychologically minded and unable to express

157

emotions easily. Some have described such patient's speech as alexithymic (Nemiah, Freyberger, & Sifneos, 1976). When verbal language
is blocked, frequently the therapy needs to address the body language
first and, after the physical symptoms have been reduced, help the
patient to make the translation from body language to talking about
his or her feelings. Self-hypnotic imagery can help to relieve phsyical
symptoms as well as to reinforce the translation of body language into
psychological language.

TEN-STEP APPROACH TO SELF-HYPNOSIS IN PSYCHOSOMATIC DISORDERS

In my practice, I use the following steps in working with psychosomatic disorders. These 10 steps reflect goals that can be realized using
hypnosis and self-hypnosis. Once the history has been taken and diagnosis has been made, the patient can experience heterohypnosis. Training in self-hypnosis and home practice of self-hypnosis can begin after
the first hypnotic session. Since the 10 steps are derived from hypnotic
phenomena, they are compatible with any number of approaches.

1. *Rationale.* The patient learns that he or she can use self-help to
feel more comfortable. Frequently, deep breathing, relaxation, and
imagery can quickly reduce discomfort.

2. *Somatic and comfort imagery techniques.* In hypnosis the patient describes imagery representing relaxation, distraction, and quiet.
The imagery can include specific somatic imagery of body parts,
vacation scenes, or both. Specific somatic imagery of body parts may
or may not be anatomically correct. The important point is that
imagery of a healthy, comfortable organ often leads to feelings of
well-being. Descriptive imagery such as beach scenes, mountain
scenes, and home scenes may be described. Because imagery is idiosyncratic, many other kinds of imagery may be produced. Whatever
the patient finds relaxing, distracting, and quiet is acceptable for
prophylaxis.

3. *Specific relaxation training.* Progressive relaxation as described
by Jacobson (1929) or autogenic training as described by Schultz and
Luthe (1959) may be used. When necessary, relaxation training may be
combined with biofeedback as a way of demonstrating physiological
change (Holroyd et al., 1982). The patient may be reassured by seeing
the tangible effects of relaxation. On the other hand, some patients
may feel even more out of control of their body when made aware of
physiological feedback. The decision is a matter of clinical judgment.

4. *Brain-storming*. The patient can think of alternative ways to feel more comfortable, that is, go on a cruise, take a vacation, succeed as with a skill, or practice self-hypnosis (Sanders, 1976). Having many ideas frequently leads to a creative change.

5. *Pacing*. The patient learns ways to alternate activity with relaxation to prevent tension buildup. The effectiveness of pacing is related to the recognition of body cues, discussed next.

6. *Self-monitoring*. The patient observes physical and emotional responses and tunes in to their causes and their effects as a way to release the tension before it builds. The self-monitoring is formalized by the maintenance of a diary or journal. Such a diary contains a description of the body cue (e.g., rapid heart rate), the time of day it was recorded, and the activity the patient was engaged with at the time. The diary is brought to the hypnotherapy session for processing, which leads to the next step.

7. *Gaining control of physiological processes*. For example, the patient learns to control finger temperature, slow down breathing, and/or reduce blood pressure. This step is enhanced by the use of biofeedback equipment or aids, such as a Biotic™ TM wrist band (Cyborg Corp., Boston: j-42 Feedback Thermometer). The biofeedback is enhanced by self-hypnotic imagery.

8. *Hypnoanesthesia*. The patient learns to numb, to dissociate, to reduce pain when appropriate, that is, after the cause of the pain has been diagnosed and treated.

9. *Cognitive restructuring*. The patient learns to think in a positive, goal-directed way that leads to success rather than frustration. With continuing practice, the person learns to prevent the tension from building, thereby preventing the symptom.

10. *Self-hypnosis home practice*. The patient learns to produce the above phenomena on his or her own during self-hypnosis practice scheduled on a regular basis. The frequency and duration of home practice is related to a wide variety of factors as discussed in Chapter 4.

Thus, the therapist's orientation, the patient's response to self-hypnosis practice, as well as the meaning of the words and images, all contribute to frequency of practice. In addition, the patient may be assigned one long practice session per day, or may use a spaced-trial model where he or she would practice 4 times a day, for 5 minutes at a time. Depending on the patient's response, the time alloted would be increased or decreased. There is no clear evidence that one long session is as effective as spaced, brief sessions. However, patients frequently report using two to three 15-minute sessions per day when practicing at home. Rossi (personal communication, March 1990) has reported some relationship between the ultradian rhythm and the 15 to 30 minutes of drowsiness during the 90-minute cycle. He believes that the 15-to-20 minute trance may be the most effective since it can be matched with the natural ultradian rhythm, particularly in the practice of self-hypnosis. If this hypothesis is confirmed, the use of self-hypnosis will be maximized since the patient can learn to tap into the natural ultradian rhythm.

As the patient learns to control the physiological response, he or she may now be able to look at the psychological factors contributing to the problem, for example, perfectionism, dependency, anger—the personality dynamics. This stage of therapy is more dynamically oriented. As the patient becomes more able to talk about his or her problems and less alexithymic, this transformation is natural. According to Blumenthal (1963), the personality dynamics are important in the treatment of patients with psychosomatic disorders.

GENERAL SELF-SUGGESTIONS

Self-suggestions in psychosomatic disorder may be general (geared at general feelings of relaxation and well-being) as well as specific, that is, directed at a specific type of phenomenon, such as numbness in the hand.

The following verbalization is an example of general self-suggestions for positive response to medical management. Hospitalized patients can be trained to restructure their thinking about discomfort. The example is adapted from Crasilneck and Hall (1985).

> I can experience a minimum of discomfort. I can be relaxed, at ease, with a feeling of well-being—sleeping when I desire and reinforcing the suggestions for comfort. I can eat well and enjoy food. I can rest well, secure in the knowledge that my unconscious mind will allow me to be free of tension and any physical or psychological discomfort. My body can respond maximally to any medical treatment that is presented. I can take care of myself best by relaxing and helping myself to feel more comfortable. At the same time, I can create a receptive healing environment to help myself to further the treatment. (p. 431)

While diverse interpretations may be made, one way of viewing these suggestions is through the window of implication: Essentially, the patient focuses on the natural relaxed and positive experience of engaging in normal and natural healing functions and participating as an active member of the treatment team. Of course, there are a diversity of alternative ways to describe the process. There is no one best way. Rather, the combined factors of patient characteristics, therapist characteristics, and contextual characteristics all interact to consolidate the patient's response to self-hypnosis.

SPECIFIC CASE EXAMPLES

This section describes the use of self-hypnosis with a variety of disorders including asthma, peptic ulcer, migraine headache, neurodermatitis, burns, hypertension, compulsive eating, anorexia nervosa, and bulimia.

Asthma

Asthma is a common psychophysiological respiratory disorder in which a variety of factors interact leading to the narrowing of the air passageways. Emotional factors can trigger an attack or exacerbate one. Anxiety heightens breathing difficulty. Self-hypnosis can be useful both prophylactically and for reducing the intensity of an attack (Collison, 1975; Maher-Loughnan, 1980; Maganet, 1960).

Jay was a 30-year-old professional male with asthma. He frequently had to go to the emergency room at a local hospital for shots to control his breathing. He was referred for hypnotherapy and proved to be a very motivated subject. Initially, he practiced deep breathing and physical relaxation. He found that the emergency room visits were decreasing. Also he found that the asthmatic wheezing would start when he was impatient, such as waiting in the checkout line at the supermarket. He began to incorporate in his home self-hypnosis practice the image of stopping time or taking time out so as to reduce his tension at having to wait. The image of controlling time was a powerful one. He found that he no longer wheezed in these situations. In self-hypnosis, he imaged his lungs. He described and experienced the narrow bronchial tubes and squeezed-in lungs while wheezing. He imaged and felt the bronchial tubes expanding as he started deep breathing and found that the wheezing stopped and his ease of breathing had returned. This image was experienced at several levels: at the cognitive level, at the level of tension reduction, and at the respiratory level. He felt more in control and more self-confident.

As we progressed, he began to brainstorm about which situations seemed to trigger wheezing. He found driving in heavy traffic, situations in which he was evaluated, and situations where people disagreed with him all tended to trigger wheezing. For each situation, he brainstormed about a specific corrective image where he felt in control. Brainstorming involves broadening conscious awareness and tapping into the unconscious for creative solutions. He spontaneously imaged the following during self-hypnosis practice twice a day: being in his den in the recliner; being in control of driving his car; opening his lungs.

He learned to pace himself, alternating activity with relaxation to prevent tension buildup. Continuously, he used self-monitoring to keep attuned to physical and emotional responses so that he could release the tension before it built.

Soon, deep breathing and finger warming alone allowed him to maintain control of his breathing. He experienced a sense of physical control. With increased control, he became more aware of triggers that set him off, especially impatience and anger. He learned to accept these feelings rather than to fight them within himself. He recognized a feeling as a communication about himself.

His self-hypnosis practice had become a part of his everyday life. The imagery, both somatic and relaxing, was prophylactic in that tension was prevented from building and fewer asthmatic attacks were triggered from emotional reactions. The self-hypnosis practice contributed to the improvement in his quality of life.

In this example, the patient progressed from an ego-passive state where he became flooded with panic to an ego-active one as he became more in control of his breathing, where he was able to reduce tension rather than to let it build. In self-hypnosis, he experienced relaxation and an opening of the bronchial tubes. He was transformed to a person more comfortable with outside frustrations as well as more receptive to his own needs.

Peptic Ulcer

An ulcer consists of an open sore in the wall of the stomach or of the duodenum. It is produced by abnormally high levels of gastric activity. In certain vulnerable individuals, the excess acid eats into the wall of the stomach, resulting in an ulcer. One explanation why gastric oversecretion occurs is based on stress (Wolf & Wolff, 1947). Self-hypnosis can be useful in management of stress (Ikemi et al., 1959). Fostering relaxation and quiet, reducing conflict, and reducing gastric secretion through accessing of the autonomic nervous system are possible images.

Wright and Wright (1989, p. 70) described a patient with a peptic ulcer who, in self-hypnosis, was asked "Do you think that you might check your remedies kit to see if you have anything that might help?"

The patient responded: "I have this large tube filled with white jelly, and it has a device like a grease gun that I can use to put it right into the center of the working mass"(Wright & Wright, 1989, p. 70).

The imagery provided a particularly relevant solution for this particular patient. The storehouse of knowledge and experience known as the unconscious contains a treasure chest just waiting to be tapped. In this example, the patient described an image, a grease gun, that provided immediate soothing relief to a specific area. It seemed to generate a quiet, soothing physiological state within while decreasing the burning sensation of excess acid. I believe that the unconscious contains all of the rich experiences and learnings necessary to facilitate a healing process in addition to empowering drives and instincts. It is the seat of our creative potential.

Migraine Headache

Painful, intractable migraine headaches of vascular origin are a common psychosomatic problem. Self-hypnosis can be an useful adjunct to treatment by alerting the patient to early cues of the possible onset of a migraine such as the aura. Self-hypnosis can be used prophylactically to prevent tension buildup. In conjunction with the 10-step approach described earlier, self-hypnosis can be an effective deterrent. Many researchers have found hypnosis and self-hypnosis to be an aid in reducing migraines (Andreychuk & Skriver, 1975; Graham, 1975; Ansel, 1977; Stambaugh & House, 1977; Daniels, 1975, 1976a). Generally, self-control techniques, whether they consist of self-hypnosis, meditation, or relaxation have all been found useful (Daniels, 1976b; Shapiro, 1982, 1984). According to Olness, the pain of migraine and other kinds of pain can be reduced and even eliminated by self-hypnosis exercises. Because different types of exercises are available, and not every exercise works with every patient, she presents several choices. As she does so, she points out that the body makes its own natural painkiller. She suggests that controlling pain is possible because the brain understands the pain signals in a new and different way (Olness & Gardner, 1988, p. 63).

The evidence has not been conclusive that a particular neurochemical process is operative in hypnosis generally or in hypnotic analgesia particularly (Sternbach, 1982). In a study to determine if atropine would disrupt hypnotic analgesia, for example, Sternbach found only a nonsignificant tendency for atropine to interfere with hypnotic analgesia in the most hypnotizable group. He wondered whether hypnotic analgesia shares the same general underlying mechanism as other trance phenomenena rather than activating a specific analgesic system. More research is necessary. In addition, the evidence has not been conclusive that one method is better than another.

Images revealed by pain patients run the gamut of creative imagery possibilities. Whereas some imagery may be very cognitive, other imagery might be quite fantastic. Still others appear to be of a metaphoric quality of the pain, such as a tight rubber band that becomes loose, a normalizing of the size of the blood vessels, a tight vice around the head that is loosened. The possibilities are limited only by the creativity of the patient. The images are spontaneous, and they emerge effortlessly from the unconscious to the patient's awareness. This description matches the concept of ego-receptivity (Fromm, 1977).

Neurodermatitis

Dermatological disorders reflect a connection between emotional factors and the skin (Kroger, 1977; Gardner & Olness, 1981; Barber, 1978; Medansky & Handler, 1981). Imagery related to warming and cooling seem particularly effective with dermatological disorders (Maher-Loughnan, 1980). Tebecos and Provins (1976) conducted studies clarifying physiological concomitants of hypnosis such as changes in skin temperature, heart rate, and skin resistance.

In my practice, I saw a woman who had developed a rash on her back and shoulders. She had been to a number of dermatologists, but nothing seemed to help. Yet use of imagery depicting walking into a cool pool of water dramatically reduced the rash. The patient practiced self-hypnosis, relishing the coolness she felt and relaxing in the quiet, peaceful experience. After she had mastered the rash, she went on to understand the interaction of complicated factors that contributed to the problem: menopause, anger at her husband who kept irregular hours, and a low frustration tolerance. The imagery and mental experience of cool water and cool skin were particularly potent for symptom relief. She felt cooler, she looked cooler, she was cooler. In addition, the dynamic understanding contributed to maintenance of improvement.

Burns

Burn victims present special problems in medical management. They are in pain. They have poor appetites and have nourishment problems. Frequently, they withdraw psychologically and resist treatment. Self-hypnosis can be a particularly helpful accompaniment to treatment

(Crasilneck et al., 1956; Wakeman & Kaplan, 1978; Burrows, Collison, & Dennerstein, 1979; Ewin, 1978, 1980).

Dabney Ewin teaches his burn patients self-hypnosis:

> What do you think will make a great deal of difference in your healing? Have you ever seen a person blush? Well, you know that nothing has happened except a thought, an idea, and all the little blood vessels in the face have opened up and turned red or clamped down and blanched. What you think is going to affect the blood supply to your skin and that affects healing, and you can start right now. Now let your inner mind lock in on that sensation of being cool and comfortable, and you can keep it that way during your entire stay in the hospital. You can enjoy going to your laugh place as often as you like, and you'll be able to ignore all of the bothersome things we may have to do today and anything negative that is said. (Ewin, 1980, pp. 269–275)

After such instruction in imagery and physiology, the patient can use this imagery as a way of being cool and comfortable. With such training, the motivated patient has the potential to remain more comfortable during even the most uncomfortable procedures.

Hypertension

The use of self-hypnosis in producing relaxation and concomitant lowering of blood pressure has been sparsely reported (Case, Fogel, & Pollack, 1980; Friedman & Taub, 1977; Stratton, 1979; Crasilneck & Hall, 1960). Although possible images are unlimited, specific imagery of a comfortable place and pleasant relaxing imagery in a stress-free environment can be useful. Metaphoric images described by some patients include imagery of blood vessels normalizing in size by widening or narrowing. Picturing a thermostat set at the perfect temperature, neither too high nor too low, can be helpful. Such images among a multitude of possibilities can provide metaphoric imagery for blood pressure change. The production of images is limited only by the creativity of the patient.

Melissa was referred for hypnotherapy by her internist because of hypertension. She described herself as being uptight and not knowing how to relax. In fact, she believed that by relaxing she would be brought closer to the inevitable heart attack that killed her father. She was able to create an image of healthy, active relaxation that insured her well-being. Her self-hypnosis practice transformed her physical perception from uptight to flexibly energetic. Subsequent blood pressure readings normalized.

Friedman and Taub (1977), in their comparative study, instructed subjects that their "only task was to sit quietly and comfortably relax as much as possible while blood pressure measurements were taken several times. They were also told to pay special attention to the last number lit on the diastolic pressure machine and to try to make the number lower and lower" (p. 336). They might or might not know how they do it, but to just keep trying. Their instructions for self-hypnosis were "Place yourself in a relaxed position and put yourself into hypnosis twice a day for a 3-minute period each time" (p. 336). They found that over time the self-hypnosis group had the best results. Generally, studies demostrate that hypnosis, meditation, and self-hypnosis can all be effective (Barabasz & McGeorge, 1978; Benson, 1975; Crasilneck & Hall, 1960; Deabler et al., 1973; Holroyd et al., 1982).

Compulsive Eating

Interest in weight control has grown because of our society's focus on health and recognition of the high risk factors in health caused by obesity, which in the past had been viewed as a single-symptom problem but is now viewed as a way of life. Across weight control programs, be their orientation behavior modification, self-help, or self-hypnosis, it is clear that in the short term, people can lose weight. Rather, problems lie in long-term maintenance. The following self-hypnosis treatment approach is based on cognitive problem-solving techniques that begin with the therapist but are continued by the patient. This approach focuses on the positive motivation of the person and essentially allows him or her to self-monitor, problem-solve, and substitute healthy eating behaviors for unhealthy ones. Self-hypnosis provides the opportunity for the person to perceive him- or herself, food, and eating behaviors in a new light (Sanders, 1986a). After experiencing heterohypnosis, the patient is instructed in self-hypnosis and asked to practice self-hypnosis before meals and at bedtime. As the patient masters self-hypnosis, self-hypnotic techniques are practiced whenever he or she is tempted to eat.

The self-hypnosis instructions are presented in the following script to be imaged in self-hypnosis practice. They are worded in the first person to encourage the patient to think in terms of him- or herself (Ruch, 1975):

> I sit down, close my eyes, and become comfortable. After five deep breaths, I relax.

I focus my attention on reasons for wanting to become more in control of my eating behavior. I see a list of reasons why I wish to become more in control.

I repeat (out loud) each reason for wanting to become more in control. I want to become a normal eating person because I will feel better. I want to become more in control because I will look better. I want to become more in control because I will have more energy.

Now I see myself looking in a mirror and seeing myself the way I want to look and the way I want to feel after I have become the boss of my eating. I repeat to myself how I look and how I feel.

I focus on the feelings I have about myself as I imagine myself more in control, looking better, feeling healthier. I repeat to myself all the good feelings and expectations I have about becoming more in control.

I can dream about becoming more in control.

I can elaborate and reward any good feelings obtained or revealed in the dream.

What can I do about preventing any problem from interfering with my goal? I can think now of possible solutions to difficulties in following a healthy eating program or remaining in control.

I can practice self-hypnosis as often as I wish, as often as is necessary. I can practice before meals and even between meals. Each day I become stronger and more motivated.

Whenever I am tempted to eat or am worried about being able to remain in control, I can relax in this way and remind myself of my reasons for wanting to be in charge and my resolve to eat normally. In this way I will be able to avoid food temptation.

I can now take three deep breaths and open my eyes to the here and now. (Sanders, 1986a, pp. 35–40)

The imagery accompanying these words varies with the patient, the problem, the motivation, and the interaction with the therapist. Nonetheless, the patient in self-hypnosis can imagine him- or herself engaging in a new way of life—a healthy way in which he or she relaxes and exercises and is good to him- or herself. The patient becomes more motivated in the self-hypnotic imagery to carry out a plan in real life.

In contrast, Kroger describes a threefold approach to weight control: (1) take in fewer calories; (2) take medication to get you started; (3) pursue self-hypnosis—the degree of success will be in direct proportion to the amount of effort you put forth in practice. "If you really wish to lose weight, you will roll the food from the front of the tongue to the back of the tongue and from side to side. Think thin. Think of the most horrible, nauseating and repugnant smell . . ." (Kroger, 1977, p. 284). The negative image serves as a noxious stimulus. It interrupts the habitual thoughts and behaviors associated with eating. Following such an interruption, new learning is possible. New learning is maximized through the power of self-hypnotic suggestions and images.

Many therapists describe programs for weight loss in which hypnotherapy can help in treating obesity (Cohen, 1979; Spiegel & Spiegel, 1978; Kroger, 1977; Crasilneck & Hall 1985; Stanton 1975). Ringrose (1979) found that 85% of his subjects lost notable amounts of weight. Mott and Roberts (1979) criticize the anecdotal nature of reports and absence of long-term follow-up. Wadden and Flaxman have found that hypnosis is not effective for long-term change in eating habits (Wadden & Flaxman, 1981). It is important to note that these studies were carried out primarily in heterohypnotic programs. If self-hypnosis were in fact a part of that program, the results from each were not differentiated.

Anorexia Nervosa

The patient with an eating disorder experiences a fear of getting fat. In addition, the patient exhibits a distorted body image and persistently strives to become ever thinner, eating less and exercising more. The patient may purge, abuse laxatives or diuretics, and overdo exercise to achieve the goal of becoming even thinner.

How Self-Hypnosis May Apply

Self-hypnosis exercises create a quiet, comfortable space in which the patient learns to use self-suggestion in a positive way. Reducing tension by progressive relaxation, the patient begins to understand the necessity of healthy food intake to provide energy, much like the ebb and flow of water in the ocean or the cash flow in a checking account that requires regular deposits in order to cover the checks that are written.

In addition, the patient learns to focus on personal power rather than on size and body proportions. Being strong requires healthy food intake. The patient uses imagery of kinesthetic power to permit reasonable food intake.[1] Gradually, the patient revises her self-image.

Case Example

The patient, Sue, is a 13-year-old intellectually gifted white female brought to psychotherapy because of food abstention. Her weight was

[1]By kinesthetic power I mean feelings of well-being.

72 pounds, her height 5 feet. The pediatrician and I agreed that if she lost 2 more pounds she would have to be hospitalized.

Initially, the patient refused to talk, demonstrating a decided lack of trust. Gradually becoming interested in knowing what I thought about her difficulty eating, she began to ask questions. In treatment, Sue initially abstained from talking, but as we continued to meet, it was possible to communicate to her through metaphors that elicited her curiosity.

The abstaining anorexic, that is, the patient who refuses to eat, may be enacting self-directed behavior aimed at blocking out normal body cues of hunger as well as altering body perception. Food refusal and altered body perception may be viewed as an indication of high interval locus of control, and both are consistent with self-direction characteristic of self-hypnotic suggestion. The patient's goal was to separate herself from her parents and enable herself to act independently and autonomously by refusing food. In school, before lunch, for example, she would tell herself that she would only eat half her lunch. She would repeat this suggestion many times until lunchtime at which point she ate a quarter of her lunch.

Hypnotic Techniques

Physical Metaphor. Initially Sue wanted to talk about not eating. The topic was accepted but reframed within a physical metaphor: "The stomach thermostat." I explained that "her stomach thermostat" was not working and that was why she was not hungry and not eating. She became interested in how this thermostat worked and what would make it work. I explained that in order for it to work she had to eat enough healthy food to increase her weight by 10 additional pounds.

Description of Self-Suggestion. Sue related that it had been difficult to lose weight at first, but she had learned that if she told herself while at school "I will eat only half of my cheese sandwich, I will eat only half of my cheese sandwich," by lunch time she only felt like eating one-fourth of it. She soon found that she was no longer hungry. Now her greatest fear was that if she ever really started to eat again, she would become too heavy. As therapy continued, her more positive self-directed suggestions included healthy choice and decision making. In addition, as she reached a more normal weight, she began to eat a broader range of foods.

Metaphor of Food as Energy. I explained that her stomach needed energy, just as the motor of a car needed gasoline to make it run. She could remain in control of what she ate by eating different things. We developed the following rules: (1) eat to be satisfied; (2) no gooey chocolate cake; (3) no snacks; (4) three regular meals a day; (5) experiment with new foods. It was important for Sue to have some prohibition over food. Prohibiting gooey chocolate cake and snacks appealed to her. It balanced out the requirement to eat three regular meals a day.

Mirroring. I mirrored her fears and reinforced her ability to follow the rules we developed. I told her that she was very bright, and even if she were frightened, she could make her own decisions. Because the rules were general, Sue was able to be the judge as to how to carry these rules out so that her needs to be in control and self-directive were affirmed.

Reframing Weight Gain. We talked about the need for the body to be at a normal enough weight to allow the stomach thermostat to operate, so that she would not have to worry about her weight. She began to believe that she could look attractive and slim at 98 pounds. Sue began to eat more balanced meals, reached 98 pounds, and has continued to do well. At this point, the therapy became more insight-oriented, as Sue was now able to talk about her feelings and was able to accept interpretations and insights. That is, she became more ego-receptive.

According to Pettinatti, anorexics are less susceptible to hypnosis than bulimics (Pettinatti & Wade, 1986). This patient was unable to use heterohypnosis but was found to use spontaneous self-hypnosis. As treatment progressed, she was able to incorporate helpful images discussed in the session into her spontaneous self-hypnotic experiences. She began to experience more control over these experiences.

Bulimia

The bulimic patient engages in binge eating and purging. During times of high stress, the binges may occur several times a day. At other times, they may be intermittent. The patient is aware that the binges are unnatural because of the amount eaten and the feeling of being out of control. During the binges, the patient is totally absorbed in the binge, but afterwards she feels considerable guilt and follows by purging or using laxatives. Frequently, the patient plans for the binge and almost as a ritual goes to the store or supermarket to buy sweets, carbohydrates, and unhealthy foods to be eaten in secret.

The use of self-hypnosis monitored by the therapist provides the general effect of creating a quiet healing environment. The patient may learn to prevent a binge by using the first thought about planning a binge as a cue to self-relaxation. The patient can then use self-suggestion to divert her attention away from food and onto some activity that would be incompatible with eating, such as taking a walk or cleaning a closet.

The patient can learn to use problem-solving techniques to find alternative solutions to stress rather than bingeing (Sanders, 1976, 1978). By practicing the experience of being in control, the patient experiences success. In addition, the patient learns various cognitive strategies to reinforce the experience of being and remaining in control.

Furthermore, the patient begins to view herself differently, to develop a more positive self-image through self-hypnotic imagery. Initially, the therapist may provide a neutral image for the patient to use during self-hypnosis practice, such as seeing herself succeed at relaxing all the muscles in the body. As treatment progresses, the patient may initiate her own neutral or positive imagery that will reinforce a more positive self-image, for instance, enjoying her friends.

Finally, the patient learns self-control through ego-building exercises (Waxman, 1989) such as telling herself that each and every day that she practices relaxation, her self-confidence will increase. She will find herself bingeing less and engaging more in productive activity. Each and every day, she will feel more in control of how she looks, how she feels, and what she eats. As she selects healthy foods and eats these foods in realistic amounts, she will feel physically stronger, more powerful, and more in control.

Self-initiated hypnotic dreams help the patient discover inner motivations, inner strengths, and creative ways to live healthier, happier, and in greater control (Schneck, 1953; Sacerdote, 1967; Sanders, 1982). Hypnoprojective techniques such as the pendulum can be used to gain insight.

As Cindy, a bulimic patient of mine, succeeded in distracting herself, she began to feel better about herself. In effect, she felt more in control. She liked herself better. With increasing success in controlling and preventing binges, Cindy began to work on the conflicts she had about growing up, becoming more independent, and knowing herself more completely. Using spontaneous imagery in the session, Cindy could experience herself as she wished to be: calm, cool, and collected. She was able to see herself sometime in the future when she had overcome the problem (age progression). She was able to use hypnotic dreams as a barometer of change and as a measure of unconscious involvement.

Home self-hypnosis practice involved entering a comfortable hypnotic state and practicing imagery related to change as well as verbal and feeling-oriented ego-building exercises:

"*I can increase my control by taking a long, slow, deep breath.*" This ego-building exercise builds confidence and positive self-esteem by stimulating the patient to be in control. When the self-control is recognized or actualized, the patient has a sense of strength.

"*I can each day feel more confident in my ability to remain in control.*" This exercise focuses on continuity of the experience. Thus, the patient realizes his or her ability to remain in control not only today but tomorrow and for however long is necessary.

"*Each and every day I feel stronger and more able to move toward my goal.*" This exercise focuses on the titration of strength, building in density each and every day.

"*Every day I am more aware of my personal power to eat in a healthy and comfortable way.*" The patient has learned the benefits of self-monitoring and how it can reinforce new behaviors.

"*I know how to become comfortable and relaxed.*" The patient may experience awe at the soothing experience of helping him- or herself to relax. Something as simple as deep breaths, letting tension go, and imagery involvement can make him or her feel so good.

Imagery of being in control of emotion and behavior is regularly experienced. Many patients are fearful of losing control of emotions. Learning how to feel emotion without being overwhelmed is a long-term process. This moderating task is complicated because the patient may feel that it is "bad to have emotions" or else feel that it is a sign of personal weakness. Each new question or myth has to be addressed. By clarifying to Cindy that she had the right to choose, she was able to contain her anxiety. She then imagined herself becoming more open with her friends, going out more, and feeling more relaxed. At this point in therapy, her weight was normal, her binges were under control, and she was engaging more in social relationships.

Because bulimics are more susceptible to heterohypnosis, more direct use of imagery could be assigned for home practice. Among others who have used hypnosis and self-hypnosis in the treatment of bulimics are Gross (1983a, 1986) and Thakur and Thakur (1984).

Neurological Disorders

Neurological impairments limit the patient's ability to communicate and to attend. Although a variety of single-case studies are presented in the literature, the degree of effectiveness over the condition is difficult to evaluate, as these are not controlled studies of self-hypnosis in neurological dysfunction (Chappell, 1964; Crasilneck & Hall, 1970; Wright, 1960; Brunn, 1966; Dorcus, 1956).

Generally, hypnosis in neurological deficit is clinically useful to help the patient to relax physically, increase span of attention, reduce anxiety, increase motivation, decrease pain perception, and enhance self-control and self-mastery. All of these goals contribute to the patient's ability to participate actively in control of sensation and in rehabilitation. Rehabilitation, according to Kroger (1977), is a relearning process that involves intellectual and emotional as well as neurological difficulties. Passive and active resistive exercises may be accelerated and enhance improvement of motor power, especially if directed toward more optimistic attitudes toward the self and the physical impairment.

Pain in many neurological conditions is variable and often chronic. The goal is to help the patient to cope. A multidimensional approach is indicated, including biofeedback, counseling, training, physical therapy or activities program, and medication (Brunn, 1966).

Spasticity results from a progressive deterioration affecting the central nervous system (Chappell, 1964). When severe, it seriously interferes with mobility. In addition, it decreases motivation. Finally, it interferes with rehabilitation. Initial training in heterohypnosis and reinforcement by home practice of self-hypnosis increase the patient's sense of self-mastery in rehabilitation therapy.

Seizures are an important diagnostic indicator. Some patients experience both true seizures and pseudoseizures. The degree of secondary gain may in fact increase the number, frequency, and duration of seizures. Stress factors also lower the seizure threshold.

According to Kroger (1977), direct hypnosis may help cerebral palsied patients develop more complex and useful patterns of movement, particularly those patients whose performance is significantly below expected and in whom emotional factors are prominent. He describes a patient who was remotivated to use muscles that were atrophying because of disuse:

A 34-year-old female had a marked weakness in both gastrocnemii muscles due to poliomyelitis during girlhood. In physical therapy, she showed some improvement but seemed to reach a plateau. Under hypnosis, she was told that she could relive all the athletic activities in which she had participated prior to the onset of her symptoms. She used sensory imagery conditioning, together with daily resistance exercises, under autohypnosis. Within 10 weeks she was able to stand on the toes of the right leg alone, something she had been unable to do prior to hypnotherapy. (p. 261)

Crasilneck and Hall (1985) describe hypnotherapy for severe cerebral deficits. In 21 of 25 patients, a marked reversal in psychological attitudes and physiological functioning occurred. Nonetheless, these results occurred slowly over an extended period of time.

I consulted with a 55-year-old woman in chronic pain from migraines, who was paralyzed on her right side. She was referred for hypnotherapy to control the pain and to increase her motivation for physical therapy. She was well able to concentrate and to enter a medium trance. In hypnosis she was asked to describe a book that she had read and enjoyed. She described *Wuthering Heights*. She was then asked to describe the sensations she experiences in her right hand and arm. She described feeling that the right hand and arm were out of control and moved in a strange, jerking manner. I asked her to imagine she was holding a heavy rubber ball in her right hand and to lift the hand and arm slowly with the heavy ball. Her arm moved in a more natural and controlled manner. This experience so moved her that she agreed to participate in physical therapy. She was given the posthypnotic suggestion that she could relax and feel more comfortable, and was told to practice holding the ball and moving her hand and arm upward very slowly four times a day. In addition, the nurses were asked to remark to the patient that she looked more comfortable and to fluff her pillow and spend some time reading to her. After just 1 day of practice, the nursing staff reported that the patient really was a very nice woman who no longer seemed irritable or depressed, who was motivated to feel more comfortable without narcotic medication, and who now looked forward to vocational rehabilitation.

Although hypnosis does not regenerate neural tissue, it appears to enhance motivation, psychological coping, and comfort. The reciprocal action of mind and body is self-evident in the unique and powerful words and images experienced by the patient. The use of self-hypnosis facilitates the creation of words and images.

Cancer

Obviously hypnosis does not attempt to treat terminally ill patients; however, it can reduce stress related to the illness and can help the patient to cope with the illness, thus improving the quality of life (Kaye, 1987). By reducing anxiety and providing a tool with which to reduce pain perception, the patient can lead a richer, fuller life during the time remaining (Gardner, 1976; Gardner & Olness, 1981; Zeltzer & LeBaron, 1986).

Acquired Immune Deficiency Syndrome (AIDS)

Although I have not seen any published studies of hypnosis and self-hypnosis in the treatment of AIDS patients, self-hypnosis may be used with these patients as with cancer patients and other terminally ill patients to improve the quality of life, and to reduce pain perception and anxiety. The physiological benefits of relaxation, the soothing quality of hypnoanesthesia, and the ability of the patient to dissociate in a helpful manner are all essential in improving the quality of life for a terminally ill patient. Also, the patient can work through feelings of grief and helplessness so that he or she can enjoy the time remaining.

Phil was a 35-year-old AIDS patient. He had been suffering significant illness for 9 months. Currently, he was fearful that he would lose his eyesight because of an eye infection. He was very frightened of what was happening to him and knew that he did not have long to live. He used hypnosis and self-hypnosis to reduce high levels of anxiety and to reduce pain. Nonetheless, Phil developed a severe respiratory infection, was hospitalized, and died within 4 months. He frequently used the self-hypnosis during this difficult time.

COMPLIANCE

Generally, clinical reports of self-hypnosis associated with the treatment of psychosomatic disorders have been favorable. Obviously, it is too soon to compare methods, techniques, and disorders. However, it is important to discuss those patients who have difficulty in complying with self-hypnosis.

Some patients have difficulty focusing on positive imagery. They seem caught in a spiral of negative imagery and failure. This response may result from resistance of the patient to regaining health. It is important to clarify what if any secondary gains contribute to the illness.

Other patients may have difficulty because they are self-destructive. They may feel that they deserve poor health or punishment. It is important to clarify the relative weight of guilt and masochistic gratification. Still others may use the defense mechanism of denial and fail to perceive the self-destructive consequences of their thinking. Some patients may fear that they cannot meet practice expectations. It is important to set realistic goals. To help the patient to promote helpful imagery, encourge him or her to describe neutral or nonaffective perceptions and experiences.

Some patients may not be suitable candidates for self-hypnosis treatment. They may have little affinity for it, lack susceptibility, or have too vulnerable ego boundaries to use it in a helpful manner.

The interactions among context, illness, goals, and subject variables are quite complex and have not yet been studied. However, in the practical, clinical situation, the use of self-hypnosis by the patient dramatically contributes to transformations of selected perceptions, affects, and a sense of self-control that facilitates the healing process. The word as experienced and the image as perceived have the power of intention.

CONCLUSIONS

Self-hypnosis can be an useful adjunct to the ongoing treatment of patients with a variety of physical, emotional, and psychophysiological disorders. Particularly, it is helpful in reducing anxiety and pain and in increasing comfort and motivation. It is important to monitor the patient's use of self-hypnosis in order to maintain realistic goals that can be realized. The teaching of self-hypnosis does not provide a clearly predictable outcome, as the patient may be able to integrate and transform his or her own response to the teaching. What is learned is generally more than what is taught; that is, the patient's response to self-hypnosis, being a complicated interaction among numerous factors, leads to a remarkable, frequently dramatic, and meaningful conclusion. As research further clarifies these interactions and the body of knowledge expands, the heightened imagery generated in self-hypnosis will provide grist for the mill of transformation of meaning and experience that can enhance and foster improvement in quality of life and foster self-control of pain and anxiety. The verbalization of helpful suggestions can serve to reinforce newly learned behaviors and to focus attention on positive self-help techniques. Finally, the words and images generated in self-hypnosis can reflect the basis of a new self-integration.

CHAPTER 10

Children, Psychotherapy, and Hypnosis: A Therapeutic Triad

What wound did ever heal but by degrees?
—Shakespeare, *Othello* (II, 5)

This chapter describes examples of self-hypnosis with children. The play therapy situation provides a naturalistic environment that enables the child to use hypnosis as a form of play to control physical reactions such as tension, psychological reactions such as anxiety, and hypnotic behaviors such as dissociation. As a form of play, self-hypnosis reinforces the psychotherapy that enables the child to improve, by degrees, via daily practice. The combination of children, psychotherapy, and hypnosis comprises a therapeutic triad. Erickson (1958b; as well as Olness & Gardner, 1988; Kohen, 1987; LaBaw, 1975; LaBaw et al., 1975) reported that self-hypnosis in the psychological treatment of children is a useful adjunct to other forms of treatment.

PLAY THERAPY

Play therapy is defined as a bridge to hypnosis. Play therapy for the child permits the expression of feelings. In addition, the absorption in play during the psychotherapy hour leads to spontaneous alterations of consciousness. Consciousness, as I am using the term, is a tool, a coping mechanism for dealing with agreed upon reality. In the child's world, agreed upon reality is a mystery that he or she is just learning, but the world of make believe or pretend is less mysterious to the child because it is more under his or her control. In this pretend world, the child studies, practices, and becomes for the moment a king, a doctor, or a parent. The child expresses through action, metaphor, and play experience ways of being and feeling in the world.

The major tool in the psychotherapy of children is play. The child selects toys and becomes involved in the drama of play and hypnotic experience; his or her life space at that moment reflects the child's life, feelings, situations, and characteristic ways of responding to life.

The hypnotherapist serves a specific role leading to an integration of permissiveness and directedness. The therapist is a guide, a helper, a parent figure who models, instructs, sets limits, compromises, and provides feedback and choices. Although the therapist may present interesting imagery rewards that the child can assimilate or fit in with prior experience, he or she also is receptive to the child's unique, curious, and idiosyncratic imagery that can be used as a source for new learning.

INDICATIONS FOR HYPNOTHERAPY

Self-hypnosis is useful for many problems both recent and of long duration. It is particularly helpful when discomfort is experienced repeatedly or when undesirable habits need to be changed. Specific goals include ego support, symptom amelioration, and uncovering (Olness & Gardner, 1988; Hilgard & LeBaron, 1982).

Just as with adults, hypnosis and self-hypnosis should be used for a specific goal agreed upon by the therapist and the patient. Similar to other forms of therapy, successful outcomes are achieved when the child is motivated, the problem is treatable by hypnosis, and the child responds to hypnotic induction.

In addition, it is important to meet with both child and parents in order to clearly define a therapeutic contract in which the child participates and in which the parents are involved. Hypnosis appears to provide a method by which both parents and child can participate to control painful and debilitating symptoms such as vomiting and pain during the terminal phase of illness. A contract or consensual agreement permits the child freedom to explore hypnosis. The child needs to feel the unity of purpose shared by therapist and parents.

CONTRAINDICATIONS

Self-hypnosis is not indicated when the use of an altered state could lead to physical danger such as the risk of peritonitis when appendicitis is ignored. The origin of the problem always requires a differential diagnosis.

Self-hypnosis is not indicated when using it could aggravate emotional problems, such as deprivation when strong secondary rewards are denied. For example, if losing weight leads to less attention from the family, the child may become quite depressed.

Self-hypnosis is not indicated if the problem can be more effectively treated by some other modality.

GUIDELINES

After diagnosis, the pediatric hypnotherapist follows many of the same guidelines as the adult hypnotherapist. Initially, it is important for the therapist to establish rapport and to determine the child's interests. The specific interests and activities that the child enjoys provide the common ground from which to introduce hypnosis and self-hypnosis. Discussing the child's interests maximizes rapport (Gardner, 1981; Olness, 1977; Olness & Gardner, 1988).

As treatment progresses, the pediatric hypnotherapist validates the child's experience by using the child's own words and responses. Such mirroring of words and responses maximizes communication. He or she maintains the child's experience as continuous; that is, he or she provides sustained and continued input to the child and provides concrete suggestions on which to build the child's confidence. He or she provides immediate rewards and praise to the child. Such feedback contributes to confidence and maintenance of the experience. The child's self-esteem builds as his or her efforts are recognized and his or her experiences are validated.

INDUCTIONS

The first step in teaching self-hypnosis is to provide a positive heterohypnotic induction. Hypnotic inductions for children, as with adults, require that the level of communication be appropriate to the child. Because hypnotic inductions can be given kinesthetically as well as verbally, it is possible to use a continuum of inductions appropriate for that child's level of understanding.

Early verbal inductions involve simple storytelling, such as describing a favorite activity, and pretending to be a teddy bear. These inductions work for children aged 2 to 4 years. Preschool inductions involve pretending to be at a favorite place or with a favorite pet, or sitting under a mighty oak tree and finger lowering. These imaginal inductions work for children aged 4 to 6. Latency-age inductions involve cloud gazing, flying on a blanket, riding a bicycle, and arm lowering. These more active fantasy inductions are for children aged 7 through 11. From age 11 on, any adult induction can be used, for example, arm catalepsy, deep breathing, or eye fixation. For a more detailed discussion of hypnotic inductions for children, see Olness and Gardner (1988).

Example of Induction

Gardner described a three-step method for teaching children self-hypnosis that is easily accomplished in one session.

> In step 1, the therapist uses various induction and deepening methods, usually emphasizing imagery and ideomotor techniques. After allowing time to enjoy imagery the therapist asks the child to count silently up to five, eyes opening at three, fully alert at five. The therapist comments that the child now knows how to come out of hypnosis and return to the alert state without help.
>
> In step two, therapist and patient discuss which of the induction techniques employed in step 1 were most helpful and agree to discuss the rest. The child is then asked to describe to the therapist in detail the techniques chosen for induction, to feel the same good feelings, and to go into hypnosis as easily and naturally as the description. The therapist may add details if the child's wording is too general. After another pause and a reassuring comment, the therapist asks the child to return to the normal alert state. Problems are discussed as necessary.
>
> In step 3, the child is asked to recall and to decide to experience the induction silently. Neither child nor therapist speaks. The child nods when trance is achieved. After another pause, the child returns again to the normal, waking state. Any remaining problems or questions are discussed. (Gardner & Olness, 1981, pp. 300–312)

GOALS

After being introduced to self-hypnosis, the child may be introduced to one or more goals for hypnosis, such as symptom alteration, learning self-hypnosis, habit interruption, and the uncovering of dynamics.

Hypnosis can also be used for new learning and for prevention of problems (Olness & Gardner, 1988; Hilgard & LeBaron, 1982, 1984).

STRATEGIES

Next, specific strategies for self-hypnosis can be introduced to the child. Among self-hypnotic strategies that are helpful for children as well as for adults are relaxation, imagery, time distortion, and dissociative experience. However, with children, these will be used as a game. In addition, the full range of phenomena related to pain control can be used with children (Sanders, 1981). Some of these include the following:

1. *Relaxation.* Children are capable of responding to a progressive relaxation verbal induction. They respond to the rhythm, the voice tone, as well as the words. They experience such an induction as a soothing holding environment.

2. *Imagery.* Children are closer to nonverbal imagery experiences than adults. If we trace the development of cognition and communication, we find that before the age of 11, experience is sensory–motor (Piaget, 1951). New learning accrues in conjunction with sensory experience and motor experience and the congruence between the two. Before language develops, sensory experience is nonverbal. It is experienced as imagery.

3. *Time distortion.* Children below the age of 11 also have an undeveloped sense of time. They can learn to stretch and shrink time experience as part of their play.

4. *Dissociation.* Children are able to pretend and to play as if things were different. In the child's world, agreed on reality is a mystery that he or she is just learning, but the world of make believe or pretend is less mysterious to the child because it is more under the creation of the child. In this pretend world, the child studies, practices, and becomes for the moment an explorer, a doctor, a teacher. The child expresses through action, metaphor, and play experiences of being and feeling.

5. *Time regression.* Because children have had positive anesthesia-related experiences in the past, such as going to the dentist and having to have only one cavity filled, asking him or her to remember a time when he or she experienced anesthesia under such positive circumstances is a productive method.

6. *Motivational curiosity.* Because children are growing, developing, and learning all at the same time, they are curious. They have an

ever-present motivation to seek more and better understandings of all
that is about them. Their natural drive to learn and to discover presents
an opportunity to respond in a new way. Exploring hypnosis can present such an opportunity. The limited experiential background of the
child, the hunger for new experience, and the openness to new learning all render the child a natural candidate for hypnotic experience.

7. *Guided stories.* Because children enjoy stories, guided stories
bring hope and the possibility for change. Vicariously, the child identifies with the hero or heroine of the story, as well as the conflicts,
feelings, and ways in which the story is resolved. The hypnotherapist is
well armed when he or she has a large supply of guided stories.

8. *Metaphor.* The metaphor is a bridge to understanding based on
the very limited knowledge and reflection of the child. The use of the
metaphor enables the child to affect and to master the problem on an
unconscious level. Metaphors are powerful tools of change (Mills,
Crowley, & Ryan, 1986). Working with a metaphor, such as the metaphor of an electrical switching system, is a pain control method that
children find interesting. They are taught to imagine that they can see
beneath the skin the wires that come from the fingers and join together
to form bigger wires in the arm. There are wires that go to every part
of the body: the face, the mouth, the ears, the hands, the feet. The
child is told that all the wires come together in a special fuse box in the
back of the head. The child then learns to turn off the wires in specific
places, like turning off the switch for the wires in the left finger or
turning off the switch for the wires in the right toe. The child is asked
to practice at home turning the wires on and off. Soon, the child
becomes very proficient at turning the switches on and off.

Specific techniques of pain control via hypnosis and self-hypnosis,
include as previously mentioned, hypnoanesthesia—the experience of
reduced sensitivity to pain as a consequence of hypnotic suggestion
(Bartlett, 1963); glove anesthesia, which involves focusing the patient's
attention on a neutral nonpainful part of the body, such as the hand,
and asking the patient to imagine that the hand will soon become
insensitive to pain; amnesia, or the forgetting of pain; displacement of
pain, or changing the location of the pain from its original place to a
less critical place; and finally, conversion, or changing the quality of
experienced pain.

How does this relate to psychotherapy? Certainly, the major tool
in the psychotherapy of children is play. The child selects toys and
play activities. He becomes involved in the play, and in his or her life
space at that moment, the pretend play reflects important aspects of

the child's life: feelings, situations, and characteristic ways of responding and reacting to life. Using hypnosis with children, in my view, is an
extension of the use of interesting imagery that is novel and a source of
new learning. For children it is play.

Many of these techniques are quite familiar. Child psychotherapists have used hypnotic techniques with children, although they were
not recognized as hypnotic: distraction, pretend games, imagination,
remembering, and explaining. All these can be hypnotic techniques.

Importantly, children are growing, developing, curious, and persistent by nature. They have an ever-present motivation to seek more
and better understandings of all that is about them. Indeed, they have
a natural drive to learn and to discover. Every new object and event
potentially presents an opportunity to respond in some new way.
Exploring hypnosis can present such an opportunity. The limited
experiential background of the child, the hunger for new experience,
and the openness to new learning render the child a natural candidate
for hypnotic experiences (Erickson, 1958b). Indeed, the child is close
to imagery in thought, is willing to pretend, and enjoys pretend experiences. The task of the therapist is to present ideas in a manner that
fits the level of communication of the child so that the child can
understand.

According to Gardner and Olness (1981), the use of hypnosis
permits mastery. Josephine Hilgard and Samuel LeBaron believe that
both hypnosis and self-hypnosis may be successful in dealing with
recurrent problems and anxiety (Hilgard & LeBaron, 1984).

A KINESTHETIC INDUCTION

Lullabies convey a pleasing sense of sound and rhythm in association
with pleasing physical sensations. Every mother can tell you of her
successes in calming her child by rocking and crooning. This form of
sensory–motor communication is in keeping with the infant and young
child's mode of learning and communication, which is sensory–motor.
Any touch that serves to stimulate an expectation of pleasure consti-
tutes an important communication. And important communications
can be most helpful if they serve to reduce tension and stimulate an
expectation that this effect will be continued. In hypnosis, there is a
need for a continuity of stimulation that combines a willingness and
cooperation of the child in working together to reach simple, good,
and pleasing stimuli that serve in everyday life to elicit normal behavior pleasing to everyone.

Case Studies

One frequent problem that leads parents to seek help for their children is functional enuresis, a condition that involves repeated involuntary voiding of urine during the day or at night, after a successful resolution of toilet training. In the majority of cases after age 5 there is no discernable organic cause.

Olness explains that treatment depends on the child's involvement and commitment to practice self-hypnosis. The practice is the child's responsibility. Details regarding time and place for practice of self-hypnosis are discussed with the child. Practice is recommended just after dinner and at bedtime. The path to the bathroom from the child's bed is reviewed. The child is encouraged to decide on a specific reminder for practice such as a string around the toothbrush handle, a ribbon around the neck of a favorite stuffed toy, a sign on the door. An emphasis is placed on the bladder as a muscle and on the fact that the patient has previously learned control of many muscles. In addition, the therapist is viewed as a coach asking the patient to practice muscle control, thereby placing responsibility firmly on the child.

The choice of induction is determined on the basis of the child's likes and dislikes, such as hobbies, interests, favorite colors, and favorite dreams. Ideomotor signaling is used to evoke an answer to questions such as "Would you like to have all dry beds?" or "Are you ready to work on solving the problem of wet beds today?" Once the child agrees to try, the following suggestions are then given:

> "Tell yourself that you will sleep well tonight. Tell your bladder to send a message to your brain to awaken you when it is full of urine. When you awaken, tell yourself to get out of your dry bed, walk across the room through the door, down the hall to the bathroom, turn on the light, urinate in the toilet, turn the light off, return to your dry bed and go back to sleep. Then think of yourself, awakening in a dry bed, knowing you will have a good day. Enjoy knowing your bed is dry because of your efforts, because you're the boss of your bladder muscle. Enjoy the good feeling of waking up in a dry bed as long as you like. Then, when you're ready, you can open your eyes and enjoy the rest of the day." The child is to practice this exercise daily. (Olness & Gardner, 1988, pp. 135–137)

The child's self-hypnosis practice incorporates imagery, instruction, feeling body messages, and success. It is a very real experience leading to emotional growth and mastery.

Olness also has described hypnotherapy for functional megacolon (Olness, 1976). She cites as advantages for using self-hypnosis: an increase in control and mastery and the fact that desired behavior is more frequently reinforced by repetition of appropriate imagery exercises. She taught four children with functional megacolon self-hypnosis, and they gave themselves daily suggestions regarding their ability to control bowels in appropriate ways. Olness concluded that success was chiefly the result of the children's being given responsibility for their own solution. Parents were involved only to the extent that they praised the child for improvement and reinforced feelings of mastery (Olness, 1976, pp. 28–32).

The following case studies are presented from my practice to illustrate some varied uses of hypnosis in the treatment of children.

George is a 13-year-old asthmatic who was covered from head to toe with eczema. There is not a clear spot on him. Because of his fragile asthmatic condition and his uncomfortable skin condition, George was hospitalized on a children's psychiatric inpatient unit in order to achieve control of his asthma and his skin.

Even in the hospital, George was emotionally unavailable. The intern assigned to work with him was disappointed that George was not more verbal. He seemed quite alexithymic. In therapy, he removed himself from interaction and withdrew behind a shell of apathy. We decided to use hypnosis as a way to help George to get out from this shell.

The first hypnotic session focused on teaching George how to enter hypnosis. We used a progressive relaxation and deep breathing induction described and modeled by the intern. First the therapist described progressive relaxation; then he began to engage in progressive relaxation, describing his own experiences of looseness, lightness, and comfort to George. Such role modeling was employed with both children and parents as a way of improving communication (Sanders, 1975). Then it was George's turn to carry out progressive relaxation. The therapist gave the instructions, and George was asked to take deep breaths and to let the different parts of his body become loose and comfortable and relaxed.

Even in this first session, George showed a remarkable response. From continuously scratching his arms and his legs before hypnosis, as he became more engrossed in the relaxation exercises, he became increasingly quiet all over. The constant scratching stopped. The therapist provided George with recognition that now everything was quiet because he was relaxed. George was given a posthypnotic suggestion that he could practice the deep breathing and relaxation exercises on his own and make his whole body quiet, just as it was now. He was to practice this exercise four times per day.

The second session progressed to associating body language to affects of anger. The therapist role-modeled how to recognize anger by a body signal. The therapist told George that when he, the therapist, felt angry, his chest became tight, and he found it hard to breathe. When he recognized that his chest was tight, he began to take long, slow, deep breaths and to relax. When he did this, his chest became looser, and his breathing returned to normal.

When it was George's turn, hypnosis was induced, and then the therapist asked George what happened when somebody did something that he did not like. George replied that he did not like it when somebody told him what to do. The therapist asked George what his body said when that happened. George replied that he felt itchy all over and had to scratch.

This admission provided the therapist with the opportunity of giving George an alternative way to respond to anger. The technique of symptom substitution or displacement was used. The therapist told George essentially that whenever he felt itchy, he could take a plastic hammer and nail and hit the nail with the hammer instead of scratching. And he could close his eyes and relax with deep breathing as his arms and legs relaxed and became quiet. In just a few days, George's skin began to clear.

During the third session, the therapist role-modeled how to put one's anger into words and tell the person toward whom one felt anger the reason for the anger. This lesson was carried out in hypnosis and practiced in imagery. George practiced telling the nurse that he was mad at her when she wanted him to put some things away.

Between the Thursday when he learned how to use words of power in fantasy and Tuesday, the time of his next appointment, George began to speak up on the unit. The nurses were pleased as George became more vocal and "assertive." In their words, he was becoming a holy terror. They liked him better this way. Before, George had been a nonperson, nonresponsive and robotlike. Now he was perceptive and didn't miss a trick. He was indeed a person.

In family sessions not involving hypnosis but involving role-modeling, both George and his parents were introduced to varbalizing angry feelings. The parents had considerably more difficulty with this exercise than did George. However, as the sessions helped improve the family communication, George began to gain greater control over his asthma. This success was reinforced in his hypnosis sessions with his therapist.

In retrospect, George's hypnotherapy taught him how to relax physiologically. Deep breathing and relaxation enabled George to begin to become more confortable. They provided the opportunity for a success experience.

In addition, George learned to identify feelings of anger within himself by associating his physical symptoms with an affect of anger. By concretizing the meaning of the symptom, George was able to gain control of the symptom by externalizing the anger, first physically, hitting a plastic nail with a plastic hammer, and later by transforming his anger into powerful words spoken to the person he was angered by. Finally, the entire family began to verbalize feelings of anger more directly. After 4 months, George was able to leave the hospital and return home, his skin completely clear and his asthma under control.

This example has illustrated some of the very intricate interactions that occur among the child, the environment, the parents, and the expression of affect. The child learned to recognize and label his emotions, which in turn reduced the psychophysiological problems.

TRICHOTILLOMANIA

Trichotillomania is a form of compulsive behavior whereby the patient pulls his or her hair. Fabbri (1976) has described a behavioral approach that incorporates hypnosis to treat this condition. Because of the automaticity of this behavior, a multi-faceted approach is necessary.

Also using a multi-faceted approach, I treated Joan, a 9-year-old, highly controlled, anxious, and pseudomature young lady. Her parents brought her to outpatient therapy because she pulled out her hair, and there were so many bald spots she had to wear a wig. Joan had been hair-pulling since she was 3. Joan's behavior was constantly compared to her 15-year-old adolescent sister, who was outgoing, outspoken, and the apple of her mother's eye. Joan, on the other hand, just never seemed to do anything right.

Joan was eager to learn how to control her hair-pulling, as she was very embarrassed at having to wear a wig. Her motivation was quite high. During the first hypnotic session, Joan learned the rag doll game: She learned to become like a rag doll. She became loose, without bones, and very relaxed. She could become a rag doll at the count of three. Once she had become a rag doll, she learned to recognize the quiet place where she felt comfortable and where no one nagged at her to clean the house or do other chores. She liked the quiet peacefulness of the relaxation created by becoming a rag doll.

She explored the kinesthetic feelings of heaviness in her hands when she was a rag doll. This heaviness would intrude into her thinking whenever her right hand was moving up to her head. That recognition would trigger becoming a rag doll, so that her hand would fall into her lap and prevent any hair-pulling.

In addition, Joan began to keep a diary recording when she felt like pulling her hair, what was happening at the time, and what reinforcements or punishments there were that would influence the hair-pulling. As she became more in control of the hair-pulling, that is when she could begin to interrupt it and later prevent it, she began to feel good about herself. She became more interested at school and at home. She carried out her assigned tasks. However, she became aware of being angry with her older sister, the apple of her mom's eye, who had no assigned chores because she was older. Joan felt like she was Cinderella, having to do all the work while her sister got to have all the fun. As she worked on interrupting her symptom, simultaneously with gaining insight and understanding about the reasons for her behavior, her hair began growing thicker and longer. Within 3 months, she no longer needed a wig.

At home, in addition to maintaining the diary, Joan became the rag doll four times a day and whenever her right hand moved toward her hair. She told herself that (1) she could be in control of her hand; (2) she could be aware of her anger; and (3) she could talk about her anger with the therapist. In addition, several family sessions were held to clarify progress and the need to allow Joan to express her anger.

The hypnosis training in the office enabled Joan to escape an essentially hostile and critical emotional environment. In this time-out place, Joan was able to focus more on the dissociated hand as it began to move to her hair. She learned to use this kinesthetic cue to enter self-hypnosis both as a way of aborting the hair-pulling and as a way of maintaining a more comfortable emotional environment. The journal enabled Joan to work more dynamically on the problems by exploring those situations that triggered self-consciousness, guilt, and anger. Thus, the use of self-hypnosis and self-monitoring reinforced by an eclectic hypnotherapy approach enabled Joan to master her problem.

As with adults, self-hypnosis, to be effective, must be practiced. Forgetting to practice, lack of motivation to practice, or negative attitudes of the parents may discourage practice. Tapes can be useful to assist the child in practice. Phone calls too can help motivate the child. Even a letter to the patient can have a motivating effect.

Olness and Gardner (1981) stress the importance of working with the parents to whom they give the following instructions:

> Your child is practicing autosuggestion for control of bedwetting, and it is important that you enhance your child's self-confidence and learning in the following ways:

You should ensure that there will be a quiet spot available every evening where your child can practice relaxation.

In general, the best time for practice is shortly before bedtime; however, if your child is one who is exceedingly tired and ready to fall asleep as soon as he or she gets into bed, practice would be immediately after supper or at some other convenient time between suppertime and bedtime. (pp. 300–312)

Self-hypnosis is helpful when recurrent experiences of discomfort occur or when undesirable habits need to be changed. LaBaw has discussed self-hypnosis in the sense that the child now knows how to come out of hypnosis and return to the alert state without help. The child is then ready for fully independent use of self-hypnosis (LaBaw, 1975, pp. 103–110).

Hypnotherapy can be useful for many problems of both recent and of long duration. Poor results are associated with lack of motivation, conflicts, severe underlying pathology, significant secondary gain, and premature termination of treatment. Parental attitudes also play an important role. However, hypnosis and self-hypnosis are not a panacea, in fact, in some situations hypnosis should not be used, as in the case of the following example. I received a phone call at home on a Saturday at 6:30 P.M. from a woman whom I had never seen who wanted me to "hypnotize her daughter." I asked her why. She replied that her daughter would not mind her. I asked the age of her daughter. The woman replied 13. I would never hypnotize a child to mind the parent. This use of hypnosis is inappropriate as it is one that interferes with normal development, that is, becoming adolescent and more autonomous, and it is in the service of relationship control within the family. These problems are much better worked with in family therapy.

Secondly, I would not use hypnosis to mask a pain that has not yet been diagnosed, since this would interfere with the child getting needed medical help.

Also, I would not use hypnosis as a substitute for a lie detector test. One parent, worried about her daughter's lies, wanted her to be hypnotized to find out the truth. I extended an invitation for parent and child to come to my office to discuss their communication problem, but I let them both know that hypnosis was not indicated in this situation.

Hypnosis and self-hypnosis should be used for a specific purpose, agreed upon by the therapist and the patient. Not everyone should use hypnosis. The teaching of self-hypnosis is best left to the trained professional in order to integrate the self-hypnotic work with the ongoing treatment.

Research in the area of self-hypnosis and children is virtually nonexistent. A few studies are just beginning to appear (Kohen, 1986; Olness, 1976). Usually, the reports are anecdotal in nature. It will be interesting to see the growth and development of a cohesive theory of self-hypnosis in children.

SUMMARY

This chapter has presented a sampling of how hypnosis may be used in the hypnotherapy of children. Space does not permit an exhaustive discussion of every possible use of self-hypnosis with children. Rather, the focus is on a few specific clinical examples that illustrate the power of words and images in the hypnotic experience of children.

CHAPTER 11

Self-Hypnosis for the Professional

The power of thought—the magic of the mind.
—Byron, "Corsair"

This chapter presents a variety of areas in which self-hypnosis may be of interest in the everyday life of the therapist. The first section addresses ways of using self-hypnosis in the office. The second area of interest is the use of self-hypnosis in surgery for the therapist. The third area of interest lies in the development of creativity, and last, the use of self-hypnosis in sports and leisure. This chapter, although not focused on the importance of expectations, demands, motivations, and orientations, is not exempt from their influences. These factors operate even in the realm of practicing self-hypnosis on one's own.

SELF-HYPNOSIS IN THE OFFICE

The busy psychotherapist undergoes stress from several sources during work time. Patients are waiting to be seen; phone calls are waiting to be initiated and returned. Correspondence is waiting to be read and to be responded to. Decisions are waiting to be made. Emergencies need to be handled. The demands of limited time available and the extent of the work to be done can take their toll on the professional in the form of burnout, exhaustion, and psychosomatic dysfunction. In this age of multiple simultaneous stimulus barrage, the professional needs quiet, reflective time to become aware of a void in which there is no time. Within a still, expansive, and timeless self-hypnotic state that is deliberately demand-free, the professional can relax— breathing deeply, feeling comfortable and secure—and thereby prevent the buildup of stress as well as make it easier to maintain a heavy work load. This primary goal is a prophylactic one. In addition, such a time-out experience provides renewal of both energy and motivation.

While the professional guards his or her time, and understandably so, taking the time for self-renewal is a vital activity. Renewal fosters a balance between the physical condition and mental operations. It increases one's endurance.

In this chapter, examples of brief self-hypnotic exercises are described and offered as examples that can be experienced individually, or may be combined depending on one's goals. They are worded in the first person to establish a mind-set. These exercises have been developed from a pooling of the images and words of many patients over the span of many years. They are not examples from personal experience. The best exercises, you will find, come from your own images, words, and thoughts matched to a specific goal to be achieved. There is no one exercise that is absolutely right for everyone. Indeed the best exercise for a given individual is one that is tailor-made for him or her.

These exercises consist of specific cognitive strategies that are further enhanced by the altered state of consciousness in which self-hypnosis occurs. The themes focus on the following: (1) time stopping or learning to experience a still, quiet void; (2) reenergizing or learning to perceive an increase in natural energy; (3) refocusing or learning to expand and to narrow the focus of consciousness; (4) reorganizing or learning to use the mind's natural ability to organize, sort, and understand; (4) preparing or readying oneself to begin a task; (5) relaxing or experiencing a general sense of comfort and well-being; (6) tranforming a passive stance to an active one; (7) problem solving or brainstorming, that is, preparing a list of possible solutions; and (8) creating or devising something new or different. According to Carl Rogers (1959), "The mainspring of creativity appears to be man's tendency to actualize himself, to become his potentials, whether it be to solve problems in life, in therapy, or to produce symbolic works of art" (p. 153). In this view, everyone has creative potential that can be elicited under the proper conditions. The degree to which you become involved in the imagery will color your individual response to self-hypnosis. The exercises or scripts that are presented are worded in the first person to provide self-direction (Ruch, 1975). The words generate images, personal meanings. The grammatical presentation is necessary for readability since the personal experience may be quite nonverbal.

Time Stopping

As I close my eyes and take a deep breath, I become aware of a void in which time doesn't exist. Breathing deeply, I feel comfortable, comfortable and secure, comfortable and safe, in a place where there are no clocks, no demands, only a satisfying quiet that is mine for as long as I want, as long as I need, when I need it. Time is eternal, boundless, and as I breathe deeply, I participate in the experience of eternity, even if only for a moment. Now that time has stopped, I can return to the flux of every-changing time, recognizing that I can restore the void of eternity when I want, how I want, when I need to.

Reenergizing

As my arm floats upward, and my eyes close, I become aware of the powerful machinery in the body. The body is a factory that produces chemicals, natural chemicals that heal, natural chemicals that calm, and natural chemicals that reenergize. Just as the car needs gasoline to keep the engine running, my body needs to create the energy to maintain my activity. I take the car to the gasoline station; in like manner, I take my mind and body to a quiet place to procure its natural energy. I am amazed at the rapid increase in natural energy, even as I sit here, feeling stronger, having more endurance, feeling my body respond to the reenergizing process. When I am ready to return, I will do so, stronger and more energized and prepared.

Refocusing

Closing my eyes and taking a long, slow, deep breath, I deliberately allow the focus of my attention to expand and to blur. As I exhale, I begin to narrow the breadth of attention so that soon, my perception of whatever I am attending to leaps into graphic relief, much like focusing a macrolens for a close-up shot on a camera. The clarity and precision of my image are dazzling, like gems and jewels. I can see so clearly, so precisely. I know that I understand more clearly and more precisely than ever before. I can now return to the task at hand with the newly found clarity and precision.

Reorganizing

As I sit in my office, confronted by papers, papers everywhere, I realize it is time to reorganize. I sit quietly, taking a long, slow, deep breath, my signal to initiate trance, and find myself far away, in a special place that has wonderful possibilities for organizing. I decide it is time to organize a particular task, such as a particular chapter, and I take another deep breath to inhale focus and direction and to exhale disorganization. My mind contains the tools to organize, to sort, to order, and to understand. I can use these tools now to sort, to order, to understand, and to organize my thoughts, my ideas, and my understanding. I see my thoughts enacted in my mind's eye, I hear my ideas resonating, and I am aware that I know, that I understand. The reorganization has occurred. I can return to make use of my new understanding and reorganization.

Preparation

The time has come for a new project. There are so many ideas, so many trains of thought, it is difficult to know where to begin. I close my eyes to clear the thoughts and breathe deeply to start preparing for what is to come. As I exhale, I see the necessary tools: paper, pencil, eraser. These tools become a vital part of me, an extension of my thoughts, my ideas, my very being. I view an idea that emerges from every possible direction, so that I can see it, hear it, feel it, touch it. The idea comes to brilliant animation, and I interact with it, following it first down one path and then another until I am fully prepared to begin the translation from private perception to public realization. I realize that preparation is only creating a pathway from the multitude of possibilities to first one promise, then to another. Just as it is necessary to clear away extraneous trees, flowering plants, and other obstacles to set the foundation of a house, the task of preparing for any activity is to remove extraneous perceptions, sensations, and ideas to set forth the essence of the venture in all its vibrant potentialities. Now I see the path cleared, and I can begin the journey down it to the final destination while allowing myself to scan the path along various intersections. I am now prepared to begin.

Relaxation

It has been a long day. I am aware of a tension that has accumulated during the day and recognize the utility of relaxation. I breathe in the quality of relaxation while exhaling the kinesthetic image of tension so that I am aware of a lightening, a tingling, a general sense of comfort and ease. I continue to inhale relaxation and exhale tension, setting up a rhythm, much like the ebb and flow of the ocean's waves at the shoreline. Now I focus my attention on particular muscle groups to relieve any specific tension areas. I relax my feet. I let them become comfortable. I relax my ankles. I relax the calves of my legs, and I feel a sense of lightness and untroubled awareness. I relax the hips and the abdomen, the back and the chest. The relaxation affects me directly, normally, naturally, and comfortably. I relax the fingers and hands, the arms and shoulders. And in particular, I relax the neck and the face. I am aware now that I am remarkably comfortable, at ease and can enjoy the soothing quality of this wonderful experience, which I can enjoy again and again, if I wish.

Transformation

There are times I feel stuck. The image that appears does not match the sensation I experience. I feel the need for a transformation of the image to mirror the sensation. Just as oxygen and hydrogen when mixed in appropriate amounts are transformed into water, so images, ideas, feelings, thoughts, and perceptions can be transformed into different images, different ideas, different feelings, different thoughts, and different perceptions. The metamorphosis I seek is much like the metamorphosis of the caterpillar into a butterfly. I want to transform the sensation of feeling stuck into a sensation of motion. Rather than experiencing the sense of sticking to fly paper, I prefer to experience now the sense of freedom to move, freedom to express, freedom to choose. Suddenly the image and the sensation match. The transformation has occurred. I feel free to move in whatever direction I choose.

Problem Solving

I have a specific problem. My desk is overcrowded with papers, memos, telephone messages, brochures, and other assorted papers. I can image this overcrowded desk, seeing how inefficient and confusing it can be. It serves as a blockade to any goals I may wish to accomplish. I take a deep breath and list in my mind's eye a number of different solutions to this problem. I can take all the papers, memos, telephone messages, brochures, and other assorted papers and simply dump them into the wastepaper basket. Or I can sort through the stacks of papers and set up separate files for each. Or I can prepare myself for this task by reviewing the preparation exercise. Or I can first reenergize myself and activate my body's natural energizing chemicals so that I feel stronger and ready to begin the sorting process. When I am aware of the first increase in natural energy, I will begin to resolve the problem and will have the satisfaction of having a clear desk.

Creativity

I wish to tap into my creative potential. I can do this most efficiently by clearing my mind and taking a deep breath, while setting aside questions, critiques, and distractions, so that for a moment my mind is like a blank page. Every emergent thought is now a possible step in the creative process. Every emergent image is a link within the creative process. Every emergent feeling reflects important information from the unconscious. These verbal and nonverbal messages permit me to go beyond my usual ways of thinking. I can experience in my imagination each and every possibility that comes to mind until I know that I have met my goal. And I know that some things need time to incubate, to develop, to ripen before they emerge into conscious awareness. I will permit this incubation process, confident that the ripening process is proceeding in my unconscious and that when maturation has occurred, the fruit of the creative incubation will appear, much like the spring harvest after the fall planting. I can now return to my usual state of awareness knowing that the incubation process is continuing.

Exercises for Serenity

The following exercises can be used for calming and achieving self-control. They can be used effectively for pain control as well as for anxiety control. Essentially, these words are a form of distraction from stress, disease, and anxiety. The images generated can lead to a dissociative experience.

Close your eyes.
Think of a comfortable place.
Think of the beauty of autumn.
Breathe in the fresh cool air.
Listen to the song of the birds.
This is my experience to enjoy.

The following exercise provides a way of temporarily storing painful feelings, experiences, thoughts until a later time when they can be sorted and worked through.

Storage

Think of pleasant things.
Put all negative thoughts and ideas in a box or filing cabinet until a later
  time.
Now is the time to be more comfortable.
If I like, I can allow myself to drift off to sleep for a while.
I imagine that I am in a warm soothing place.
A comfortable wall of comfort surrounds me.
I now experience the wall of comfort: how it looks, feels, sounds, is.
I describe the colors that capture it: red, black, purple.
I am absorbed.

Procrastination interferes with completing good works. The following exercise is one person's way of getting into action, of doing something right now.

Doing

I list pleasant ways to occupy my time.
I knit, crochet, read. The list enlarges.
I explore each activity absorbing myself. I become the activity.

The following exercise captures the expansion of experience in self-hypnosis for one person and how that person attempts to communicate that experience.

Experience

I become my experience. My experience becomes my entire awareness. Closing my eyes permits me to experience the ever deepening of experience. I simply translate those sensory images and sensory perceptions into words, cognition, and feelings. This translation is a literal one. I just bring into the experience every sensory modality. I see, feel, hear, touch, move with the experience.

SELF-HYPNOSIS STRATEGIES FOR PAIN CONTROL

The use of self-hypnosis in surgery can enhance one's power to tolerate and/or diminish the experience of pain. In addition, it can decrease the necessity for high levels of anesthesia and in some situations, it can actually be used as the primary anesthesia. It is very important that one be adequately prepared for the surgical procedure in terms of its identification, familiarity with the sequence, and permission to block out the sounds and the areas in which the surgery will be performed.

Since the perception of pain can be minimized or maximized psychologically, self-hypnosis can provide an useful adjunct when used in a positive, healing, relaxing manner.

Approaches to using self-hypnosis for this purpose can include any of the hypnotic procedures used in hypnotherapy as well as those used for reduction of pain. A direct suggestion that I can feel comfortable and heal normally and naturally is an useful one.

The following scripts were designed for a patient who wanted to use self-hypnosis as an adjunct to reduce anxiety, to keep pain to a basic minimum, and to speed healthy healing functions. The script was to be read to the patient by the nurse in the patient's room before surgery. The second script was to be read to the patient by the anesthesiologist in the operating room before anesthesia was administered. The third script was to be read to the patient in the recovery room as the oxygen mask was applied by the nurse. The patient would reinforce these scripts by self-talk suggestions. That is, the patient would image the suggestions and repeat them.

Script 1: The Start of the Journey

(After the nurse has administered any medications) Now that you have taken the medication, you can allow yourself to relax. There is nothing that you need to do or think about. The really important task is to provide a calm, cool, healing environment within your body to maximize the benefits of the therapy. You know that healing occurs best under conditions of calm, cool relaxation. And you know just how easy and natural it is to relax in a cool, calm manner. Soon you will begin to feel the effects of the medication. Your job is to help by simply remaining cool and calm. By remaining cool, calm, and relaxed you will also become increasingly calm, confident, and secure. By maintaining this state, you are helping the doctor to do his job and helping your body to do its job of providing a healing internal environment with a minimum of bleeding and a minimum of discomfort.

Script 2: In the Operating Room

You are feeling comfortable and relaxed. This is natural. You begin to pay more attention to your own thoughts and pleasant images and to allow the sounds around you to fade into the background because what these sounds mean or sound like is not really important at this time. While you are experiencing the anesthetic, you can focus even more clearly on a pleasant script of Jamaica, where the sea is Carolina blue and the air is cool and clear. And you can continue to feel cool, comfortable, and relaxed, knowing that soon you will awake in the recovery room still in an altered state of consciousness, but aware that this alteration is temporary. With each minute, your body will continue to process the anesthetic agent, and you will gradually return to your normal state of awareness, calm, relaxed, with a minimum of bleeding and a minimum of discomfort. You know that the anesthetic that you receive is administered carefully and safely, and that the procedure is performed skillfully; and that when you awaken quietly and comfortable, it will seem as though you have awakened from a pleasantly long, deep, peaceful health-restoring sleep.

Script 3: In the Recovery Room

As you open your eyes you recognize the signs of an altered state of consciousness. The oxygen mask is a way to help you to awaken more easily, more quickly, and more efficiently. You recognize that you become more and more awake as a pleasant healing process proceeds within your body and that your bodily functions are returning to normal so that before long you will feel pleasantly hungry, your energy will slowly return, and the entire healing process will come to a natural, normal, and healthy conclusion smoothly, safely, rapidly. Very soon you will be up and around, feeling at ease, becoming more wide awake, rested, and calm. You are curious about this natural healing process and watch it occur with great interest. You need not pay any attention to any sounds and persons who are not talking directly to you. The really important thing is to allow your body now to do its job by remaining as comfortable, relaxed, and curious as you are now.

Script 4: In the Hospital Room

The journey has been completed successfully. Now to enhance healing, you can continue to relax and to feel calm, cool, and comfortable. You are aware that your body functions are continuing to return to normal and that the healing process is well under way. You may sleep as you wish, go to the beach in your imagination, or simply drift. The nurses will be here to help you if you have any needs or questions. The important thing is to maintain a healthy, comfortable, healing environment as you are now.

Discussion

As you can see, a specific stimulus was used to trigger self-hypnosis: The initial journey was triggered by the administration of medication, which in the case of this patient was penicillin. In the preop, the critical stimulus was the intravenous connection. In the O.R., the critical stimulus was the administration of anesthetic. In the recovery room, the critical stimulus was the administration of oxygen. These critical stimuli were selected ahead of time and involved clear expectations. They were chosen because they were an integral part of the surgical procedure.

The exercise includes (1) critical stimuli, (2) permission not to pay attention, (3) comfortable imagery or dissociation, and (4) future-oriented suggestions looking toward the end of surgery, returning by degrees to a normal natural condition.

Outcome

The patient was surprised to find how quickly and smoothly everything went. She was awake very quickly after surgery. Her vital functions returned to normal very quickly, and she was hungry in 2 hours. The nurse told her that there had been little bleeding.

SELF-HYPNOSIS AND
RECONSTRUCTIVE FOOT SURGERY

A professional woman who had used self-hypnosis in her practice since 1967 was scheduled for reconstructive foot surgery. A double osteotomy of both feet was to be performed to correct bunions and a misaligned metatarsal. The procedure was expected to take 5 hours. The patient decided to combine self-hypnosis with anesthesia, deciding to stay awake for part of the procedure and, if she tired, to use nitrous oxide to sleep. She asked the surgeon and the anesthesiologist, who both agreed. She made a tape that she could play on the way to the O.R. and during the surgery while she was awake. The microcassette tape and recorder were in her hands as she prepared to go to the O.R.

The patient listened to the tape on the way to the O.R. To get there, she was taken down one elevator to a small train that ran from one hospital wing to another and then up another elevator. The patient, not comfortable with being treated like an object by the aide and nurse who were taking her, decided to "leave." She paid no further attention to anything but the tape until she arrived at the O.R. The tape consisted of suggestions for comfort, healing, relaxation, and body monitoring.

The procedure will correct my foot problem. I can simply relax and feel comfortable as the team works together to correct my feet. My executive observers will monitor the site to insure that healing is taking place. If there is any question, the monitor will notify the armed forces to come to my defense by killing any untoward aliens. Then the sanitation crew will sweep up the remains of the aliens so there will be no risk of infection. It is important to know that I have executive observers, armed forces, and a sanitation crew at my disposal, so that I can relax and feel comfortable.

Once in the O.R., the patient and the anesthesiologist talked about the wonders of epidural anesthesia and how it differed from other kinds of anesthesia. This discussion went on and on when the patient asked, "When are they going to start the surgery?" The anesthesiologist told the patient that the surgery had started some time ago and had been ongoing even as they talked. The patient was amazed. She then tried to listen once more to the tape, but could not find it. She was only able to hear some dictation from earlier that week in the office. Her first thought was "Oh, no, what am I to do now?" Then she remembered the basics of the tape: the observer, the army, the sanitation crew. Now she began to image the important characters and felt comfortable once again. In the distance she heard the sounds of an electric saw and decided that it was time to sleep, pronto. She asked the anesthesiologist if she could sleep. He administered nitrous oxide, and she had no further thoughts until she awakened in the recovery room. She realized too late that she had not been prepared for the sound of the saw. Nonetheless, she imaged the monitors, the army, and the sanitation crew busily at work in her body as she became more and more alert. She continued to use these images throughout the recovery period of 6 weeks. Her surgeon was pleased at her progress. She was able to walk in 4 weeks and was free of any infection.

Clearly, there are both benefits and risks of using self-hypnosis in such a surgical procedure, yet for this patient the combination approach worked very well. By using self-hypnosis, she had established herself as a part of the surgical team. She knew that she had impacted on the team because this change in procedure was atypical. She felt a sense of power in regulating her mind-set. On reviewing the vital signs, I found that she had maintained a comfortable, stable pattern throughout the surgery. And she had not been overwhelmed by pain. She continued to use the imagery up to 4 months after surgery, assuring herself that no infections would occur. She considered the outcome of surgery to be successful.

Victor Rausch (1980) described his own use of self-hypnosis for a cholecystectomy. Rausch in 1980 used self-hypnosis in his own major abdominal surgery as the sole agent to control muscle relaxation, pain, bleeding, pulse rate, and blood pressure. During his surgery he had eye contact with one nurse throughout. It was as if they were inextricably drawn together. His vital signs remained stable throughout the surgery, and he did not have to go to the recovery room since no anesthesia had been used.

SPORTS

The use of self-hypnosis in sports addresses the reduction of anxiety and the facilitation of attention. It falls under the rubric of performance anxiety. There is considerable interest in sports facilitation and self-hypnosis (Gallwey, 1974; Stanton, 1983; Unestahl, 1979; Young, 1986). In addition, it heightens motivation for practice. Physical relaxation techniques help players to move freely and easily. Lowered anxiety levels enable them to perform effortlessly. Focused attention permits mental rehearsal in preparation for actual rehearsal. Restructuring of thoughts and expectations from negative to normal becomes effortless, natural, and pleasurable.

A Bike-Riding Script

As your calmness and confidence increase, and as you become able to bring tension under conscious control whenever you wish to by relaxing, breathing deeply, and filling your mind with pleasant memories, you will find that you are able to produce exactly the right amount of tension needed for a particular task or event; while you are riding your bike in competition, for example, you will have just the right amount of tension to allow you to perform at your very best—neither too little nor too much.

> Your powers of concentration will increase steadily, day by day, until very soon you will be able to exclude everything from your attention—everything except things that are vital for you to attend to. Everything else will be excluded from your attention. Things that are around you and things passing through your mind will recede right into the distance—you will pay no attention to them and concentrate solely on your bike-riding. Remember, from now on

you will concentrate intensely on your riding to the exclusion of everything except that which is vitally important. . . . " (from Young, 1986, pp. 217–218)

Dog Obedience Competition[1]

An ever-increasing popular sport is that of dog obedience competition. Training and showing a dog in competition can take its toll on the owner because of performance anxiety. Unfortunately, if the owner or handler is anxious, the anxiety travels down the lead, and the dog becomes anxious too. The use of self-hypnosis is useful in this situation. Just prior to going in the ring, the owner (handler) kneels down to the dog and whispers aloud so that both the dog and the owner can hear and respond to the tone, the meanings, and the rhythm of the suggestions:

Now we have to work together, a team, to demonstrate what we have been practicing. We know the routine, we can do this, together, easily, normally, naturally, and comfortably. We can heel and do the figure eight. We can stand for examination. We can do the recall so that it is fun. The important thing now is that we work together as a team, normally, naturally, comfortably, and easily.

The dog responds to this verbalization by sitting at attention, looking the owner directly in the eye, licking him or her on the face, and appearing eagerly to await their turn in the ring. The owner responds to this verbalization by deep breathing, calming, and a sense of increased confidence and control. This self-suggestion prepares the owner/handler for the competition.

Another popular sport where hypnosis can be helpful is long-distance running or marathon racing. Callen (1983a, 1983b) describes the use of autohypnosis in long-distance running, as well as addresses the mental and emotional concomitants of long-distance running.

SELF-HYPNOSIS AND CREATIVITY

Creativity is an attribute of personality that almost everyone would like to have. To write creatively, to work creatively, to live creatively are all positive goals. In order to use self-hypnosis as an instrument to stimulate creatively, we first must define it.

[1]The meanings of this self-hypnotic suggestion were important to the handler, but the timing, rhythm, and tone of voice were important to both the handler and the dog.

Creativity is a process that involves the transformation of things known into something new or unknown. Rather than mere genius, it is an attribute of life. A sizable pool of research exists in an effort to understand creativity (Bowers, 1968, 1971, 1979; Bowers & Bowers, 1979). Raikov (1977), in a theoretical analysis of deep-trance creative activity, observed a transformation from self-conscious state to a more confident one. Sanders (1976) found that when a support group of professional women used self-hypnosis over the course of 6 months, group members became more imagery-oriented, more flexible in their thinking, and seemed to solve difficult life problems more easily. Refining her approach, Sanders later (1978) developed a short-term hypnotherapy model in which the tenants of creativity were used along with other cognitive strategies.

Life provides us with the power of the senses. We see, hear, feel, taste, touch, smell. The possible ways in which we use these sensory powers are numerous. In addition, we possess an imagination that can transcend the banalities of the everyday world, opening ever new possibilities. Rather than placing limits on our skill and productivity, imagination can reorganize, reassociate, and recombine the everyday ingredients of experience into a new whole, a new experience. This imaginative power enables us to rethink, restructure, reorder, and reconceptualize.

In order to improve your creativity production, you need to know how you view your own creativity potential, how creative you believe yourself to be, and how you have used this ability in the past.

On a 10-point scale where 1 is not creative and 10 is very creative, how creative would you rate yourself to be?

            1   2   3   4   5   6   7   8   9   10

Rate your belief about the possibility of transcending your current level of creative potential.

            1   2   3   4   5   6   7   8   9   10

Rate your willingness to take risks.

            1   2   3   4   5   6   7   8   9   10

Rate your willingness to deliberately make creative things happen.

            1   2   3   4   5   6   7   8   9   10

Rate the vividness of your imagery.

1 2 3 4 5 6 7 8 9 10

Rate the extent to which you actively perform self-suggestion.

1 2 3 4 5 6 7 8 9 10

Rate the extent to which your perception of outside reality decreased.

1 2 3 4 5 6 7 8 9 10

Rate the extent to which you experienced yourself letting go.

1 2 3 4 5 6 7 8 9 10

Rate the degree to which you worked on a personal problem.

1 2 3 4 5 6 7 8 9 10

Rate the degree to which you experienced self-revelation.

1 2 3 4 5 6 7 8 9 10

Rate the degree to which you were self-hypnotized.

1 2 3 4 5 6 7 8 9 10

By such self-ratings, you can track your progress. As you go along you may notice ever higher ratings until you reach a plateau. Also, keeping a journal will enable you to recognize specific experiences that may be particularly important in your self-hypnotic practice.

REFLECTIONS

When the exercise is finished and you return to the here and now, some of you might wonder, for example, why the papers are still everywhere. The self-hypnosis exercise prepares the subject via imagery suggestion to begin to clear the clutter upon returning. Hypnotic and self-hypnotic suggestion provides a preparatory set for action. It enables the subject to view the problem, imagine solutions, and heighten personal motivation for change.

As I reflect on this process of self-hypnosis, I am further convinced that self-hypnosis, practiced in a positive, goal-directed way, is a powerful ego function permitting some changes in the existing interplay of dynamic forces within the personality. These changes within the relative intensity of ego inhibition and ego receptivity enable the individual to transform passivity into activity, inhibition into action, and stillness into flux, at least in regard to a particular task or goal. The power of words and images within self-hypnosis engenders change of experience, meaning, and perception. Perhaps the interplay lies between ego-activity and ego-receptivity. I believe this hypothesis could be put to the test. At this time, however, we can safely say that the transformation of meaning through imagery and suggestion affects the person profoundly.

PART IV

Summary

CHAPTER 12

Conclusions and Directions

> One must learn by doing the thing; though you think
> you know it, you have no certainty until you try.
> —Sophocles, *Trachiniae*

Our journey to the past has placed self-hypnosis in relief. This journey has shown us that self-hypnosis has roots in the natural, normal instinct for survival and, through the centuries, has been an important part of holistic health.

Although it took centuries for man to believe in his own ability to be self-directive, he used words and images as important tools to affect himself, even if those words and images were presumed to be mediated by an outside force, that is, the gods. I believe that the major difference between self-hypnosis and heterohypnosis is that of self-direction. Both states demonstrate the power of words and images. However, it is the self-hypnotic state that highlights the potential of the individual to move, transcend, and transform his world and himself, by himself. Whereas self-initiation is important in the already high-functioning individual, self-direction is a reasonable first step in that direction for the person who is seeking help.

We have seen that the notion of transformation of self, the goal of psychotherapy, is by no means a new idea. Transformation from a lesser good (feeling overwhelmed) to a greater good (self-control) has its roots in early religious and scientific practices. By performing acts, the individual was purified, cleansed, and healed. The concept of sacrifice might well serve as a metaphor for psychotherapy. Both sacrifice and psychotherapy involve transformation, a change from one form to another, a change leading to the better. Both involve some action. In sacrifice, the act is symbolic of change. In psychotherapy, the act is symbolic of meaning. The act of talking goes beyond the act because of the meaning the words have to that individual. Thus, both sacrifice and psychotherapy entail transcendence (going beyond where one is and changing).

Dream analysis, so popular today, has roots in the early sleep temples. It was there that the first description of separate mind–body experiences were described—the separation of soul and body during sleep (see Chapter 2).

Words in the form of mantras, meditation, and prayer all revealed the power that words could effect. The power of words goes far beyond verbal language, for one is transformed physically, psychologically, and spiritually, that is, holistically. The transformation leads to mastery, a transcendence of the problem (see Chapter 2).

For example, a woman has completed painting a picture and has submitted the picture to an art contest. She wins the first prize and is told: "Congratulations." That one word has myriad effects on her. She feels physically stimulated, her heart rate quickens, her breathing rate increases, she feels a rush of adrenalin. Psychologically, she feels wonderful and believes that that uplifting feeling could last forever. And yet, there is another level of transformation that is ineffable. She feels in touch with a greater knowledge—a greater understanding of experience than ever before. This level of transformation is transcendent, going beyond conscious knowledge. It produces a symbol that contains the mutual participation of both the conscious and the unconscious, which leads to a more fully integrated and comprehended experience. Jung has described this experience as the transcendent function that leads to a higher level of integration and understanding, symbolically speaking, in the language of the unconscious (Jung, 1958, p. 2). This experience is transcendent because it encompasses broader and more flexible boundaries; theoretically it has no limits except that of the conscious unknown. The transformation within of words and images, whether self-directed or other-directed, leads to a higher level of differentiation and integration—a transcendence of the conscious word to the "creation of a living symbol (Jung, 1958, p. 2). I am not speaking here of the supernatural; rather, I am speaking of the individual's power to participate in the healing process by the way of words and images that tap new meanings and understandings, and lead to higher-order integrations.

THE FUTURE

The future of self-hypnosis depends on the study of the subjective experience itself while the subject is experiencing self-hypnosis. Our dilemma is that whereas subjective experience is a fact of life, we cannot know another person's experience without some way of translating that experience into a modality that the outside observer can know, understand, and experience. The translation of subjective experience into words is a necessity for understanding. The phenomenological method described by Shor opens some doors to the study of self-hypnosis, as does the use of clinical interviews and, in particular, the use of a subject-maintained journal. I believe that a more rigorous use of the phenomenological method would open even more doors. Additional ways of tapping subjective experience are needed.

This study of self-hypnosis leads to the recognition that self-hypnosis is more than a simple on–off response, that there is a continuum of experiences that are self-hypnotic in nature. This continuum of experience includes:

1. Archetypal self-hypnosis: an instinctive protective process.
2. Self-initiated and undirected self-hypnosis: opening a window to the unconscious.
3. Self-directed hypnosis: brief practice exercises to improve skills, achieve specific goals.
4. Therapist-guided self-hypnosis: this reinforces helpful words and images and strengthens the power of these words and images to produce change.
5. Specific tape recordings: these are given to the patient by the therapist for home practice.
6. Specific scripts: these are given to the patient by the therapist for home practice.

Some theorists may believe that there is only one type of self-hypnosis; for example, Weitzenhoffer (1989) views posthypnotically suggested self-hypnosis as pseudohypnosis. He believes that pure self-hypnosis is quite limited.

I believe that the limitation is in the eye of the beholder. To the degree that the patient becomes absorbed in the experience of entering self-hypnosis and uses the trance state, he or she may indeed subjectively experience self-hypnosis even with a tape. Although a tape does not guarantee self-hypnosis, the essence of self-hypnosis appears to involve the patient initiating the self-hypnotic state and self-directing it by choosing to do it. As Sophocles said, "One must learn by doing the thing; though you think you know it, you have no certainty until you try."

Unfortunately, many people come to the hypnotherapist not to learn self-direction but to be given "magic" as a way of being transformed. They do not want self-direction but psychic surgery in which the hypnotherapist is expected to excise the problem for the client as a surgeon may excise a tumor. Clinical self-hypnosis is not psychic surgery. Rather, it is a catalyst for transformation to occur. It provides the patient with an opportunity to tap into his or her own abilities, strengths, motivations, that is, power. For this transformation to occur, ego activity is required, that is, the active participation by the client through ego-receptivity (Fromm, 1972a) and ego direction.

Like an important enzyme, words and images interact with ego receptivity. These are the winds that move, that arouse. If the winds are too calm, no movement takes place; if too strong, too much movement leads to damage. The winds need to be moderate to be effective. The power of words and images must be strong enough to move but not too strong lest the client be overwhelmed.

The power of words and images must be catalyzed within the structure of future goals as well as the structure of past and present personal meanings, experience, and feelings. The transformation can only occur within a meaningful context that can separate the past from the present and the present from the future. The integration of primary process thinking and secondary process organization is necessary for growth and direction.

Time perception plays a really important role in permitting or blocking change or transformation. If a client is tied to the past by dissociative flashbacks and is unable to separate past from present, little if any learning can occur. The client can learn with help from the therapist to differentiate what is in the past from what is happening in the present. Research needs to clarify the operation of time perception and ways to separate past, present, and future.

In addition, research needs to focus on measurement of the power invested in the personal meanings of words and images: power to motivate; power to feel; power to transform.

And research must look at the context itself, what interactions occur among expectations, realistic boundaries, therapist expectations, and the use of self-hypnosis.

Although self-hypnosis is a self-directed state with potentials for self-initiation, the clinical use of self-hypnosis presents some limitations on the pure spontaneous experience. To the extent that the therapist participates in the treatment, to the extent there is a compromise between self-hypnosis and the expectations, goals, and demands of treatment. This compromise must be recognized.

One question that must be raised is: How is it possible that words and images are empowered to generate actions and reactions, to transform, and to transcend the most difficult, the most painful, and the most seemingly impossible situation? Although no hard data exist, it is possible to hypothesize. In my view, it is possible because of the manner in which our brain processes language. Language triggers a choreography of brain cells to fire synergistically, in harmony, rather than in any single connection. It choreographs simultaneously the potentials for response through comprehension, feeling, and motor response potentials. The brain works in an integrated manner. That is the way the brain is hard wired. A word is more than a word; it contains a multitude of possibilities. An image is more than an image; it is a potential waiting to be fulfilled. The meaning and power attributed to the word and the image are generated by the patient.

This view of self-hypnosis as a means for individuals to transform themselves from within through their own potentials holistically, that is, physically and mentally, is consistent with the currently accepted philosophy of science. It will be interesting to follow future developments leading to other ways of construing self-hypnosis and the phenomena of words and images as these unfold with the evolution of the philosophy of science.

And so we have come to the end of this journey. We have pulled out some weeds of distortion and see the developmental progression of self-hypnosis over the course of 3,000 years. But the journey continues on this continuum of time, for there is more to be explored, learned, and understood. Our journey from past to present has placed self-hypnosis in relief, raising still more important questions.

Appendix

PAS SCALE 2

The following statements have been put together because we think they may provide information about a phenomenon which can be considered common and very normal in many cases, unusual in others, but which happens to most people at some time.

It is difficult to get honest reports on how often behaviors such as these occur in normal people, because these behaviors are very personal and not often spoken about. For this reason you are being asked to take this Scale seriously and respond to the sentences truthfully by circling the appropriate number. It is important that your answer describes experiences which have happened spontaneously in the natural course of living, and not as a result of hypnosis, drugs or an experiment.

Please respond to every statement.

PAS	Never	Sometimes	Often	Almost Always
1. At times I feel as if I were dreaming.	1	2	3	4
2. I can't understand why I can become irritable.	1	2	3	4
3. I feel out of touch with my body.	1	2	3	4
4. I automatically consume large amounts of food.	1	2	3	4
5. I find I cannot sit still.	1	2	3	4
6. I cannot control my laughing and crying.	1	2	3	4
7. When I am tired it feels like an outside force comes in to control my actions.	1	2	3	4
8. My body is too heavy.	1	2	3	4
9. I find myself in situations in which I do not wish to be.	1	2	3	4
10. I feel compelled to eat even when I am not hungry.	1	2	3	4
11. I don't want to feel angry.	1	2	3	4
12. My mind wants one thing but my body is determined to do another.	1	2	3	4

13. Time passes too quickly.	1	2	3	4
14. My attention is divided by several things at once.	1	2	3	4
15. I feel uncomfortable eating with others.	1	2	3	4
16. I feel the urge to shoplift.	1	2	3	4
17. In some situations my mind and my self just are not "together."	1	2	3	4
18. My moods can really change.	1	2	3	4
19. There are times I do things without thinking.	1	2	3	4
20. I forget right away what people say to me.	1	2	3	4
21. When I really want to do something, I don't think about the consequences.	1	2	3	4
22. I sometimes blank out in the middle of an activity.	1	2	3	4
23. After doing something, I wish I hadn't.	1	2	3	4
24. I am glad that I can forget what I look like.	1	2	3	4
25. I really want to do something, but afterwards I regret it.	1	2	3	4
26. Television really absorbs me.	1	2	3	4
27. I seem to lose time.	1	2	3	4
28. Upon awakening, I am surprised at how much time has passed.	1	2	3	4
29. I feel very happy, even when there is no reason.	1	2	3	4
30. I don't know how to stop myself from doing something.	1	2	3	4
31. I find myself in a strange place without knowing how I got there.	1	2	3	4
32. I find myself torn between doing one thing or another.	1	2	3	4
33. I find myself doing things without knowing why.	1	2	3	4
34. At times, I have to think and act in a way that is out of character for me.	1	2	3	4
35. Thoughts come into my mind that I cannot stop.	1	2	3	4
36. I find myself watching my every move.	1	2	3	4
37. Even when I have missed several meals I find that I am not hungry.	1	2	3	4
38. I find my mind blank.	1	2	3	4
39. I must fight giving in to bad habits.	1	2	3	4
40. I find myself in social situations when I don't want to be there.	1	2	3	4
41. Loud noises do not disturb me.	1	2	3	4
42. I wish I had more control.	1	2	3	4
43. I feel compelled to exercise much of the time.	1	2	3	4
44. Time passes too slowly.	1	2	3	4
45. When walking, I am aware of every step.	1	2	3	4
46. When I eat I am aware of every bite.	1	2	3	4
47. After eating, I find it difficult to keep my food down.	1	2	3	4
48. I lose track of time.	1	2	3	4
49. I want to do two conflicting things at once and find myself arguing with myself.	1	2	3	4
50. My mind feels divided.	1	2	3	4

51. I find I can tune out unpleasant sounds.	1	2	3	4
52. I have to pretend that I remember things.	1	2	3	4
53. I feel that there are two of me.	1	2	3	4
54. I do things without thinking.	1	2	3	4
55. I am not aware that I am eating.	1	2	3	4
56. I start to do one thing, only to drop it to do something else.	1	2	3	4
57. I am less aware of physical pain than others.	1	2	3	4
58. I find myself more aware of pain than other people.	1	2	3	4
59. I enjoy the cold.	1	2	3	4
60. I see myself differently than other people see me.	1	2	3	4

References

Abroms, G. M. (1969). The new eclecticism. *Archives of General Psychiatry, 20* (5), 514–523.

Aja, J. H. (1977). Brief group treatment of obesity through ancillary self-hypnosis. *American Journal of Clinical Hypnosis, 19* (4), 226–230.

American Psychiatric Association. (1980). *Diagnostic and statistical manual of mental disorders* (3rd ed.). Washington: Author.

Andreychuk, M. S., & Skriver, C. (1975). Hypnosis and biofeedback in the treatment of migraine headache. *International Journal of Clinical and Experimental Hypnosis, 23* (3), 172–183.

Ansel, E. L. (1977). A simple exercise to enhance response to hypnotherapy for migraine headaches. *International Journal of Clinical and Experimental Hypnosis, 25* (2), 68–71.

Araoz, D. (1985). *The new hypnosis.* New York: Brunner/Mazel.

August, R. V. (1961). *Hypnosis in obstetrics: Obstetric hypnoanesthesia.* New York: Blakeston, McGraw-Hill.

Aurelius, M. (1945). Meditations IV, 3. In *Marcus Aurelius and his times.* Roslyn: Walter J. Blackman.

Bacon, F. O. (1986). Religious meditations, of heresies, (1561–1626). Quoted in H. Rawson & M. Miner (Eds.), *The new international dictionary of quotations* (p. 82). New York: Mentor.

Baker, E. L. (1983a). State of the art of clinical hypnosis. *International Journal of Clinical and Experimental Hypnosis, 31* (2), 82–89.

Baker, E. L. (1983b). The use of hypnotic techniques with psychotics. *American Journal of Clinical Hypnosis, 25* (4), 283–288.

Baker, E. L. (1985). Ego psychology and hypnosis: Contemporary theory and practice. *Psychotherapy in Private Practice, 33* (3), 115–122.

Balsam, P., Dempster, C. R., & Brooks, C. R. (1984). Autohypnosis as a defense against coercive persuasion. *International Journal of Clinical and Experimental Hypnosis, 26* (4), 246–251.

Bandler, R., & Grinder, J. (1975). *The structure of magic, Vol. 1: Patterns of the hypnotic techniques of Milton H. Erickson, M.D.* Cupertina, CA: Meta Publications.

Banyai, E. I., & Hilgard, E. R. (1976). A comparison of active alert hypnotic induction with traditional relaxation induction. *Journal of Abnormal Psychology, 85,* 218–224.

Barabasz, A. F., & McGeorge, C. M. (1978). Biofeedback, mediated biofeedback and hypnosis in peripheral vasodilation training. *American Journal of Clinical Hypnosis, 21* (1), 28–37.

Barber, T. X. (1969). *Hypnosis: A scientific approach.* New York: Van Nostrand Reinhold.

Barber, T. X. (1975). Responding to "hypnotic" suggestions: An introspective report. *American Journal of Clinical Hypnosis, 18* (1), 6–22.

Barber, T. X. (1978). Hypnosis, suggestions and psychosomatic phenomena: A new look from the standpoint of recent experimental studies. *American Journal of Clinical Hypnosis, 21* (1), 13–27.

Barber, T. X. (1979). Suggested ("hypnotic") behavior: The trance paradigm versus an alternative paradigm. In E. Fromm & R. E. Shor (Eds.), *Hypnosis: Developments in research and new perspectives* (2nd ed., rev., pp. 217–271). New York: Aldine.

Barber, J. (1982a) Incorporating hypnosis in the management of chronic pain. In J. Barber & C. Adrain (Eds.), *Psychological approaches to the management of pain* (pp. 40–59). New York: Bruner/Mazel.

Barber, J. (1982b). Managing acute pain. In J. Barber & C. Adrian (Eds.), *Psychological approaches to the management of pain* (pp. 168–185). New York: Brunner/Mazel.

Barber, T. X. (1984). Changing unchangeable bodily processes by (hypnotic) suggestions: A new look at hypnosis, cognitions, imagining and the mind-body problem. *Advances, 1* (2), 7–40.

Barber, T. X., Spanos, N. P., & Chaves, J. F. (1974). *Hypnotism: Imagination and human potentialities.* New York: Pergamon.

Barber, T. X., & Wilson, S. C. (1978). The Barber Suggestibility Scale and the Creative Imagination Scale: Experimental and Clinical Applications. *The American Journal of Clinical Hypnosis, 21* (2 & 3), 84–108.

Bartlett, E. E. (1963). Control of postoperative pain with autohypnosis. *American Journal of Clinical Hypnosis, 6,* 166–167.

Baudouin, C. (1922). *Suggestion and autosuggestion* (E. Paul & C. Paul, Trans.). London: Allen & Unwin.

Beahrs, J. (1971). The hypnotic psychotherapy of Milton H. Erickson, *American Journal of Clinical Hypnosis, 14,* 73–90.

Benson, A. H. (1975). *The relaxation response.* New York: William Morrow.

Benson, A. H., Arns, P. A., & Hoffman, J. W. (1981). The relaxation response and hypnosis. *International Journal of Clinical and Experimental Hypnosis, 29* (3), 259–270.

Benson, H. A., Frankel, F., Apfel, R., Daniels, M. D., Schniewind, H. F., Nemiah, J. C., Sifneos, P. E., Crassweller, K. D., Greenwood, M. M.,

Kotch, J. B., Arns, P. A., & Rosner, B. (1978). Treatment of anxiety: A comparison of the usefulness of self-hypnosis and a meditational relaxation technique—an overview. *Psychotherapy and Psychosomatics, 30,* 229-242.

Bernheim, H. (1980). *Bernheim's new studies in hypnotism.* (R. S. Sandor, Trans.). New York: International Universities Press. (Original work published 1891)

Bernstein, E., & Putnam, F. (1986). Development, reliability and validity of a dissociation scale. The dissociative experiences scale (DES). *Journal of Nervous and Mental Disease, 174* (12), 727-735.

Black, S., Humphrey, J. H., & Niven, J. S. (1963). Inhibition of Mantoux reaction by direct suggestion under hypnosis. *British Medical Journal, 6,* 1649-1652.

Bliss, E. L. (1983). Multiple personalities, related disorders and hypnosis. *American Journal of Clinical Hypnosis, 26* (2), 114-123.

Bliss, E. L. (1986). *Multiple personality, allied disorders, and hypnosis.* New York: Oxford University Press.

Bloomfield, M. T. (1964). *Hymns of the Atharva-veda.* Delhi: Motilal Banarsidirs.

Blumenthal, L. (1963). Hypnotherapy of a headache. *Headache, 2* (3), 197-203.

Bowers, K. (1968). Hypnosis and creativity: A preliminary investigation. *International Journal of Clinical and Experimental Hypnosis, 16* (1), 38-52.

Bowers, K. S. (1971). Sex and susceptibility as moderator variables in the relationship of creativity and hypnotic susceptibility. *Journal of Abnormal Psychology, 78* (1), 93-100.

Bowers, P. (1979). Hypnosis and creativity: The search for the missing link. *Journal of Abnormal Psychology, 88* (5), 564-572.

Bowers, P. G., & Bowers, K. S. (1979). Hypnosis and creativity: A theoretical rapproachment. In E. Fromm & R. E. Shor (Eds.), *Hypnosis: Research developments and new perspectives* (rev., pp. 351-379). New York: Aldine.

Bowers, M. K., & Glasner, S. (1958). Auto-hypnotic aspects of the Jewish cabbalistic concept of Kavanah. *International Journal of Clinical and Experimental Hypnosis, 6,* 50-70.

Bramwell, J. M. (1956). *Hypnotism: Its history, practice and theory.* New York: Institute for Research in Hypnosis publication Society. (Original work published 1903)

Breuer, J. B., & Freud, S. (1957). *Studies on hysteria* (J. Strachey, Trans.). New York: Basic Books. (Original work published 1893)

Brown, D. P. (1977). A model for the levels of concentrative meditation. *International Journal of Clinical and Experimental Hypnosis, 25* (3), 236-273.

Brown, D. P. (1985). Hypnosis as an adjunct to the psychotherapy of the severely disturbed patient: An affective development approach. *International Journal of Clinical and Experimental Hypnosis, 33* (4), 281-301.

Brown, D. P., & Fromm, E. (1986). *Hypnotherapy and hypnoanalysis.* Hillsdale: Erlbaum.

Brown, D. P., & Fromm, E. (1987). *Hypnosis and behavioral medicine.* Hillsdale: Erlbaum.

Brunn, J. T. (1966). Hypnosis and neurological disease: A case report. *American Journal of Clinical Hypnosis, 8,* 312–313.

Byron, G. (1966). "Corsair." In L. C. Henry (Ed.), *Best quotations for all occasions* (p. 228). Greenwich, CT: Fawcett.

Bulfinch, T. (1979). *Bulfinch's mythology.* New York: Avenal Books.

Burrows, G. D., Collison, D. R., & Dennerstein, L. (Eds.). (1979). *Hypnosis 1979.* New York: Elsevier/North Holland Biomedical Press.

Callen, K. E. (1983a). Auto-hypnosis in long distance runners. *American Journal of Clinical Hypnosis, 26* (1), 30–36.

Callen, K. E. (1983b). Mental and emotional aspects of long-distance running. *Psychosomatics, 24* (2), 133–151.

Campbell, J. (1976). *Primitive mythology.* New York: Penguin.

Cannon, W. (1953). *Bodily changes in pain, hunger, fear and rage* (2nd ed.). Boston: Charles T. Branford.

Carrington, P. (1977). *Freedom in meditation.* New York: Doubleday.

Case, D. B., Fogel, D. H., & Pollack, A. A. (1980). Intrahypnotic and long-term effects of self-hypnosis on blood pressure in mild hypertension. *International Journal of Clinical and Experimental Hypnosis, 28* (1), 27–38.

Cautela, J. R. (1967). Covert sensitization. *Psychological Reports, 20* (4), 459.

Cautela, J. R. (1975). The use of covert conditioning in hypnotherapy. *International Journal of Clinical and Experimental Hypnosis, 23* (1), 15–27.

Chaisson, S. W. (1981). *Sorry I'm late: A day in the life of an obstetrician and gynecologist.* Youngstown, OH: Youngstown Lithographing.

Chappell, A. T. (1964). Hypnosis and spasticity in paraplegia. *American Journal of Clinical Hypnosis, 7* (1), 33–36.

Charcot, J. M. (1877). *Lectures on the diseases of the nervous system.* London: The New Sydenham Society.

Cheek, F. B., & LeCron, L. M. (1968). *Clinical hypnotherapy.* New York: Grune & Stratton.

Clarke, J. C., & Jackson, J. A. (1983). *Hypnosis and behavior therapy: The treatment of anxiety and phobias.* New York: Springer.

Coe, W. C., St. Jean, R. L., & Burger, J. M. (1980). Hypnosis and the enhancement of visual imagery. *American Journal of Clinical and Experimental Hypnosis, 28* (3), 225–243.

Cohen, S. B. (1979). Hypnosis for obesity. *American Journal of Clinical Hypnosis, 22* (1), 1–2.

Collison, D. R. (1970). Cardiological applications of the control of the autonomic nervous system by hypnosis. *American Journal of Clinical Hypnosis, 12* (2), 150–156.

Collison, D. R. (1975). Which asthmatic patients should be treated by hypnotherapy. *Medical Journal of Australia, 1,* 776–781.

Coué, E. (1922). *Self-mastery through conscious autosuggestion.* New York: American Library Service.

Crasilneck, H. B. (1979). Hypnosis in the control of chronic low back pain. *American Journal of Clinical Hypnosis, 22* (2), 71–78.

Crasilneck, H. B. (1982). The use of hypnosis in the control of chronic pain. *International Journal of Clinical and Experimental Hypnosis, 30* (2), 189–230.

Crasilneck, H. B., & Hall, J. A. (1960). Blood pressure and pulse rates in neutral hypnosis. *International Journal of Clinical and Experimental Hypnosis, 8* (3), 137–139.

Crasilneck, H. G., & Hall, J. A. (1970). The use of hypnosis in the rehabilitation of complicated vascular and post-traumatic neurological patients. *International Journal of Clinical and Experimental Hypnosis, 18,* 149–159.

Crasilneck, H., & Hall, J. (1985). *Clinical hypnosis: principles and applications* (2nd ed.). New York: Grune & Stratton.

Crasilneck, H. B., Stirman, J., Wilson, B. J., McCranie, E. J., & Fogelman, J. M. (1957). Use of hypnosis in the management of patients with burns. *Journal of the American Medical Association, 162,* 1606–1608.

Crawford, H. J. (1981). Hypnotic susceptibility as related to gestalt closure tasks. *Journal of Personality and Social Psychology, 40* (2), 376–383.

Crawford, H. J. (1982). Cognitive processing during hypnosis: Much unfinished business. *Research Communications in Psychology, Psychiatry and Behavior, 7* (2), 169–179.

Culbertson, F. (1989). A four step hypnotherapy model for de La Tourette's Syndrome. *American Journal of Clinical Hypnosis, 31* (4), 252–256.

Daniels, L. K. (1975). The treatment of psychophysiological disorders and severe anxiety by behavior therapy, hypnosis and transcendental meditation. *American Journal of Clinical Hypnosis, 17* (4), 267–270.

Daniels, L. K. (1976a). The effects of automated hypnosis and hand warming on migraine: A pilot study. *The American Journal of Clinical Hypnosis, 19* (2), 91–94.

Daniels, L. K. (1976b). The treatment of acute anxiety and postoperative gingival pain by hypnosis and covert conditioning: A case report. *The American Journal of Clinical Hypnosis, 19* (2), 116–119.

Das, J. P. (1965). The Pavlovian theory of hypnosis: An evaluation. In R. E. Shor & M. T. Orne, (Eds.), *The nature of hypnosis: Selected basic readings* (pp. 255–266). New York: Holt, Rinehart & Winston.

Davenport-Slack, B. (1975). A comparative evaluation of obstetrical hypnosis and antenatal childbirth training. *International Journal of Clinical and Experimental Hypnosis, 23* (4), 266–281.

Davidson, R. J., & Goleman, D. J. (1977). The role of attention in meditation and hypnosis: A psychobiological perspective on transformations of consciousness. *International Journal of Clinical and Experimental Hypnosis, 25* (4), 291–308.

De Puysegur, A. M. (1837). *An essay of instruction on animal magnetism* (J. King, Trans.). New York: J. C. Kelley.

Deleuze, J. P. F. (1982). *Practical instruction in animal magnetism*. New York: Da Capo Press. (Original work published 1825)

Dengrove, E. (1973). The uses of hypnosis in behavior therapy. *International Journal of Clinical and Experimental Hypnosis, 21* (1), 13–17.

Dorcus, R. M. (1956). *Hypnosis and its therapeutic applications*. New York: Blakiston Division, McGraw-Hill.

Durant, C. F. D. (1982). *Exposition of a new theory of animal magnetism*. New York: Da Capo Press. (Original work published 1837)

Easton, M. G. (1989). *The illustrated bible dictionary*. New York: Crown.

Edelstein, G. (1981). *Trauma, trance and transformation: A clinical guide to hypnotherapy*. New York: Bruner/Mazel.

Edmonston, W. E. (1981). *Hypnosis and relaxation: Modern verification of an old equation*. New York: Wiley.

Edmonston, W. E. (1986). *The induction of hypnosis*. New York: Wiley.

Eisen, M. R. (1989). Return of the repressed: Hypnoanalysis of a case of total amnesia. *International Journal of Clinical and Experimental Hypnosis, 37* (2), 107–119.

Eisen, M. R., & Fromm, E. (1983). The clinical use of self-hypnosis in hypnotherapy: Tapping the functions of imagery and adaptive regression. *The International Journal of Clinical and Experimental Hypnosis, 31* (4), 243–255.

Elkins, G. B. (1987). Hypnotic treatment of anxiety. In W. C. Wester (Ed.), *Clinical hypnosis: A case management approach* (pp. 142–157). Cincinnati: Behavioral Science Center.

Ellenberger, H. F. (1970). *The discovery of the unconscious: The history and evolution of dynamic psychiatry*. New York: Basic Books.

Emerson, R. W. (1986). The American scholar. In H. J. Rawson & M. Miner (Eds.), *International dictionary of quotations* (p. 214). New York: Mentor.

Erasmus, D. (1966). Adagio. In L. C. Henry (Ed.), *Best quotations for all occasions* (p. 206). Greenwich, CT: Fawcett.

Erickson, M. H. (1943). Hypnotic investigation of psychosomatic phenomenon, III: A controlled use of hypnotic regression in the therapy of an acquired food intolerance. *Psychosomatic Medicine, 5,* 67–70.

Erickson, M. H. (1948). Hypnotic psychotherapy. In *The medical clinics of North America* (pp. 571–583). New York: W. B. Saunders.

Erickson, M. H. (1958a). Naturalistic techniques of hypnosis. *American Journal of Clinical Hypnosis, 1* (1), 3–8.

Erickson, M. H. (1958b). Pediatric hypnotherapy. *The American Journal of Clinical Hypnosis, 1* (1), 25–29.

Erickson, M. H. (1966). The interspersal technique for symptom correction and pain control. *The American Journal of Clinical Hypnosis, 8,* 198–209.

Erickson, M. H. (1980a). *The Collected Papers of Milton Erickson* (E. L. Rossi, Ed.). New York: Irvington.

Erickson, M. H. (1980b). Hypnotic alteration of sensory, perceptual and psychophysical process. In E. L. Rossi (Ed.), *The collected papers of Milton H. Erickson on hypnosis, Volume II*. New York: Irvington.

Erickson, M. H. (1983). *Healing in hypnosis, Vol. I* (E. R. Rossi, M. O. Ryan, & F. L. Sharp, Eds.). New York: Irvington.

Erickson, M. H. (1985). *Life reframing in hypnosis: The seminars, workshops and lectures of Milton H. Erickson, Vol II* (E. L. Rossi & M. O. Ryan, Eds.). New York: Irvington.

Erickson, M. H., Hershman, S., & Sector, I. I. (1981). *The practical application of medical and dental hypnosis*. Chicago, IL: Seminars on Hypnosis Publishing Co. (Original work published in 1961)

Erickson, M. H., & Rossi, E. (1975). Varieties of double bind. *American Journal of Clinical Hypnosis, 17* (2), 143–157 .

Erickson, M. H., & Rossi, E. (1977). *Hypnotic realities*. New York: Irvington.

Estabrooks, G. H., & May, J. A. (1965). Hypnosis in integrative motivation. *American Journal of Clinical Hypnosis, 7* (4), 346–352.

Ewin, D. (1978). Clinical use of hypnosis for attenuation of burn depth. In F. H. Frankel & H. S. Zamansky (Eds.), *Hypnosis at its bicentennial*, (pp. 155–162). New York: Plenum Press.

Ewin, D. (1980). Hypnosis in burn therapy. In G . D. Burrows & L. Dennerstein (Eds.), *Handbook of hypnosis and psychosomatic medicine*. Amsterdam: Elsevier/North Holland Biomedical Press.

Fabbri, J. R. (1976). Hypnosis and behavior therapy: A coordinated approach to the treatment of trichotillomania. *American Journal of Clinical Hypnosis, 19* (1), 4–8.

Ferenczi, S. (1956). Introjection and transference. (E. Jones, Trans.). In S. Ferenczi & O. Rank (Eds.), *The development of psychoanalysis*. New York: Dover.

Finer, B. (1982). Treatment in an interdisciplanary pain clinic. In J. B. Barber & C. Adrian (Eds.), *Psychological approaches to the mangement of pain* (pp. 186–204). New York: Brunner/Mazel.

Fordyce, W. (1978). Learning processes in pain. In A. Sternbach (Ed.), *Psychology of pain* (pp. 49–72). New York: Raven Press.

Frankel, F. H. (1976). *Hypnosis: Trance as a coping mechanism*. New York: Plenum Press.

Frankel, F., Apfel, R. J., Kelly, S. F., Benson, H., Quinn, T., Newmark, J., & Malmud, R. (1979). The use of hypnotizability scales in the clinical review after six years. *International Journal of Clinical and Experimental Hypnosis, 27* (2), 63–73.

Frankenthal, K. (1969). Autohypnosis and other aids for survival in situations of extreme stress. *International Journal of Clinical and Experimental Hypnosis, 17* (3), 153–159.

Freud, S. (1962). *Complete psychological works of Sigmund Freud* (standard edition, J. Strachey, Ed.) London: Hogarth Press.

Friedman, H., & Taub, H. H. (1977). The use of hypnosis and biofeedback procedures for essential hypertension. *International Journal of Clinical and Experimental Hypnosis, 25* (4), 335–347.

Fromm, E. (1965a). Hypnoanalysis: Theory and two case excerpts. *Psychotherapy: Theory Research and Practice, 2* (3), 127.

Fromm, E. (1965b). Spontaneous autohypnotic age regression in a nocturnal dream. *International Journal of Clinical and Experimental Hypnosis, 13* (3), 119–131.

Fromm, E. (1968a). Dissociative and integrative processes in hypnoanalysis. *American Journal of Clinical Hypnosis, 10* (3), 174–177.

Fromm, E. (1968B). Transference and countertransference in hypnoanalysis. *International Journal of Clinical and Experimental Hypnosis, 16* (1), 77–84.

Fromm, E. (1972a). Ego activity and passivity of the ego in hypnosis. *International Journal of Clinical and Experimental Hypnosis, 20* (3), 238.

Fromm, E. (1972b). Quo vadis hypnosis? Predictions of future trends in hypnosis research. In E. Fromm & R. E. Shor (Eds.), *Hypnosis: Research developments and perspectives* (pp. 575–586). Chicago: Aldine-Atherto.

Fromm, E. (1975a). Autohypnosis. In L. E. Unestahl (Ed.), *Hypnosis in the seventies* (pp. 24–28). Orebro, Sweden: Veje Forlag.

Fromm, E. (1975b). Self-hypnosis: A new area of research. *Psychotherapy: Theory, Research and Practice, 12,* 295–301.

Fromm, E. (1977). An ego-psychological theory of altered states of consciousness. *International Journal of Clinical and Experimental Hypnosis, 25* (4), 372–387.

Fromm, E. (1978–1979). Primary and secondary process in waking and in altered states of consciousness. *Journal of Altered States of Consciousness, 4,* 115–128.

Fromm, E. (1981). Ego-psychological parameters of hypnosis and their clinical applications. In H. Wain (Ed.), *Theoretical and clinical aspects of hypnosis.* Miami, FL: Symposia Specialists.

Fromm, E. (1984), The theory and practice of hypnoanalysis. In W. C. Wester, & A. H. Smith (Eds.), *Clinical hypnosis: A multidisciplinary approach* (pp. 142–154). Philadephia: J. B. Lippincott.

Fromm, E., Brown, D. P, Hurt, S. W. Oberlander, J. Z., Boxer, A. M., & Pfeifer, G. (1981). The phenomena and characteristics of self-hypnosis. *International Journal of Clinical and Experimental Hypnosis, 29* (3), 189–246.

Fromm, E., & Eisen, A. M. (1982). Self-hypnosis as a therapeutic aid in the mourning process. *American Journal of Clinical Hypnosis, 25* (1), 3–14.

Fromm, E., & Gardner, G. G. (1979). Ego psychology and hypnoanalysis: An integration of theory and technique. *Bulletin of the Menninger Clinic, 43* (5), 413–423.

Fromm, E. & Shor, R. E. (Eds.). (1979). *Hypnosis: Developments in research and new perspectives* (2nd ed.). New York: Aldine.

Fromm E., & Kahn, S. (1990a). *Self-hypnosis: The Chicago paradigm.* New York: Guilford Press.

Fromm, E., & Kahn, S. (1990b). The relation of self-reports of hypnotic depth in self-hypnosis to hypnotizability and imagery production. In *Self-hypnosis: The Chicago paradigm* (pp. 147–159). New York: Guilford Press.

Fromm, E., & Kahn, S. (1990c). Representations of self-hypnosis in personal narratives. In *Self-hypnosis: The Chicago paradigm* (pp. 115–121). New York: Guilford Press.

Fromm, E., & Kahn, S. (1990d). The role of imagery in self-hypnosis: Its relationship to personality characteristics and gender. In *Self-hypnosis: The Chicago paradigm* (pp. 135–146). New York: Guilford Press.

Gallwey, W. T. (1974). *The inner game of tennis.* New York: Random House.

Gardner, G. G. (1976). Childhood, death, and human dignity: Hypnotherapy for David. *International Journal of Clinical Experimental Hypnosis, 24* (2), 122–129.

Gardner, G. G. (1981). Teaching self-hypnosis to children. *International Journal of Clinical and Experimental Hypnosis, 29* (3), 300–312.

Gardner, G. G., & Olness, K. (1981). *Hypnosis and hypnotherapy for children.* New York: Grune & Stratton.

Garver, R. B. (1984). Eight steps to self-hypnosis. *American Journal of Clinical Hypnosis, 24* (4), 232–235.

Ghalioungui, P. (1973). *Magic and medical science in ancient Egypt* (2nd ed.). Amsterdam: Israel Press.

Gill, M., & Brenman, M. M. (1959). *Hypnosis and related states: Psychoanalytic studies in regression.* Nw York: International Universities Press.

Glasner, S. (1951). A note on allusions to hypnosis in the Bible and Talmud. *International Journal of Clinical and Experimental Hypnosis, 13* (1), 34–39.

Glucksman, M. L. (1981). Physiological measures and feedback during psychotherapy. *Psychotherapy and Psychosomatics, 36* (3–4), 165–199.

Graham, G. W. (1975). Hypnotic treatment for migraine headaches. *International Journal of Clinical and Experimental Hypnosis, 23* (3), 165–171.

Gross, M. (1983a). Correcting perceptual abnormalities, anorexia nervosa and obesity by use of hypnosis. *Journal of the American Society of Psychosomatic Dentistry and Medicine, 30* (4), 142–150.

Gross, M. (1983b). Hypnoanalytic approach to bulimia. *Medical Hypnoanalysis, 4* (2), 77–82.

Gross, M. (1986). Use of hypnosis in eating disorders. *New Directions for Mental Health Services, 31,* 109–118.

Gruber, L. N. (1983). Hypnotherapeutic techniques in patients with affective instability. *American Journal of Clinical Hypnosis, 25* (4), 263–266.

Gruen, W. (1972). Successful application of systematic self relaxation and self suggestions about postoperative reactions in a case of cardiac surgery. *International Journal of Clinica and Experimental Hypnosis, 20* (3), 143–151.

Gruenewald, D. (1982a). Problems of relevance in the application of laboratory data to clinical situations. *International Journal of Clinical and Experimental Hypnosis, 30* (4), 345–353.

Gruenewald, D. (1982b). A psychoanalytic view of hypnosis. *American Journal of Clinical Hypnosis, 24* (3), 185–190.

Gruenewald, D., Fromm, E., & Oberlander, M. (1979). Hypnosis and adaptive regression: An ego psychological inquiry. In E. Fromm & R. Shor (Eds.), *Hypnosis: Research developments and perspectives* (619–635).

Gur, R. C., Reyher, J. (1976). Enhancement of creativity via free-imagery and hypnosis. *American Journal of Clinical Hypnosis, 18* (4), 237–249.

Haley J. (Ed.). (1967). *Advanced techniques of hypnosis and therapy: Selected papers of Milton H. Erickson, M.D.* New York: Grune & Stratton.

Hall, H. R. (1983). Hypnosis and the immune system: A review with implications for cancer and the psychology of healing. *American Journal of Clinical Hypnosis, 25* (2), 75–103.

Hamilton, E. (1940). *Mythology: Timeless tales of gods and heroes.* New York: New American Library.

Hammond, C. D. (1987). The use of fractionation in self-hypnosis. *American Journal of Clinical Hypnosis, 30* (2), 119–124.

Hardy, J. D., Wolff, H. G., & Goodell, H. (1952). *Pain sensations and reactions.* New York: Williams & Wilkins.

Hathaway, S. R., & McKinnon, J. C. (1956). *The Minnesota Multiphasic Personality Inventory.* New York: Psychological Corporation.

Heidegger, M. (1962). *Being and time.* New York: Harper & Row.

Henry, L. C. (1966). *Best quotations for all occasions.* Greenwich, CT: Fawcett Publications.

Heraclitus (1986). *Lives of eminent philosophers.* In H. Rawson, & M. Miner, (Eds.), *The new international dictionary of quotations* (p. 50). New York: Mentor.

Hilgard, E. R. (1965). *Hypnotic susceptibility.* New York: Harcourt, Brace & World.

Hilgard, E. R. (1969). Altered states of awareness. *Journal of Nervous and Mental Disease, 149* (1), 68–79.

Hilgard, J. R. (1970). *Personality and hypnosis: A study of imaginative involvement.* Chicago: University of Chicago Press.

Hilgard, E. R. (1975). Self-induction of hypnosis by inexperienced subjects and self-deepening perspectives. In L. E. Unestahl (Ed.), *Hypnosis in the seventies* (pp. 61–65). Orebro, Sweden: Veje Forlag.

Hilgard, E. R. (1977). *Divided consciousness.* New York: Wiley.

Hilgard, E. R. (1979a). Divided consciousness in hypnosis: The implications of the hidden observer. In E. Fromm & R. E. Shor (Eds.), *Hypnosis: Developments in research and new perspectives* (2nd ed., pp. 45–80). New York: Aldine.

Hilgard, J. R. (1979b). *Personality and hypnosis: A study of imaginative involvement* (2nd ed.). Chicago: University of Chicago Press.

Hilgard, E., & Hilgard, J. (1975). *Hypnosis in the relief of pain.* Los Altos: William Kaufman & Sons.

Hilgard, J. R., & LeBaron, S. (1982). Relief of anxiety and pain in children and adolescents with cancer: Quantitative measures and clinical observations. *International Journal of Clinical and Experimental Hypnosis, 30* (4), 417–442.

Hilgard, J. R., & LeBaron, S. (1984). *Hypnotherapy of pain in children with cancer.* Los Altos: William Kaufmann.

Hilger, W. (1912). *Hypnosis and suggestion, their nature, action, importance and position amongst therapeutic agents* (R. W. Felkin, Trans.). New York: Rebman.

Holroyd, J. (1987). How hypnosis may potentiate psychotherapy. *American Journal of Clinical Hypnosis, 29* (3), 194–200.

Holroyd, J. C., Nuechterlein, K. H., Shapiro, D., & Ward, F. (1982). Individual differences in hypnotizability and effectiveness of hypnosis or biofeedback. *International Journal of Clinical and Experimental Hypnosis, 30* (1), 45–65.

Hull, C. L. (1933). *Hypnosis and suggestibility: An experimental approach* (pp. 391–400). New York: Appleton-Century-Crofts.

Ikemi, Y., Akagai, M., Maeda, J., Fukumoto, T., Kaate, K., Hirakawa, K., Gondo, S., Nakagawa, T., Honda, T., Sakamototo, A., & Kumagai, M. (1959). Hypnotic experiments on the psychosomatic aspects of gastrointestinal disorders. *International Journal of Clinical and Experimental Hypnosis, 7* (3), 139–150.

Jacobson, E. (1929). *Progressive relaxation: A physiological and clinical investigation of muscular states and their significance in psychology and medical practice.* Chicago: University of Chicago Press.

Jaynes, J. (1976). *The origin of consciousness in the breakdown of the bicameral mind.* Boston: Houghton Mifflin.

Johnson, L. S. (1979). Self-hypnosis: Behavioral and phenomenological comparisons with heterohypnosis. *International Journal of Clinical and Experimental Hypnosis, 27* (3), 240–264.

Johnson, L. S. (1981). Current research in self-hypnotic phenomenology: The Chicago Paradigm. *International Journal of Clinical and Experimental Hypnosis, 29* (3), 247–258.

Johnson, L. S., Dawson, S. L., Clark, J. L., & Sikorsky, C. (1983). Self-hypnosis versus hetero-hypnosis: Order effects and sex differences in behavioral and experiential impact. *International Journal of Clinical and Experimental Hypnosis, 31,* 139–145.

Johnson, L. S., & Weight, D. G. (1976). Short report self-hypnosis versus heterohypnosis: Experiential and behavioral comparisons. *Journal of Abnormal Psychology, 85* (5), 523–526.

Jung, C. G. (1958). *Psyche and symbol* (V. S. deLaszlo, Ed.). Garden City: Anchor Books.

Kant, E. (1926). *The critique of pure reason* (Max Muller, Trans.). New York: Macmillan. (Original work published in 1781)

Kaye, J. M. (1987). Use of hypnosis in the treatment of cancer patients. *Journal of Psychosocial Oncology, 5* (2), 11–22.

Kierkegard, S. (1954). *The sickness unto death* (Walter Lowrie, Trans.). New York: Doubleday & Co.

Kihlstrom, J. F. (1980). Personality correlates of hypnotic susceptibility: Needs for achievement, and autonomy, self-monitoring and masculinity-feminity. *American Journal of Clinical Hypnosis, 22* (4), 225–230.

Kline, M. V. (1958). *Freud and hypnosis: The interaction of psychodynamics and hypnosis.* New York: Julian Press.

Kline, M. V. (1967). *Psychodynamics and hypnosis: New contributions to the practice and the theory of hypnotherapy.* Springfield, IL: Charles C. Thomas.

Kline, M. V. (1972). Freud and hypnosis: A reevaluation. *International Journal of Clinical and Experimental Hypnosis, 20* (4), 252–263.

Kohen, D. P. (1987). Application of relaxation, mental imagery (self-hypnosis) in pediatric emergencies. *American Journal of Clinical Hypnosis, 34* (4), 283–294.

Kroger, W. S. (1977). *Clinical and experimental hypnosis* (2nd ed.). Philadelphia: J. B. Lippincott.

Kroger, W. S., & Fezler, W. D. (1976). *Hypnosis and behavior modification: Imagery conditioning.* Philadelphia: J. B. Lippincott.

Kumar, V. K., & Pekala, R. J. (1987). Hypnotizability, absorption and individual differences in phenomenological experience. *International Journal of Clinical and Experimental Hypnosis, 36* (2), 80–95.

LaBaw, W. L. (1975). Autohypnosis in hemophilia. *Haemotologia, 9,* 103.

LaBaw, W., Holton, C., Tewe, L., & Eccles, D. (1975). The use of self-hypnosis by children with cancer. *American Journal of Clinical Hypnosis, 17* (4), 233–238.

Leuner, H. (1969). Guided affective imagery. *American Journal of Psychotherapy, 23,* 4–22.

Lewis, E. (1982). The use of headphones and tape recording with selected patients in hypnotherapy. *International Journal of Clinical and Experimental Hypnosis, 30* (2), 189–230.

Lieberman, L. R., Fishers, J. R., Thomas, R., & King, W. (1968). Use of tape recorded suggestions as an aid to probationary students. *American Journal of Clinical Hypnosis, 11* (1), 35–41.

London, P. (1963). *Children's Hypnotic Susceptibility Scale.* Palo Alto, CA: Consulting Psychologist Press.

Ludwig, A. (1983). The psychobiological functions of dissociation. *The American Journal of Clinical Hypnosis, 26* (2), 93–99.

Lusebrink, V. B. (1986–1987). Visual imagery: Its psychophysiological components and levels of information processing. *Imagination, Cognition and Personality, 6* (4), 205–218.

Lynn, S. J., Nash, M. R., Rhue, J. W., Frauman, D., & Stanley, S. (1983). Hypnosis and the experience of nonvolition. *International Journal of Clinical and Experimental Hypnosis, 31* (4), 293–308.

Lynn, S. J., Neufeld, V., & Matyi, C. L. (1987). Inductions vs. suggestions:

Effects of direct and indirect wording on hypnotic responding and experience. *Journal of Abnormal Psychology, 96,* 76-79.

Lynn, S. J., & Rhue, J. W. (1985). The fantasy prone person: Hypnosis, imagination and creativity. *Journal of Personality and Social Psychology, 51* (2), 404-408.

Lynn, S. J., Snodgrass, M., Rhue, J. W., & Hardaway, R. (1987). Goal-directed fantasy, hypnotic susceptibility and expectancies. *Journal of Personality and Social Psychology 53* (5), 933-938.

MacCulloch, J. A. (1911). *The religion of the ancient Celts.* Edinburgh: T. & T. Clark.

Machovic, F. J. (1981). Shakespeare on hypnosis: The tempest. *American Journal of Clinical Hypnosis, 24* (2), 73-78.

Magonet, A. P. (1960). Hypnosis in asthma. *International Journal of Clinical and Experimental Hypnosis, 2,* 121-127.

Maher-Loughnan, G. P. (1970). Hypnosis and autohypnosis for the treatment of asthma. *International Journal of Clinical and Experimental Hypnosis, 18* (1), 1-14.

Maher-Loughnan, G. P. (1980). Applications of hypnosis in medicine. *British Journal Hospital Medicine, 23,* 447-448.

Margolis, C. G. (1982-1983). Hypnotic imagery with cancer patients. *American Journal of Clinical Hypnosis, 25,* 128-134.

McConkey, K. M., & Sheehan, P. W. (1982). Effort and experience on the creative imagination scale. *International Journal of Clinical and Experimental Hypnosis, 30* (3), 280-288.

Meares, A. (1978). Vivid visualization and dim visual awareness in the regression of cancer in meditation. *Journal of the American Society of Psychosomatic and Dental Medicine, 25* (3), 85-88.

Medansky, R. S., & Handler, R. M. (1981). Dermatopsychosomaticas: Classification, physiology, and therapeutic approaches. *Journal of the American Academy of Dermatology, 5* (2), 1125-1136.

Melzack, R. (1973). *The puzzle of pain.* New York: Basic Books.

Merleau-Ponty, M. (1963). *The structure of behavior* (A. Fisher, Trans.). Boston: Beacon Press.

Mersky, H., & Spear, F. H. (1967). *Pain: Psychological and psychiatric aspects.* London: Balliere Tindall.

Meszaros, I., Banyai, E. I., & Greguss, A. C. (1985). Evoked potential correlates of verbal versus imagery coding in hypnosis. In D. Waxman, P. C. Misra, M. V. Gibson, & M. A. Basker (Eds.), *Modern trends in hypnosis.* New York: Plenum.

Miller, R. D. (1984). The possible use of auto-hypnosis as a resistance during hypnotherapy. *International Journal of Clinical and Experimental Hypnosis, 32* (2), 236-247.

Mills, J. C., Crowley, R. J., & Ryan, M. O. (1986). *Therapeutic metaphors for children and the child within.* New York: Brunner/Mazel.

Morgan, A. H., & Hilgard, J. R. (1979). The Stanford Hypnotic Clinical Scale: Adult. *American Journal of Clinical Hypnosis, 21* (2 & 3), 134-147.

Mott, T. (1982). The role of hypnosis in psychotherapy. *American Journal of Clinical Hypnosis, 24* (4), 241–248.

Mott, T. J., & Roberts, J. (1979). Obesity and hypnosis: A review of the literature. *American Journal of Clinical Hypnosis, 22* (1), 3–7.

Murray-Jobsis, J. (1984). Hypnosis with severely disturbed patients. In W. C. Wester & A. H. Smith, Jr. (Eds.), *Clinical hypnosis: A multidisciplinary approach* (pp. 368–404).

Muthu, D. C. (1930). *A short account of the antiquity of Hindu medicine and civilization.* London: Balliere, Tindall and Cox.

Nemiah, J., Freyberger, H., & Sifneos, P. (1976). Alexithymia: A view of the psychosomatic process. In D. Hill (Ed.), *Modern trends in psychosomatic medicine, Vol III.* London: Butterworth.

Nietzsche, F. (1909). *Thus spake Zarathustra* (T. Common, Trans.). In O. Levy (Ed.), *The complete works of Frederich Neitzsche.* Edinburgh: T. N. Foulis.

Nugent, W. R., Carden, N. A., & Montgomery, D. J. (1984). Utilizing the creative unconscious in the treatment of hypodermic phobias and sleep disturbance. *American Journal of Clinical Hypnosis, 26* (3), 201–205.

Olness, K. (1976). Autohypnosis in functional megacolon in children. *American Journal of Clinical Hypnosis, 19* (1), 28–32.

Olness, K. (1977). In-service hypnosis education in a children's hospital. *American Journal of Clinical Hypnosis, 20* (1), 80–83.

Olness, K., & Culbert, T. (1989). Voluntary regulation of salivary immunoglobulin. *Pediatrics, 83* (1), 66–71.

Olness, K., & Gardner, G. G. (1988). *Hypnosis and hypnotherapy for children* (2nd ed.). New York: Grune & Stratton.

Orne, M. T. (1965). The nature of hypnosis: Artifact and Essence. In R. E. Shor & M. T. Orne (Eds.), *The nature of hypnosis: Selected basic readings* (pp. 89–123). New York: Holt, Rinehart and Winston. (Original work published in 1959)

Orne, M. T., & McConkey, K. M. (1981). Toward convergent inquiry into self-hypnosis. *International Journal of Clinical and Experimental Hypnosis, 29* (4), 313–323.

Pattie, F. (1967). A brief history of hypnotism. In J. E. Gordon (Ed.), *Handbook of clinical and experimental hypnosis* (pp. 10–43). New York: Macmillan.

Paul, G. L., & Trimble, R. W. (1970). Recorded vs. live relaxation training and hypnotic suggestion: Comparative effectiveness for reducing physiological arousal and inhibiting stress response. *Behavior Therapy, 3,* 285–302.

Pavlov, I. P. (1941). *Lectures on conditioned reflexes* (W. H. Gantt, Trans.). New York: International Publications.

Persinger, M. A., & De Sano, C. F. (1986). Temporal lobe signs: Positive correlations with imaginings and hypnosis induction profiles. *Psychological Reports, 58,* 347–350.

Pettinatti, H. M., & Wade, J. H. (1986). Hypnosis in the treatment of anorexic and bulimic patients. *Seminars in Adolescent Medicine, 2* (1), 75–79.

Piaget, J. (1951). *Play, dreams, and imitation in childhood.* New York: Norton.

Raginsky, B. B. (1963). Hypnosis in internal medicine and general practice. In J. M. Schneck (Ed.), *Hypnosis in modern medicine* (2nd ed.). Springfield: Charles C. Thomas.

Raikov, V. L. (1977). Theoretical analysis of deep hypnosis: Creative activity of hypnotized subjects into transformed self-consciousness. *American Journal of Clinical Hypnosis, 19* (4), 214–220.

Rappaport, D. (1967). States of consciousness: A psychopathological and psychodynamic view. In M. M. Gill (Ed.), *The collected papers of David Rapaport* (pp. 385–404). New York: Basic Books.

Rausch, V. (1980). Cholecystectomy with self-hypnosis. *American Journal of Clinical Hypnosis, 22* (4), 547–551.

Rawson, H., & Miner, M. (1986). *The new international dictionary of quotations.* New York: New American Library.

Ringrose, C. A. D. (1979). The use of hypnology as an adjunct in curbing smoking, obesity and hypertension. In G. D. Burrows & L. Dennerstein (Eds.), *Handbook of hypnosis and psychosomatic medicine* (pp. 223–238). Amsterdam: Elsevier Biomedical Press.

Risenberg, D. E. (1986). Can mind affect body defenses against disease? Nascent specialty offers a host of tantalizing clues. *Journal of the American Medical Association, 256,* 313–317.

Rogers, C. (1959). Toward a theory of creativity. In H. H. Anderson (Ed.), *Creativity and its cultivation.* New York: Harper Press.

Romen, A. S. (1981). *Self-suggestion and its influence on the human organism.* Armonk, NY: M. E. Sharpe.

Rosenhan, D. L. W. (1969). Hypnosis and personality: A moderator variable analysis. In L. Chertok (Ed.), *Psychophysiological mechanisms of hypnosis* (pp. 193–198). New York: Springer-Verlag.

Rossi, E. L. (1986). *The psychobiology of mind–body healing: New concepts of therapeutic hypnosis.* New York: W. W. Norton.

Ruch, J. (1972). A study of self-hypnosis under alternative procedures. *Dissertation Abstracts International, 33* (5–8), 2381–2382.

Ruch, J. C. (1975). Self-hypnosis: The result of heterohypnosis or vice versa? *International Journal of Clinical and Experimental Hypnosis, 23* (4), 282–304.

Sacerdote, P. (1967). *Induced dreams* (2nd ed.). Brooklyn: Theo Gaus.

Sacerdote, P. (1972). Eclectic approaches to hypnotherapy. *American Journal of Psychotherapy, 26* (4), 511–520.

Sacerdote, P. (1978). Teaching self-hypnotism to patients with chronic pain. *Journal of Human Stress, 4* (1), 18–21.

Sacerdote, P. (1981). Teaching self-hypnosis to adults. *International Journal of Clinical and Experimental Hypnosis, 29* (3), 282–299.

Sacerdote, P. (1982). Techniques of hypnotic intervention with pain patients. In J. Barber & C. Adrian (Eds.), *Psychological approaches to the management of pain* (pp. 60–83). New York: Brunner/Mazel.

Salter, A. (1951). Three techniques of autohypnosis. *Journal of General Psychology, 24,* 423–438.

Salter, A. (1961). *Conditioned reflex therapy*. New York: Capricorn.

Sanders, S. (1975). Corrective social interaction therapy (role modeling). *Journal of Orthopsychiatry, 45* (5), 875–883.

Sanders, S. (1976). Mutual group hypnosis as a catalyst in fostering creative problem solving. *American Journal of Clinical Hypnosis, 19* (1), 622–626.

Sanders, S. (1978). Creative problem solving and psychotherapy. *International Journal of Clinical and Experimental Hypnosis, 26* (1), 15–21.

Sanders, S. (1981). Hypnotic self-control strategies in hemophiliac children. *Journal of the American Society of Psychosomatic Dentistry and Medicine, 28* (1), 11–21.

Sanders, S. (1982). Hypnotic dream utilization. *American Journal of Clinical Hypnosis, 25* (1).

Sanders, S. (1986a). Self-hypnosis and problem solving in the treatment of obesity. *Psychotherapy in Private Practice, 4* (3), 35–41.

Sanders, S. (1986b). The perceptual alteration scale: A scale measuring dissociation [Special issue: Dissociation]. *American Journal of Clinical Hypnosis, 29* (2), 95–102.

Sanders, S. (1987). Styles of clinical self-hypnosis. In W. C. Wester (Ed.), *Clinical hypnosis: A case management approach* (pp. 29–39). Cincinnati: Behavior Science Center Publications.

Sanders, S., & Boswell, J. (1974). Corrective social interaction therapy. *Psychiatric Forum, 4* (2), 11–13.

Sarbin, T. R. (1950). Contributions to role-taking theory. I: Hypnotic behavior. *Psychological Review, 57*, 255–270.

Sarbin, T., & Coe, W. (1972). *Hypnosis: A social–psychological analysis of influence communication*. New York: Holt, Rinehart and Winston.

Sarbin, T. R., & Slagel, R. W. (1979). Hypnosis and physiological outcomes. In E. Fromm & R. Shor (Eds.), *Hypnosis: Developments in research and new perspectives* (2nd ed.). New York: Aldine.

Scagnelli, J. (1980). Hypnotherapy with schizophrenic and borderline patients: The use of trance. *American Journal of Clinical Hypnosis, 22*, 164–169.

Schneck, J. M. (1953). The therapeutic use of self-hypnotic dreams. *International Journal of Clinical and Experimental Hypnosis, 1* (2), 28–31.

Schneck, J. M. (1963). *Hypnosis in modern medicine* (3rd ed.). Springfield, IL: Charles C. Thomas.

Schneck, J. M. (1965). *Principles and practice of hypnoanalysis*. Springfield, IL: Charles C. Thomas.

Schneck, J. M. (1966). A study of alterations in body sensations during hypnoanalysis. *International Journal of Clinical and Experimental Hypnosis, 14* (3), 215–231.

Scholem, G. G. (1941). *Major trends in Jewish mysticism*. Jerusalem: Schocken.

Schultz, J. H., & Luthe, W. (1959). *Autogenic training: A psychophysiological approach to psychotherapy*. New York: Grune & Stratton.

Shakespeare, W. (1945). *The complete works of William Shakespeare*. Roslyn, NY: Walter J. Blackman.

Shapiro, D. H. (1982). Overview: Clinical and physiological comparison of meditation with other self-control strategies. *American Journal of Psychiatry, 139* (3), 267-274.

Shapiro, D. H., Jr. (1984). Overview: Clinical and physiological comparison of meditation with other self-control strategies. In *Meditation: Classic and contemporary perspectives.* New York: Aldine.

Shengold, L. 1978). *Autohypnotic watchfulness. Psychoanalytic Quarterly, 47* (1), 113-115.

Shor, R. (1959). Hypnosis and the concept of the generalized reality-orientation. *American Journal of Psychotherapy, 13,* 582-602.

Shor, R. (1962a). Three dimensions of hypnotic depth. *International Journal of Clinical and Experimental Hypnosis, 10* (1), 23-38.

Shor, R. (1962b). *Inventory of self-hypnosis, Form A.* Palo Alto, CA: Consulting Psychologists Press.

Shor, R. (1979a). The fundamental problem in hypnosis research as viewed from historic perspectives. In E. Fromm & R. Shor (Eds.), *Hypnosis: Developments in research and new perspectives* (2nd ed., rev.). New York: Aldine.

Shor, R. (1979b). A phenomenological method for the measurement of variables important to an understanding of the nature of hypnosis. In E. Fromm & R. Shor (Eds.), *Hypnosis: Developments in research and new perspectives* (2nd ed.). New York: Aldine.

Shor, R., & Easton, R. D. (1973). Preliminary report on research comparing self and hetero-hypnosis. *American Journal of Clinical Hypnosis, 16* (1), 37-44.

Shor, R., Orne, M., & Orne, E. C. (1962). *The Harvard Group Scale of Hypnotic Susceptibility, Form A.* Palo Alto: Consulting Psychologists Press.

Shor, R., & Orne, M. T. (Eds.). (1965). *The nature of hypnosis: Selected basic readings.* New York: Holt, Rinehart & Winston.

Singer, J. L., & Pope, K. S. (1981). Daydreaming and imagery skills as predisposing capacities for self-hypnosis. *International Journal of Clinical and Experimental Hypnosis, 29* (3), 271-281.

Sophocles (1986). *Trachinae.* In H. R. Rawson & Miner, M. (Eds.), *The new international dictionary of quotations* (p. 79). New York: Mentor.

Soskis, D. (1986). *Teaching self-hypnosis: An introductory guide for clinicians.* New York: Norton.

Soskis, D. A., Orne, E. C., Orne, M. T., & Dinges, D. F. (1989). Self-hypnosis and meditation for stress management: A brief communication. *International Journal of Clinical and Experimental Hypnosis, 37* (4), 285-289.

Spinoza, B. (1960). Ethics. In J. M. Cohen & M. J. Cohen (Eds.), *The Penguin dictionary of quotations* (p. 372). London: Penguin Books.

Spiegel, D. (1983). Hypnosis with medical/surgical patients. *General Hospital Psychiatry, 5,* 265-277.

Spiegel, D. (1986a). Dissociating damage. *American Journal of Clinical Hypnosis, 2* (2), 123-131.

Spiegel, D. (1986b). Vietnam grief work using hypnosis. *The American Journal of Clinical Hypnosis, 24,* 33–40.

Spiegel, H. (1972). An eye-roll test for hypnotizability. *American Journal of Clinical Hypnosis, 15,* 25–28.

Spiegel, H., & Spiegel, D. (1978). *Trance and treatment: Clinical uses of hypnosis.* New York: Basic Books.

Spinhoven, O. (1987). Hypnosis and behavior therapy: A review. *International Journal of Clinical and Experimental Hypnosis, 35* (1), 8–31.

Stambaugh, E. E., & House, A. E. (1977). Multimodality therapy of migraine headaches: A case study utilizing biofeedback, relaxation, autogenic and hypnotic therapy. *American Journal of Clinical Hypnosis, 19* (4), 235–240.

Stanton, H. E. (1975). Weight loss through hypnosis. *American Journal of Clinical Hypnosis, 18* (2), 94–97.

Stanton, H. E. (1983). Helping sportsmen to help themselves. *Australian Journal of Clinical and Experimental Hypnosis, 11* (1), 33–38.

Stein, M., Schleifer, S., & Keller, S. (1982). The role of the brain and neuro-endocrine system in immune modulation: Potential links in neoplastic disease. In S. Levy (Ed.), *Biological mediators of behavior and disease.* New York: Elsevier.

Sternbach, R. A. (1982). On strategies for identifying neurochemical correlates of hypnotic analgesia. *International Journal of Clinical and Experimental Hypnosis, 30* (3), 251–256.

Sternbach, R. A., & Tursky, B. (1965). Ethnic differences among housewives in psychophysical and skin potential responses to electric shock. *Psychophysiology, 1,* 241.

Stratton, R. (1979). Behavioral therapy in the treatment of hypertension: The state of the art. *Biological Psychology Bulletin, 5* (3), 104–112.

Stutman, R., & Bliss, E. L. (1985). Posttraumatic stress disorder, hypnotizability and imagery. *American Journal of Psychiatry, 142* (6), 741–743.

Summers, J. K. (1982). Hypnosis and relaxation training in a group setting with adolescents who are emotionally and behaviorally disturbed. *International Journal of Clinical and Experimental Hypnosis, 30* (2), 189–230.

Tart, C. T. (Ed.). (1969). *Altered states of consciousness: A book of readings.* New York: Wiley.

Tart, C. T. (1970). Self-report scales of hypnotic depth. *International Journal of Clinical and Experimental Hypnosis, 8* (2), 105–125.

Tart, C. T. (1975). *States of consciousness.* New York: Dutton.

Tart, C. T. (1978–1979). Quick and convenient assessment of hypnotic depth: Self-report scales. *American Journal of Clinical Hypnosis, 21* (2 & 3), 186–207.

Tebecis, A., & Provins, K. A. (1976). Further studies of physiological concomitants of hypnosis: Skin temperature, heart rate and skin resistance. *Biological Psychology, 4* (4), 249–258.

Tebecis, A., Provins, K., Farnback, R., & Pentony, P. (1975). Hypnosis and the EEG: A quantitative investigation. *Journal of Nervous and Mental Disease, 161* (1), 1-17.

Tellegen, A., & Atkinson, G. (1974). Openness to absorbing and self-altering experiences ("absorption"): A trait related to hypnotic susceptibility. *Journal of Abnormal Psychology, 83,* 268-277.

Teyler, T. J., & Discenna, P. (1984). The topological anatomy of the hippocampus: A clue to its function. *Brain Research Bulletin, 12,* 711-719.

Thakur, A., & Thakur, K. (1984). Hypnotherapy in bulimia. In William C. Wester (Ed.), *Clinical hypnosis: A case management approach.* Cincinnati: Behavioral Science Center Publications.

Tinterow, M. M. (1970). *Foundations of hypnosis: From Mesmer to Freud.* Springfield, IL: Charles C. Thomas.

Toomey, T. C., & Sanders, S. (1983). Group hypnotherapy as an active self-control strategy in chronic pain. *American Journal of Clinical Hypnosis, 26* (1), 20-25.

Torem, M. (1987). Hypnosis in the treatment of depression. In W. C. Wester (Ed.), *Clinical hypnosis: A case management approach* (pp. 288-301). Cincinnati, OH: Behavior Science Center.

Unestahl, L. E. (1979). Hypnotic preparation of athletes. In G. D. Burrows, D. R. Collison, & L. Dennerstein (Eds.), *Proceedings of the 8th International Congress of Hypnosis and Psychosomatic Medicine.* Amsterdam: Elsevier/North Holland Biomedical Press.

Van Nuys, D. (1973). Meditation, attention and hypnotic susceptibility: A correlational study. *The International Journal of Clinical and Experimental Hypnosis, 21* (1), 59-69.

Vergil (1986). The Aeneid. In H. Rawson & M. Miner (Eds.), *The new international dictionary of quotations* (p. 335). New York: Mentor.

Vlastos, G. E. (1971). Plato: Ethics, politics and philosophy of art and religion. Garden City, NY: Doubleday Anchor.

von Dedenroth, T. E. A. (1962). Trance depth: An independent variable in therapeutic results. *American Journal of Clinical Hypnosis, 4,* 174-176.

Wadden, T. A., & Anderson, C. H. (1982). The clinical use of hypnosis. *Psychological Bulletin, 91,* 215-243.

Wadden, T. A., & Flaxman, J. (1981). Hypnosis and weight loss: A preliminary study. *International Journal of Clinical and Experimental Hypnosis, 29* (2), 162-173.

Wain, H. (1980). *Theoretical and clinical aspects of hypnosis.* Miami, FL: Symposia Specialists.

Wakeman, J. R., & Kaplan, J. Z. (1978). An experimental study of hypnosis in painful burns. *American Journal of Clinical Hypnosis, 21* (1), 3-12.

Walker, W. L., Collins, J. K., & Krass, J. (1982). Four hypnosis scripts from the Macquarie weight control programme. *Australian Journal of Clinical and Experimental Hypnosis, 10* (2), 125-133.

Walrath, L. C., & Hamilton, D. W. (1975). Autonomic correlates of meditation and hypnosis. *American Journal of Clinical Hypnosis, 17* (3), 190-197.

Watkins, J. G. (1971). The affect bridge. *International Journal of Clinical and Experimental Hypnosis, 19* (1), 21–27.

Waxman, D. (1989). *Hartland's medical and dental hypnosis* (3rd ed.). London: Bailliere Tindall. (Original work published in 1961)

Weitzenhoffer, A. M. (1957). *General techniques of hypnotism.* New York: Grune & Stratton.

Weitzenhoffer, A. (1989). *The practice of hypnotism.* New York: Wiley.

Weitzenhoffer, A. M., & Hilgard, E. R. (1962). *Stanford Hypnotic Susceptibility Scale, Forms A and B.* Palo Alto, CA: Consulting Psychologists Press.

Weitzenhoffer, A. M., & Hilgard, E. R. (1963). *Stanford Hypnotic Susceptibility Scale, Form C.* Palo Alto: Consulting Psychologists Press, 1963.

Wilson, S. C., & Barber, T. X. (1978). The creative imagination scale as a measure of hypnotic responsiveness: Applications to experimental and clinical hypnosis. *American Journal of Clinical Hypnosis, 20,* 235–249.

Winnicott, D. W. (1953). Transitional objects and transitional phenomena. *International Journal of Psychoanalysis, 34* (1), 89–97.

Wolberg, L. R. (1945). *Hypnoanalysis.* New York: Grune & Stratton.

Wolberg, L. R. (1948). *Medical hypnosis* (2 vols.). New York: Grune & Stratton.

Wolf, S., & Wolff, H. G. (1947). *Human gastric functions.* New York: Oxford University Press.

Wolff, W. (1951). *Changing concepts of the bible: A psychological analysis of its words, symbols, and beliefs.* New York: Hermitage House.

Wolpe, J. (1958). *Psychotherapy by reciprocal inhibition.* Stanford: Stanford University Press.

Woolson, D. A. (1986). An experimental comparison of direct and Ericksonian hypnotic induction procedures and the relationship to secondary suggestibility. *American Journal of Clinical Hypnosis, 29* (1), 23–28.

Wright, M. E. (1960). Hypnosis and rehabilitation. *Rehabilitation Literature, 21,* 2–12.

Wright, M. E., & Wright, B. A. (1989). *Clinical practice of hypnotherapy.* New York: Guilford Press.

Young, P. (1986). *Personal change through self-hypnosis.* Eden Park: Angus and Robertson.

Zeig, J. S. (1980). Symptom prescription and Ericksonian principles of hypnosis and psychotherapy. *The American Journal of Clinical Hypnosis, 22,* 16–22.

Index

Acting, stage, self-hypnosis in, 4
Adolescents, 101–102, 189
Affect in self-hypnosis, 13–15
  thought/action balance, 13, 14
Age regression
  and depression, 136
  and pain control, 145–146
  self-hypnosis, 53
AIDS, 175
Airplane phobia, treatment of, 76–77
Amnesia, psychogenic, 129–131
  and self-hypnosis, 130, 131
Anesthesia, surgical, self-hypnosis in, 152.
  See also Pain control; Surgery, pain
  control in
Animal magnetism, 30, 32
Anorexia nervosa
  abstinence in, self-suggestion for,
    169
  food as energy, metaphor, 169–170
  as independence drive, 169
  mirroring, 170
  self-hypnosis for, 168
  stomach thermostat metaphor, 169
  weight gain, reframing of, 170
Anxiety
  comfort trigger, 128
  imagery for treatment of, 127–128
  learning to enter hypnosis, 127
  prevention, 77
  self-control techniques for, 127
  treatment goals, 127
  validation of in real life, 128
Arm levitation, 48
Asthma
  ego-passive to ego-active
    transformation, 162
  lung imagery, 161
  triggers for, 161–162
Atropine, and pain research, 163
Attention focus, 50–51
Attention span, 51
Autogenic training, 45–46
Autohypnosis. See also entries under
  Self-hypnosis
  autosuggestions, 33

repetition, 33
and will, 33
Autonomic functioning, in relaxation, 94

Back injury, pain control in, 150–151
Bedwetting. See Enuresis
Behavioral orientation of therapist,
  76–78
Bias of therapist, vs. therapy, 52
Bingeing, eating disorder, and self-
  hypnosis, 12–13
Birth pangs
  hypnosis for, 154
  imagery about, 154–155
  research, 151
  teaching of self-hypnosis for, 154
Body functions, use of hypnosis to
  control, 149–150
Body parts, focusing hypnosis on, 40
Body, self-perception of, 11
Borderline patients
  self-hypnosis for, 134–135
  and strong affects, 103
Brain, language processing of, 213. See
  also Words
Bulimia
  age progression for, 171
  attention diversion techniques, 171
  binges in, 170
  ego-building exercises, 171
  emotions, fears about, 172
  food choice and control, 171, 172
  pendulum technique for, 171
  purging in, 170
  self-control, 171, 172
  self-image improvement, 171
  and stress, 170
Burns, hypnosis for, 164–165
  blood-supply image, 165

Cancer, 174
Cerebral deficits, 174
Cerebral palsy, 173–174
Charcot, J.-M., 35
Charms, as transitional objects, 23

Children, hypnotherapy for
  age of child, 180
  contraindications, 179
  curiosity of child, 181, 182, 183
  dissociation, 181
  and goals, 178, 180-181
  guided stories, 182
  guidelines, 179
  imagery, 181
  indications for, 178
  inductions for, 179-180, 183
  metaphor in, 182
  mirroring of words, 179
  as play, 182-183
  reinforcements, 183
  relaxation, 181
Children's Hypnotic Susceptibility Scale,
  124
Cholecystectomy, self-hypnosis in, 202
Cognitive problem solving, 153-154
  mental engagement of patient, 154
Communication methods of patient, 109
Compliance problems
  denial, 175
  negative images, problems with, 175
  realism in goals, 17
  self-destructiveness, 175
Consciousness in hypnosis, 92
Coué, formulas of, 41
Creative Imagination Scale, 122
Creative reorganization, hypnotic
  concept, 44-45
Creativity
  defined, 99
  ego-analytic concept of adaptive
    regression, 100
  and hypnosis, 204
  imaginary identification with famous
    person, 100
  nonverbal hemisphere, 100
  regression in service to ego, concept, 100
  and self-hypnosis, 99-101
  self-rating scale, 204-205
  tests for, 100-101
Cues
  explicit, 51
  indirect, 50-51
  for patients in self-hypnosis, 47, 48
  self-relaxation, 171, 172

Daydreams, association of with hypnosis,
  96
Deep breathing, 79, 114, 116-117, 172
Depression episodes, 135-136
  affect bridge, 136
  screen method, 136
  signs of, 135
  suicidal tendencies, 135

Depth of hypnosis, clinical interview for,
  91-92
Dissociation, 35, 99, 103-104
  as defense mechanism, 103-104
  in self-hypnosis, 99
Dreams, 20, 22-23, 210
  analysis, 210

Eating, compulsive. See also Anorexia
    nervosa; Bingeing; Bulimia
  long-term maintenance of patient,
    166
  negative images associated with food,
    167
  positive motivation of patient, 166
  research on, 168
  self-hypnotic instructions for control
    of, 166-167
Eclectic orientation of therapist
  content, 71-72
  pain treatment, 72-73
  practice, 72
Eczema, hypnosis for, 185-187
  anger, alternate response to, 186, 187
  asthma control, 186
  body language vs. anger, 185-186
  cure of, 187
  opening up of patient, 186
  posthypnotic suggestion, 185
  progressive relaxation, 185
  withdrawal of child, 185
Ego functions, 8-9
Enuresis
  bladder muscle control, 184
  ideomotor signaling, 184
  induction choice, 184
  self-hypnotic practice, 184
  suggestions for child, 184
  time for practice, 189
  work with parents, 188-189
Evaluation of patient, content of
  activities of patient, 108
  clinical history, 107
  diet, 108
  education, 107
  health, 107
  intelligence, 108
  social history, 107
  thought content, 108
Existential-phenomenological theory of
    hypnosis, 67-68
  consciousness, knowledge of, 68
  phenomena, attention to, 68
Eye catalepsy susceptibility test, 44
Eye rolls, 47, 48

Falling test, for self-suggestion, 44
Fantasy rehearsal, 76

Finger temperature, control of, 133
Fixed ideas, 35
Fractionalization, 102
Free-floating associations and images, 10
Freud, Sigmund, 35, 36, 37, 38
  abreaction, 37
  and Anna O case, 36, 37
  and free association, 37–38
  and hypnosis, 37
  and transference, 37
Functional megacolon, 184–185

Goals
  complexity, progression of, 112–113
  graded, 112
  and imagery, 9–10
  negotiation of, 112–113
  self-fulfilling prophecy effects, 9
  self-hypnosis, 45
  verbalization for learning of, 46–47

Hairpulling. *See* Trichotillomania
Healing, direction of by hypnotherapist,
    40–41
Heterohypnosis
  cognitive control structures, 61
  executive ego, 61
  ideomotor conditioning, 62
  inhibition of cortex, 62
  neodissociation theory, 61
  neurophysiological theory, 61
  as protocol for self-hypnosis by
      patients, 95
  psychoanalytic theory, 62–63
  roletaking, 63
  and self-hypnosis, 140
  state theory, 60–61
  subjective experience of patient, 61
  thinking along with therapist, 63
  trait theory, 61–62
  verbal conditioning, 62
Heteroinduction, 49
Hypermnesia, 13
Hypnosis. *See also* Heterohypnosis; Self-
    hypnosis
  early medical research, 34–38
  ego fractions in, 143
  inner states, 34
  as learning experience, 45
  neutral, 94
  patient, attitudes of to, 50–51, 59–60
  phenomena,in, 29–32
  physiology òf, 94
  positive suggestion, 34
  and psychotherapy, 60
  response to vs. patient–therapist
      interaction, 94–95
  therapist, attitudes of to, 59–60

Hypnosis, myths and misconceptions
    about, 34, 110–111
Hypnotherapists
  psychotherapeutic orientations, 98
  role of, attitudes towards, 98–99
  self-hypnosis, use of on selves by, 98
  teaching of self-hypnosis to patients
      by, 98–99
Hypnotic Induction Profile, 123
Hypertension, hypnosis for
  imagery in, 165
  research on, 166
Hysteria
  and amnesia, 36
  repetition, 36
  spontaneous autohypnotic states in,
      36–37

Ideomotor conditioning and signaling,
    48, 62, 184
Imagery associated with goals. *See also*
    Goals
  fantasy types in, 96, 97
  healthy habits, 120–121
  ideas, restructuring of, 120
  insight, 120
  negative feelings, reduction of, 120
  new solutions, generation of, 120
  pain control, 121
  positive feelings, reinforcement of, 120
  self-control, 120
  tension, release of, 119–120
Immunity control in hypnosis
  hippocampus, memory functions of, 78
  organs, imaging of, 78
Indirect suggestions, 12
Individuality of patients, 49–50
Induction, hypnotic
  conscious future, 116
  conscious here and now, 115
  conscious past, 115
  conscious vs. unconscious experience,
      conflict between, 116
  contradictory responses of patient, 114
  debriefing of patient, 117–118
  first time as learning experience, 113
  kinesthetic, 183
  parsimony in, 113–114
  positive feedback in, 114–115
  practice of by patient, 117–118
  rapport with patient, 114
  relaxation in, 117
  therapist, reactions of, 115
  unconscious future expectations, 116
  unconscious here and now, 116
Inexperienced subjects
  and heterohypnosis, 97
  self-induction of, 97

Influences on hypnosis in clinic, 50
Inner experience, absorption in, 10
Insights of patient, 110
Insomnia, 41
Interview, self-confidence in, 12
Inventory of Self-Hypnosis, 91
"Inward Light" concept, 33

Janet, Pierre, 35–36
Journals, personal, self-monitoring by,
    40, 89, 136, 188

Le Cron, scales by, 123
Liebault, Ambroise, 34, 39–40
Literature on self-hypnosis, review of,
    87

Mantras, 20–21
Meditation, 21–22
Mental health
    as aid to hypnosis, 40–41
    and self-regulation, 40
Mesmer, Anton, 30
Migraine headache
    aura in, 163
    chronic pain of, hypnotic control, 174
    imagery for, 164
    research on, 163
    and self-hypnosis, 163–164
Mind–body interactions, historical
    perspectives, 26–29
Motion, sense of in self-hypnosis, 11
Movement disorders, 131–132. See also
    Tics; Tourette's disorder
Muscle relaxation, progressive, 42

Naturalistic behaviors and hypnosis
    analogy, 81
    creativity blockage, 81–82
    metaphor, 81
    positive double bind, 80
    pupillary dilation, 80
Neurodermatitis, hypnosis for, 164
Neurological disorders, 172–174
    benefits, 173
    and pain, 173
    and rehabilitation, 173
Neutral imagery, 49
Nonownership technique for pain
    control, 151–152
North Carolina Scale, 123
Novice phase of hypnosis, 129

Orientation, theoretical, of therapist,
    aspects of, 82. See also specific
    orientation

Pain control. See also Nonownership;
    Surgery
    and affect, 144
    alarm, pain as, 143
    Barber, work of on, 147–148
    comfortable thoughts, 153
    Crasilneck, work of on, 148–149
    dental work, 146
    displacement, 147
    dissociation, 145
    distraction, 145
    "electric-wiring" gate-control image,
        148
    Erickson, work of on, 148–149
    failure to perceive pain, 143, 147
    finger raising exercise, 149
    glove anesthesia, 145
    holistic treatment, 143, 148
    hypnoanesthesia, 145
    imagery in, 146, 152
    intents of patient, 149
    in lower back, 149
    perception of, 143–144
    phantom limb, 143
    pleasant memories, association with,
        148
    and posthypnotic suggestion, 143
    requirements for, 142
    Sacerdote, work of on, 148
    self-hypnosis for, 152–153
    self-monitoring, 148
    sense of mastery, 143
    substitution, 147
    threshold alteration, 144
PAS Scale, 215–217
Past, separation of from present, 212
Patient as member of treatment team,
    160
Pendulum as hypnotic aid, 44, 171
Peptic ulcer, 162–163
Personal properties (attributes) of
    patient, 50–52
Personality vs. self-hypnosis, 95–96
    associated traits, 95
    and MMPI results, 95
Play therapy for children
    and agreed-upon reality, 178
    hypnotherapist, 178
    therapeutic triad, 178
    therapist, 178
Playfulness in self-hypnosis, 50
Prayer, 19, 23–24
Prevention by autohypnosis, 40
Psychoanalytic orientation of therapist
    automatization of behavior, 74
    defenses, 74
    dreams, induction of, 74–75
    ego-ideal technique, 75
    imagery, 74

primary process thought, 74
receptivity of ego, 74, 75
secondary process thought, 74
and self-hypnosis, teaching of, 75–76
transferences, 74
Psychosomatic disorders and self-
    hypnosis
activity/relaxation, alternation, 159
biofeedback in, 159
cognitive restructuring, 159
comfort, imagery of, 158
DSM-III code for, 157
hypnoanesthesia, 159
language block in, 157–158
learning about self-help for, 158
organs, imagery of, 158
practice of self-hypnosis, 159
relaxation training, 158–159
self-monitoring, 159
session length, 159–160
thinking of ways to feel comfortable,
    159
Psychosis, self-hypnosis in, 134–135
Puisegur, Marquis de, 30–31

Rapport in therapy, 35, 114
Reduction of reality, 10
Reflection, 205–206
Reframing, 81, 170
Relaxation
imagery for, 79
metaphors for, 79
physical effects in, 94
and self-hypnosis, 94–95
suggestions for, 94
Relaxation and reinforcement phase of
    hypnosis, 129–130
Role enactment theory, 43–44

Scripts as self-hypnosis aids, 101–102
Seeking-self phase, 129
Seizures, 173
Self, subject/object paradox in, 156
Self-healing exercise, first explicit, 29
Self-hypnosis
adaptation to, 93
as altered state, 64–65, 92
attention in, 92, 93
as biological state, 5
and change in individual, 14
clinical orientations to, 71
conditions for, 48, 50, 144
continuum in, 211
control by patient, 43
ego receptivity, 92
exercises during sessions, 47–48
imagery in, 92
limits on, 189

mastery, 47–49
participation of patient, 4
physiological, 78–79
post-hypnotic suggestion, 43
practice of, 47–48
purpose, specificity of, 189
security and reinforcement, 149
as self-mastery experience, 151
state-specific characteristics, 94
therapist's participation as partial
    block to, 213
variety in, 14
words and images for, useful set, 140–
    141
written instructions, 43
Self-hypnosis, basic research on
behavioral paradigm, 88, 91
beliefs of therapist, 85
depth assessment, 88–90
functionalism, 90
and heterohypnosis as adjunct to
    behavioral therapy, 85–86
and heterohypnosis as baseline, 88
hidden-observer method, 90
laboratory vs. clinic, 85
questions in, 89
and subjective experience of patients, 86
Self-hypnosis, clinical
cognitive styles, 6
vs. core of discomfort, 8
guidelines for, 6
motivation in, 6–7
practice of, 6–7
as taught to patient, 4, 6
unconscious input, 6
Self-hypnosis, contraindications to
lack of motivation, 126
resistance by patient, 126
Self-hypnosis, indications for
as adjunct to treatment, 126
motivation of patient, 125
posthypnotic suggestion
    reinforcement, 126
therapist availability, 126
Self-hypnosis practice
affirmative mind set, 138
change, excitement of, 138–139
mental attitudes change, 137–138
panic attacks, 136–137
perspective change, 137–139
Self-hypnosis, teaching of
amnesia evocation, 53
dehypnotizing, 54
first induction of patient, 52
open-ended suggestion, 53
practice, suggestions for, 53–54
relaxation exercises, 53
scheduling suggestion, 53–54
therapist, interactions of with patient, 52

Self-hypnosis, theories of
  in absence of hypnotist, 66
  all hypnosis as self-hypnosis, model, 64
  all self-hypnosis as hypnosis, model, 64
  altered state of consciousness, 64–65
  clinical, 67
  concentration, 65
  free-floating attention, 65
  induction, 69
  laboratory-defined, 66
  neodissociation theory, 69
  non-state theory, 69
  physical theory, 69–70
  in presence of hypnotist, 67
  psychoanalytic theory, 70
  role-taking theory, 70
  as self-directed state, 65
  as self-intended state, 65–66
  state-dependent learning theory, 69
  trait theory, 69
  verbal conditioning theory, 70
Self-magnetism, 32–33
Self-suggestion. See Suggestion
Self-talk, discovery of, 40
Sensory preferences of patient, 111
Sleep
  healing in, 36
  and self-hypnosis, 12, 41
Smoking, 112
Spasticity, 173
Sports
  bicycling, 202–203
  dog obedience competition, 203
  running, 203
Suggestions
  in conversation, 51
  direct, 51
  indirect, 12, 51
  reciprocal inhibition model of, 41
  of self, 42, 160–161
  and sleep, 41
  and will, 41
Suggestions, embedded
  inductions, 114–115
  pain control, 148, 149
Stanford Hypnotic Susceptibility Scale
  for Adults, 122
Stanford Hypnotizability Scale, 124
Stimulus deprivation, 38
Stress control, 13
Stuttering, 133–134
Subconscious, 35
Surgery, pain control in, 197–202
  direct suggestion, 198
  during surgery, 201
  in operating room before surgery, 198–199
  outcomes, 200, 201
  patient as part of team, 201–202

presurgical preparation, 198
  in recovery room, 199
  on return to hospital room, 199
  surgical procedure, knowledge of, 198
  tape, use by patient, 200
  triggers for self-hypnosis, 200
Susceptibility, 91, 124

Talking cure, 37
Tapes as aids to self-hypnosis
  adolescents, 102
  cancer patients, 102
  and cognitive exercises, 101
  probationary students, 101
  stress response, 101
Test anxiety, 11–12
Thinking along with the hypnotist, 51, 63
Tics, 131–132
Time distortion
  and children, 181
  dissociative disorders, 93
  and pain control, 146
  reasons for, 93
  and self-hypnosis, 10, 54
Timeouts, 36
Tourette's disorder, 132–133
Trances
  instinctive, 5
  overuse of, 5
  as survival aid, 5
Transcendence, 8
Transcendental Meditation, 21
Transformation of self
  feedback, 119
  imagery generation, 118
  induction, ending of by patient, 119
  positive self-suggestion, 118
  post-hypnosis, 209, 210
  self-censorship, 118
  transcendence of problem, 210
Transitional objects, 11–12
Trichotillomania
  control of, 188
  hairpulling in, 187
  rag doll image for control, 187–188
  sister rivalry, 187, 188

Ultradian rhythms, 80
Unconscious, trust in, 45, 46. See also
    Induction, hypnotic; Self-hypnosis,
    clinical

Weight loss, hypnosis for, 112
Words
  and brain activity, 20
  as powerful objects, 18–19, 20, 24, 210
  in self-hypnosis, 156